OUR WAR TOO

OUR WAR TOO

American Women Against the Axis

MARGARET PATON-WALSH

UNIVERSITY PRESS OF KANSAS

Published by the University Press of Kansas (Lawrence, Kansas 66049), which was organized by the Kansas Board of Regents and is operated and funded by Emporia State University, Fort Hays State University, Kansas State University, Pittsburg State University, the University of Kansas, and Wichita State University

Library of Congress Cataloging-in-Publication Data

Paton-Walsh, Margaret, 1965–
Our war too : American women against the Axis / Margaret Paton-Walsh.
p. cm.
Based on the author's thesis: "Brave women and fair men" : women advocates of U.S. intervention in World War II, 1939–1941 (Ph.D.—University of Washington, 1996).
Includes bibliographical references and index.
ISBN 0-7006-1183-5 (alk. paper)
1. World War, 1939–1945—Women—United States.
2. Women—United States—History—20th century. 3. World War, 1939–1945—United States. 4. Isolationism—United States—History—20th century. 5. Intervention (International law)
I. Title.
D810.W7 P33 2002
940.53'082'0973—dc21 2002002976

British Library Cataloguing in Publication Data is available.

Printed in the United States of America

10 9 8 7 6 5 4 3 2 1

The paper used in this publication meets the minimum requirements of the American National Standard for Permanence of Paper for Printed Library Materials Z39.48-1984.

For Jennifer Messick

In memory of Jim

There was a sound of revelry by night,
And Belgium's Capital had gather'd then
Her Beauty and her Chivalry, and bright
The lamps shone o'er fair women and brave men;
A thousand hearts beat happily; and when
Music arose with its voluptuous swell,
Soft eyes look'd love to eyes which spake again,
And all went merry as a marriage bell; —
But hush! hark! a deep sound strikes like a rising knell!

—Byron, *Childe Harold's Pilgrimage,*
Canto the Third, verse XXI

Let me believe that this Committee is made up of *brave women and fair men.* I misquote with malice. I hope desperately that we can all be not only good fighters but *fair* fighters. There are honest, conscientious and honorable citizens who hold that involvement in the European war will not help our national defense and will not preserve the American way of life so precious to us all. We must respect the sincerity of their opinions while differing with them. . . . "War Monger" is an unpleasant name, but "Unpatriotic" and "UnAmerican" are equally disagreeable adjectives. When it comes to motives, let us leave the role of omniscience to God.

—Elizabeth Morrow, November 21, 1941

Contents

Acknowledgments

In the nine years that this book has been in the making, I have accumulated many debts. This project began life as a doctoral dissertation. My adviser, Wilton Fowler, provided consistent enthusiasm and support, which kept me going in the darkest hours of graduate school. Susan Glenn and Richard Kirkendall added important insights and suggestions as the dissertation approached completion. I am grateful to the Arthur and Elizabeth Schlesinger Library on the History of Women in America for a grant to conduct research in their archives and to the history department at the University of Washington for numerous sources of financial aid. Various archivists were also tremendously helpful—at the Schlesinger Library; at the Sophia Smith Collection, Smith College; and particularly Nanci Young at the Seeley G. Mudd Library at Princeton University.

Two other people were a vital part of my graduate school experience and contributed both directly and indirectly, intellectually and emotionally, to the completion of the dissertation. My heartfelt thanks to Tracy McKenzie and Jennifer Alexander for all that they did and all that they gave.

The transformation of my dissertation into this book owed a great deal to two other people—my mother, who wanted me to write something rather more readable, and my editor, Nancy Jackson, who encouraged me in the same direction. My mother also has been my most dedicated reader and critic—no words could ever be sufficient thanks.

I would also like to thank my friends Thaddeus Sunseri, Elizabeth Jones, Jay Taylor, Mary Brennan, Greta Bucher, Matt Klingle, and Jennifer Alexander, for knowing what I was going through and being there when I needed them, and Jennifer Messick for always believing.

Finally, I would like to thank both of my parents for their unfailing support and encouragement of my endeavors for as long as I can remember.

1

"Does America Deserve a Miracle?"

> How can a woman ask for implements of war without being considered unwomanly, cruel, and reckless of life? . . . The only real answer is that there are some things worse than war. . . . There are some things supreme and noble that are worth fighting for.

On June 4, 1940, with these words, Elizabeth Cutter Morrow declared herself in favor of full-scale American aid to the Allies in their war with Nazi Germany.[1] Her speech was broadcast by the National Broadcasting Company and subsequently issued as a flyer by the Committee to Defend America by Aiding the Allies, which she represented. Elizabeth Morrow was not a nationally known figure in 1940, although her name had some recognition value deriving from her husband's renown. She was born in Cleveland, Ohio, and attended Smith College in the 1890s, graduating in 1896. While at Smith she met Dwight Morrow, and they were married in 1903. Dwight Morrow was first a corporate lawyer, then a partner at J. P. Morgan, then ambassador to Mexico beginning in September 1927.

In 1930, the Morrows returned to the United States, where Dwight entered the senatorial race in New Jersey. Elizabeth, or Betty as she was generally called, played an active role in the campaign, speaking to numerous women's organizations on her husband's behalf. Dwight Morrow's death at fifty-eight in October 1931 was seen by many as a terrible loss for the nation. There had been talk that he might be a suitable Republican candidate for the presidency in 1932. Elizabeth Morrow was devastated by her husband's death and experienced a period of depression before devoting herself to writing for children.

At the time that she made this appeal for aid to the Allies, Morrow was acting president of Smith College. But what made her statement so dramatic, what led interventionists to encourage her open stand, was the fact that her son-in-law Charles Lindbergh, the aviation hero, was the leading spokesman for the isolationist side. Although Morrow never explicitly criticized Lindbergh himself, it was inevitable, as her daughter Anne Morrow Lindbergh recognized, that others would understand her public statements in that way. To complicate family matters even more, Anne's sister Constance was married to Aubrey Morgan, a Welshman who worked for the Bureau of British Information Services in the United States. Although the Morrow family appears to have weathered this divisive disagreement with remarkable success, the rift is indicative of the polarizing impact of the so-called Great Debate over whether the United States should enter the war. Lindbergh was a midwesterner whose father had been strongly isolationist in the last war. The isolationist strongholds in the early years of the Second World War were also in the Midwest. The Morrow family came from the northeastern elite, which strongly identified with the British cause and produced many of the leading interventionists of the era. Thus, the family divide reflected the national one, at least in some ways.

Although leading interventionists undoubtedly saw Elizabeth Morrow's significance at least partly in terms of her relationship with Lindbergh, her significance for our understanding of American women's response to the war goes well beyond that. When the war in Europe began in September 1939, Morrow supported the revision of the Neutrality Acts to allow the sale of arms on a cash-and-carry basis, a measure designed to assist Britain and France. In the face of the devastating successes of the German blitzkrieg in the spring of 1940, she joined the Committee to Defend America by Aiding the Allies, embracing the cause of all-out aid to the Allies. In early 1941, she advocated adoption of the administration's lend-lease plan; and by the fall of 1941, she was ready to go to war. Her journey down the road to war was one traveled in company with the majority of Americans. Some were ahead of Morrow, some behind, but they were all moving in the same direction, drawn along by essentially the same conviction: that a German victory in the war would be disastrous—for America and for freedom.

The Committee to Defend America by Aiding the Allies was formed as the phony war came to an end in April and May 1940. As the German army advanced across western Europe, a group of concerned Americans, under the aegis of influential Kansas publisher William Allen White, came together to exert both public and private pressure to increase the extent and nature of American aid to the Allies. Morrow's speech was part of the committee's initial publicity efforts and laid out the core of interventionist arguments—arguments that would be rehearsed repeatedly over the next nine months, until the passage of the Lend-Lease Act in March 1941 changed the stakes in the public debate over foreign policy.

Interventionist arguments were not always entirely consistent, especially in the first years of the war as interventionists struggled to convey their conviction that Germany had to be resisted, while still claiming not to wish for U.S. entry into the war. Interventionists reconciled these rather contradictory sentiments by arguing that the Allies needed military equipment and supplies, not men, and that providing them with these things was, in fact, the best way to prevent more direct American involvement in the conflict. As Morrow argued, "The Allies do not apparently need manpower. But as the best means of avoiding this type of involvement in the conflict in Europe, I urge immediate aid to the Allies—the sending of munitions and supplies, food, money, airplanes, ships, and everything that could help them win in their struggle against Germany."[2] Thus, the very purpose of aid was to ensure that military intervention in the war would be unnecessary. It was, as many interventionists acknowledged, an argument from self-interest: "I do not advocate help to the Allies as a crusade, but as a means of defense for ourselves. It is not heroic or generous—it is a matter of self-interest."[3] Yet it was not quite as simple as that. Interventionists also believed that the war was an ideological one, and that the Allies were fighting for ideals that Americans held dear. "The French and British are fighting tonight for all the things we honor in life. Why not support them as a first line of defense?"[4]

But Morrow's significance does not lie only in her elucidation of the shifting interventionist position. Just as striking is her consciousness that her views were unexpected coming from a woman, her challenge to the argument and expectation that women would or should oppose intervention in the war. Many Americans, including President Roosevelt, accepted this idea rather uncritically.[5] Moreover, the women's peace movement encouraged the assumption that women would be more inclined to oppose war, and this was a central tenet of the right-wing mothers' movement, which emphasized mothers' opposition to war. Even many members of women's organizations accepted this idea, although usually in the context of advocating an enlarged role for women in foreign policy making and international affairs at the end of the war.

However, women's views cannot be so simply characterized. In the interwar period, women who were interested in foreign policy were excluded from positions of influence in the State Department and thus pursued that interest in forums such as the League of Nations Association, the peace movement, and the foreign policy committees of women's organizations. In these arenas, the primary concern was the prevention of another world war, and the preferred solution was generally some variety of collective security or what we might call internationalism. In an ironic twist of fate, in the context of the Second World War, internationalist ideas developed as a means to preserve peace would become the foundation of the interventionist position.

Although internationalist women were aware of the expectations associated with their gender, they either did not see or did not feel constrained by the apparent contradictions between those ideas and their views. Rather, they argued, when they referred to gender at all, that interventionism was consistent with the maternal concerns assumed to underlie women's pacifism—first by presenting interventionist policies as those most likely to keep the Unitd States out of the war, and then by arguing that Nazi victory presented a greater threat than war. Elizabeth Morrow's speech of June 1940 was a prime example of this approach: "It is little comfort to one of my generation to think that I escape suffering to have it fall upon my children and grandchildren."[6]

Morrow's view was representative of interventionist women, who favored aid not because they hoped for war or were careless of the consequences of a policy of aiding the Allies but because they hoped aid would forestall more direct U.S. involvement and because, in the last resort, they believed that war was preferable to a Nazi victory. Rather than rejecting the idea of a political authority wielded by the mothers of the nation, Morrow claimed that authority for herself through her children and grandchildren, and then redefined the danger to the nurtured—as Nazi oppression rather than war—and presented aid to the Allies as the best means of defending them.

Lest anyone doubt the power of such maternal rhetoric, a survey of the correspondence that Morrow's speech provoked shows its prevalence among Americans at the time. One correspondent from Jersey City declared that Morrow was the "ideal American woman, wife, mother and citizen."[7] However, maternal rhetoric was more commonly employed to attack Morrow, who received a wave of hate mail. Correspondents claimed the authority of motherhood to lambaste her with the familiar isolationist charge that only those who had nothing to lose advocated aid (which was assumed to mean war in isolationist thinking). Katherine Searles Pilliod, of Delta, Ohio, declared that it was a "great pity that you who believe in overseas interference can't do the dying for the young and the weeping for the mothers."[8] This line of argument carried the implicit assumption that any mother with a son to lose would be opposed to aid.

Some anonymous correspondents were much more vitriolic. The "Committee for Sound Americanism" denounced Morrow as a witch. "Right this way mothers of America! Bring the fruit of your wombs to the cauldron of Goody Morrow, witch of Engelwood. . . . If Goody Morrow must have a bloody stew let her put her own entrails into her cauldron."[9] Thus, Morrow was attacked for sacrificing the children of American women, and her own lack of personal sacrifice was suggested. This latter idea was taken up much more explicitly in another anonymous letter—"From all mothers that have Sons!!"—that was directly threatening: "Unless you recall your speech . . . it will not go well with you! 'We,' all the 'Mothers' of the United States, will see that you will be railroaded to England and France and put in the 'Front-line,' where you or the likes of you belong. How dare you speak about war!! Have you sons to give? . . . don't forget, 'We' are coming for you. . . . We are going to get you."[10] The naked hostility of these letters is not typical, but the use of what we might call the rhetoric of motherhood was fairly common, especially by the isolationist side in the debate. In fact, Morrow's speech was rather unusual for its focus on the gender issue, for it was not part of any systematic campaign on the part of interventionist organizations to counter isolationists' claims to a monopoly on women's support. Indeed, it was not until 1941 that interventionist women began to address the gender question explicitly, making direct appeals to women both on maternal grounds and on the basis of the oppression that women faced under National Socialism. Even then their efforts did not really constitute a concerted campaign. One of the results has been the relative invisibility of interventionist women in the histories of this debate.

This book seeks to remedy this gap by telling the story of how the United States became involved in the Second World War through the eyes of American women who sought this outcome. In so doing, it seeks to illuminate the ways in which women functioned as political actors even as they were excluded from the corridors of power—through activism in women's organizations, through informal women's networks, through male-dominated lobbying groups; working within, yet manipulating, assumptions about what being a woman meant for their political ideas. At the same time, this story has importance for an ongoing debate among historians about the issue of American public opinion in the years leading up to U.S. entry into the war and about the extent to which Americans understood and supported the interventionist policies of the Roosevelt administration. The women in this story clearly understood the significance and implications of the policies they advocated; they recognized the danger of war but faced it as a necessary evil. The story of the months from September 1939 to December 1941 is not just one of President Roosevelt and the U.S. government struggling to develop a meaningful foreign policy in response to the crises engulfing both Europe and Asia. It is also one of American women trying to reconcile the irreconcilable, trying to preserve both their principles and their peace.

In June 1940, Elizabeth Morrow was still a long way from advocating American entry into the war, but her speech showed her firm conviction that the United States had a responsibility and a vested interest in an Allied victory. To those who argued, "Only a miracle can save the Allies now. Let us go to church and pray," she pointed out that the Bible told of people who "earn[ed] their miracles. . . . And we the richest nation in the world, would appeal to the Most High for help in the battle of freedom—help which we could ourselves give! Does America deserve a miracle? Not unless she earns it."[11] The following chapters tell the story of the American women who struggled to earn the miracle of German defeat.

2

Imagining Neutrality

The 1930s was a decade of tremendous international instability, when treaty systems designed to maintain the peace after the Great War were challenged and crumbled. In Europe, the system was defined by the Treaty of Versailles and the League of Nations. The treaty, imposed on Germany at the end of the war, reorganized the borders of central Europe, creating a variety of new nations in the process, and attempted to prevent any resurgence of German power. The League was supposed to adjudicate disputes arising from the treaty and provide a forum for the resolution of any other international conflicts that might arise to threaten world peace. The final element of this system was the Kellogg-Briand Pact of 1928, also known as the Pact of Paris, which outlawed war and whose signatories included all the great powers of the world, and many of the smaller, weaker ones, too. In the Pacific region, the League of Nations was supplemented by the Washington Conference system, developed in 1921–22, which attempted to regulate diplomatic relations among nations with interests in China and Southeast Asia, through a naval limitation treaty and the Nine Power Pact, under which signatories agreed to respect and maintain the territorial integrity of China.

In the 1930s, against a backdrop of worldwide economic depression, three nations—Japan, Germany, and Italy—would challenge these arrangements with considerable success. That success owed a great deal to the failure of other nations to resist. Their inability or unwillingness to work together, their reluctance to defend the existing international framework with anything more than words, their desperate desire for peace: all conspired to pave the way for another great war.

The first major challenge came in Asia in September 1931. The Japanese had had troops stationed in northern China since the beginning of the century, protecting their interests in the zone around the

South Manchuria Railway. Local military commanders there saw the world economic depression as an opportunity to increase Japanese influence in China without European interference. So, on September 18, 1931, they blew up a section of the Japanese-controlled railroad a few miles north of Mukden and blamed the Chinese. With the Mukden incident as an excuse, they then launched a military expedition against China in Manchuria, beyond the railway zone. These steps appear to have been taken without prior authorization from the civilian Japanese government, but it had no desire to repudiate a popular and successful military adventure. On October 24, the League of Nations took action, demanding that the Japanese pull back into the railway zone by November 16, but when the deadline passed with no signs of Japanese withdrawal, the League lacked the resolve to take more active measures. Instead, the League Assembly voted, on December 10, to send an investigatory mission to China to consider the situation. Meanwhile, the Japanese army continued its conquest of Manchuria.

The Hoover administration in the United States was no more inclined to confront Japan, confining its response to a note delivered to the Japanese on January 7, 1932. The note expressed what would become known as the Stimson Doctrine, after Hoover's secretary of state, Henry Stimson. It condemned Japanese actions and declared that the United States would not recognize any territory seized through the use of force. Japan appeared unconcerned, establishing the puppet state of Manchukuo on March 9, 1932. The League of Nations adopted Stimson's nonrecognition policy in the same month. The League's inquiry also condemned Japan, and in response the Japanese delegation withdrew from the League in February 1933. Thus, both the League of Nations and the United States failed signally to act in defense of two important treaties—the Nine Power Pact and the Kellogg-Briand Pact—allowing aggression to pay. It was a bad omen for the rest of the decade.

The year 1933 was a crucial one in Europe. At the end of January, the Weimar Republic in Germany finally collapsed, overwhelmed by the crisis of the depression and the millstone of the Versailles treaty. Adolph Hitler, recently appointed chancellor of Germany, pushed the Enabling Act through the Reichstag, giving himself dictatorial powers and inaugurating the Nazi state. In October, Hitler pulled Germany out of both the League of Nations and the disarmament talks under way in Geneva. Committed to rewriting the postwar settlement, Hitler dispensed with negotiations and prepared to take what he wanted. German withdrawal from these international forums presaged a determined assault on the postwar system.

In the early 1930s, as these disturbing events transpired in Europe and Asia, most American women, indeed most Americans in general, paid little attention to foreign policy questions. Instead, they focused on the domestic concerns raised by the Great Depression. However, some women devoted considerable time and effort to the study of international questions, in particular the question of maintaining peace in the world. These women were part of a larger movement embracing what we might call liberal-internationalist ideals. The fundamental characteristic of these ideals was the belief in some kind of system for collective security—in other words, internationalists believed that peace could only be secured through cooperation and consultation among the nations of world. This conviction reflected their belief in the interdependence of nations in the modern world. Nevertheless, within these shared values there was room for considerable disagreement, and the onset of war would help to expose the differences both in terms of philosophy and in terms of their stomach for war.

Many of these women were involved in peace organizations, notably the Women's International League for Peace and Freedom (WILPF). WILPF was founded at the International Congress of Women, an international gathering of peace activists, which met in Zurich in May 1919. In November 1919, the Woman's Peace Party in the United States voted to reconstitute itself as the U.S. Section of WILPF. Its agenda was ambitious and wide-ranging, focusing on issues of human rights and international peace. WILPF condemned the Versailles settlement as an invitation to further war, because of what it saw as the unjust treatment of Germany, and advocated strong support for the League of Nations and universal disarmament.[1] The women of the League shared a common goal of a world without war, but there were frequent disagreements about the best means of attaining that goal. They believed in collective security but had different ideas about how the collective might function to ensure its security. They did not see such disagreements, however, as representing significantly different moral perspectives, and the open discussion and democratic processes used to resolve them were generally seen as a source of strength: a manifestation of the democracy and justice they sought for the whole world.

Peace organizations were not, however, alone in their interest in international relations. Among the many women's groups in the United States in the interwar era, a number stand out—national groups with permanent foreign policy committees—offering a means to explore and understand American women's views on foreign policy. These organizations, founded with a variety of goals and identities, spent the interwar years debating foreign policy, often developing sophisticated foreign policy platforms within their agendas. Women's organizations generally served as an educational forum for their members, providing information and an arena for discussion of the vital issues affecting their interests, from child care and welfare policies through immigration, citizenship, and many other questions.

The League of Women Voters (LWV) was formed in 1920 at the National American Woman Suffrage Association's victory convention. Its primary objective was "to promote the political education of newly enfranchised women citizens."[2] This was a very broad agenda, encompassing many issues, including international relations. The LWV's early membership was, naturally enough, dominated by suffragists, many of whom still occupied leadership positions in the 1930s. The National Council of Jewish Women (NCJW), founded in 1893, was initially intended to increase immigrant Jewish women's understanding of Judaism so that they could work to prevent the erosion of their religious traditions in the New World. Although the character of local chapters varied from place to place, in the early twentieth century the NCJW increasingly took on the role of a social welfare agency, serving the immigrant Jewish community. Its interest in peace arose from concerns about the role of war in creating refugees.[3] The National Women's Trade Union League (WTUL), formed in 1903, was an alliance between middle-class progressive reforming women and working-class women. Although it was the smallest and least national of the groups considered here (its largest and most active local branches were predominantly in the East and Midwest), I have included it because by the 1930s its leadership was dominated by women who had begun their working lives in factories and thus provide a window on working-class attitudes toward foreign policy that is difficult to find elsewhere. Of the groups considered here, it was also the only one with a clear political stand; the others all attempted to pursue a nonpartisan course, but the WTUL was always on the left wing of the American political spectrum, by virtue of its interest in labor questions. The American Association of University Women (AAUW) was created in 1921 with the merger of several women's alumnae associations. These associations had formed over the past thirty years or so with a dual purpose: to promote higher education for women and to provide women graduates with a forum in which to continue to pursue and develop their intellectual interests.

Among the hundreds of American women's organizations of all political persuasions and interests, the groups included here were not necessarily *representative* of American women *generally.* Indeed, the women considered here were predominantly white, educated, middle-class Americans. What all these women's organizations shared, however, was the conviction that world peace could be secured only through a system of international cooperation and law. Participation by the United States in such an international system was, they believed, vital for its success. These assumptions served as the foundation for all their foreign policy positions in the interwar period.

As such, they were typical of interwar liberal internationalist women, pursuing world peace through a commitment to collective security, broadly defined. At its very first convention, in 1920, the LWV supported U.S. membership in the League of Nations. When the U.S. Senate rejected the Treaty of Versailles and membership in the League of Nations in 1920, the LWV temporarily abandoned the idea, but the 1932 convention added the cause of U.S. membership to the program once again, as well as endorsing continued support for U.S. involvement in the World Court.[4] Throughout the 1930s, the LWV emphasized the importance of international cooperation and consultation to preserve peace. Its 1936–38 program called for "a foreign policy of this country, as a non-belligerent nation, which will not obstruct the efforts of other nations to achieve peace" and U.S. "participation in the collective system for the prevention of war, including implementation of the Pact of Paris, and membership in the Permanent Court of International Justice and the League of Nations."[5]

Other women's organizations shared the LWV's faith in and commitment to international cooperation. Rose Schneiderman, president of the WTUL, declared in her report to the national convention in 1936, that "the will for peace without definite establishment of instruments for collective security is a delusion. In the establishment of collective security the United States must play a courageous and definite part. Isolation will not save us from the next war. On the other hand our cooperation with the nations of Europe may save civilization."[6] Schneiderman was an immigrant from Russian Poland who had organized her fellow cap makers into the first female local of the Jewish Socialist United Cloth Hat and Cap Makers' Union in 1903. She quickly developed a reputation as a charismatic speaker, despite her diminutive size—she was only five feet tall—and would play a significant role in the interventionist movement of the late 1930s.[7]

The AAUW also supported collective security. Item 13 of its 1939 program announced its support for the "development of an immediate and long-range foreign policy for the United States based on international cooperation and directed toward . . . support of machinery and measures, both national and international, to promote a world of law and order."[8] Moreover, Dr. Esther Brunauer, associate for international education, was closely involved with the activities of Clark Eichelberger's Committee for Concerted Peace Efforts, an organization formed to promote collective security in 1937. Brunauer, who had a doctorate from Stanford in history and political science, with an emphasis in international relations, had been hired by the AAUW in 1927 to direct the program in international education.[9] Her involvement with the Committee for Concerted Peace Efforts presaged an active part in many interventionist groups as the international crisis deepened in the late 1930s and early 1940s.

Leading members of other organizations that supported collective security were also invited to serve on the Committee for Concerted Peace Efforts in an individual capacity. They included Josephine Schain, chairman of the National Committee on the Cause and Cure of War, and Margaret Forsyth of the Young Women's Christian Association (YWCA). The committee, which became the American Union for Concerted Peace Efforts in 1939, promoted a "peace platform" based on the principles of international cooperation and collective security. Its agenda included economic sanctions against treaty violators, support for the Stimson nonrecognition doctrine, international arms reduction, and reciprocal trade agreements.[10]

The foreign policy committees of women's organizations not only provided educational materials and guidance to members on questions of foreign policy but also liaised with organizations that focused wholly on the issue of peace, such as the National Peace Conference, the National Council for the Prevention of War, and the National Committee on the Cause and Cure of War. These organizations, which were designed to serve as clearinghouses for ideas on peace, united a wide variety of organizations with a common interest in outlawing war. For example, the National Committee on the Cause and Cure of War, led by suffragist Carrie Chapman Catt, brought together eleven different women's organizations to study the reasons for wars and to develop alternative solutions to the international disputes that had traditionally led to war.[11] The centerpiece of its activities was the annual Conference on the Cause and Cure of War held in January of each year, but it also produced a series of informational study kits, named marathon round tables, which covered the major foreign policy questions of the interwar years. The Conference on the Cause and Cure of War attracted delegates from the rank and file of member organizations as well as their foreign policy experts and was intended primarily as an educational forum, although delegates also voted on a program of action to be recommended to the member organizations for the coming year.

Together, these groups provide a fascinating glimpse of the ideas of internationalist American women as the international system began to crumble in the 1930s and the United States hosted an increasingly bitter contest between internationalism and a long-standing American impulse toward isolationism for control of American foreign policy. In the context of deep economic depression and growing international tension, many American legislators sought to isolate the United States from the contagion of foreign wars. This was a particularly popular cause, given the disillusionment and alienation so many Americans felt with the results of their involvement in the Great War.

This disillusionment is perhaps best exemplified by the congressional investigation into allegations that U.S. entry into the war had been engineered by arms manufacturers and financiers in pursuit of profits and protection for their investment in the Allied cause. WILPF, long an advocate of disarmament, had been pushing for such an investigation since the early 1920s. In 1933–34, Dorothy Detzer, national secretary of the U.S. Section of WILPF, played a vital role in lobbying for the establishment of the Nye Committee, charged with investigating the munitions industry and named for its chairman, Gerald P. Nye of North Dakota.[12] She was doubtless assisted by a rush of exposés appearing in print in 1934, including Helmuth Engelbrecht and Frank Hanighen's *The Merchants of Death*, a Book-of-the-Month Club selection, which served to give the accusations a national audience.

The Nye Committee, which met in late 1934 and early 1935, heard testimony from businessmen, historians, and diplomats and concluded that, although there was no hard evidence of a conspiracy to get the United States into the war, American neutrality had been fatally compromised by financial dealings with the belligerent countries. This conclusion would provide a vital foundation for developing a congressional strategy for keeping the United States out of future wars.

Prompted by President Roosevelt, in a meeting on March 19, 1935, the Nye Committee set about drafting legislation based on its findings.

A few days earlier, on March 16, Adolf Hitler had announced plans for full-scale German rearmament, including universal conscription, in defiance of the Versailles treaty, which imposed severe limitations on the size of the German military. At the same time, a crisis was brewing in East Africa. Following a bloody encounter between Italian and Ethiopian forces in December 1934, the League of Nations persuaded Mussolini and the Ethiopian emperor Haile Selassie to agree to arbitration, and the spring and early summer of 1935 saw a series of very tense negotiations that never seemed likely to produce a viable resolution—not least because Mussolini was determined to win military glory for Italy.

In the United States, these events provoked considerable anxiety that another war was brewing across the Atlantic—an anxiety that gave Congress a special incentive to act quickly to protect the nation from the dangers of involvement. In April and May 1935, a series of resolutions were introduced to Congress, designed to keep the United States out of any war that might develop in Europe. They would prohibit American citizens from traveling on belligerent ships or entering war zones; ban loans to belligerent nations; and impose an impartial arms embargo on all nations involved in a war. Cordell Hull, Roosevelt's internationalist secretary of state, was extremely unhappy with these legislative proposals and hoped to prevent their reaching the floor of the Senate. However, Senator Key Pittman, chairman of the Senate Foreign Relations Committee, was less than cooperative, bringing a slightly modified measure to a vote on August 21, 1935. The bill required the president to institute an embargo on the export of arms to all belligerent nations in the event of a war. It also created the Munitions Control Board, with authority to regulate the peacetime traffic in arms, and gave the president the authority to warn U.S. citizens against travel on belligerent ships, if he chose. The Senate passed the bill unanimously. Although his administration had been pressing for executive discretion over imposition of the arms embargo, President Roosevelt accepted the bill, adding only a six-month time limit. Historian Robert Divine has argued that Roosevelt did this in the knowledge that the embargo would operate against Italy in its conflict with Ethiopia and in the hope and expectation that when the bill came up for renewal, he would be able to persuade Congress to allow him discretion over the embargo's application.[13]

The Italian conflict with Ethiopia came to a head in early October, when Italian forces invaded the African country on October 3. Two days later, the Roosevelt administration invoked the Neutrality Act, embargoing arms sales to either side. Since the Ethiopians had little, if any, trade with the United States and none in arms, the embargo did not do much to alter their situation. In Europe, in a final desperate attempt to give the League of Nations some meaning, the League Assembly voted to impose economic sanctions against Italy, prohibiting the export of various important raw materials. Unfortunately, the League's list did not include oil—Italy's most significant requirement. Although the Neutrality Act did not provide for American participation in these sanctions, the Roosevelt administration attempted to support the League's action by calling for a "moral embargo" against raw material exports to the belligerents. None of this was sufficient to undercut the Italian war effort, however, and by May 1936, the conquest of Ethiopia was complete. The abject failure of the League's sanctions demonstrated that organization's impotence in the face of aggression, greatly increasing the likelihood of a future war and reinforcing American determination to isolate the United States from any such conflict.

Even before the final denouement in Ethiopia, the Neutrality Act was set to expire, necessitating a renewed debate over the policy at the start of 1936. The administration developed a new version of the legislation, which kept the impartial arms embargo but added a new measure permitting the president, at his discretion, to limit other trade with the belligerents to prewar levels. This would allow the United States to punish aggressor nations—by imposing the limitations, if that would most affect the aggressor, or not, if the impact would largely fall on the victim. The administration's proposals also included a ban on loans to belligerent nations, to sweeten the pill for the advocates of mandatory measures. However, the new bill faced attack both from opponents of executive discretion and from economic nationalists who opposed any infringement on America's traditional neutral rights to trade freely with nations at war. Throw into the mix angry Italian-Americans, critical of the administration's attitude toward the Ethiopian conflict, and the ranks of the opposition were too strong. Roosevelt had to settle for simple renewal of the existing legislation, with the addition of the ban on loans. This second Neutrality Act was set to expire on May 1, 1937.

Internationalist women shared the administration's concerns about the mandatory character of the neutrality law, but they did not immediately decide to call for revision or repeal. The primary goal of the legislation—to keep the United States out of war—was still a high priority for them. In March 1936, the LWV sent out a "Reference Memorandum on Neutrality," which explained the various developments in neutrality legislation and noted the split among "peace groups" between those favoring mandatory embargoes and those supporting some degree of executive and/or congressional discretion.[14] The memorandum also described the extent and nature of League study and opinion on the neutrality question. Some 1,650 study kits had been distributed in forty states, Hawaii, and the District of Columbia. Each kit contained a short questionnaire which was used to create a picture of League opinion about neutrality.

The results were revealing. There seemed to be a good deal of doubt regarding whether neutrality legislation would actually serve to keep the United States out of war. Members were also concerned that U.S. policy should not obstruct the peace efforts of other nations and that some kind of international consultation to uphold the Kellogg-Briand Pact was desirable. Nevertheless, they also favored the extension of the arms embargo to cover loans, credits, and war materials as a means of keeping the United States out of war. In addition to these areas of consensus among members, the memorandum noted two related questions upon which there was disagreement: whether the executive should have some discretion in the application of neutrality legislation and whether the United States should pursue a policy of discriminating against aggressor nations.[15] These disagreements reflected the split that would emerge between the isolationists and the interventionists once the war had started; between those who placed a higher priority on support for collective security—that is, discriminating against aggressor nations—and those whose first concern was keeping the United States out of war.

The significance of the survey results was pointed out by Anne Hartwell Johnstone, author of the memorandum and secretary of the Department of Government and International Cooperation: "The apparent contradiction among the various study group conclusions as listed above undoubtedly results from the attempt to obtain two ends, first to keep the United States out of war by refusing to have anything to do with other people's quarrels; and second, to continue support of the collective system without willingness to make the fundamental decisions involved which would result in active cooperation for the prevention of war."[16]

Here Johnstone got right to the heart of the matter. In the late 1930s, American internationalists faced an awkward dilemma as they pursued two increasingly incompatible goals—maintaining international peace and keeping the United States out of war. The problem for internationalists was that they believed that U.S. cooperation with other nations for collective security purposes was the best way to accomplish the first goal; but they feared it might also drag the nation into war if collective security failed. The neutrality acts of the mid-1930s began the process of dividing internationalist forces in America into two distinct groups—those for whom collective security was the primary goal and those for whom keeping the United States out of war was most important. The latter group, exemplified by the U.S. Section of WILPF, faced with the looming war in Europe and Asia, would gradually move toward an isolationist stance. In 1936, the LWV was just beginning to come to terms with this dilemma—making the choice for an emphasis on collective security. The memorandum ended by noting that, at the start of 1936, the League had endorsed the administration's neutrality bill, which gave the president the discretion to apply embargoes against aggressors.

A week after the second Neutrality Act was signed into law, Hitler announced that he was sending troops into the Rhineland, an area of Germany along the border with France that the Versailles treaty had established as a demilitarized zone. Neither the British nor the French challenged this decision. The British were preoccupied with their domestic economic problems and were disinclined to object to German revisions of a treaty that they agreed had been too harsh. The French, left out on a limb in 1923 when they had tried to force German fulfillment of their treaty obligations, were disinclined to act without British support. The principles of national sovereignty and self-determination seemed to be on Germany's side in these revision efforts, and so the British government accepted Hitler's changes in the spirit of appeasement. Additionally, some British Conservatives sympathized with Hitler's anti-Semitism and hoped that Germany would serve as a buffer against the Soviet Union, further increasing British disinclination to act.

An apparently much greater threat to the peace of Europe developed a few months later when, on July 18, 1936, a civil war broke out in Spain, initiated by an army rebellion against the left-wing Republican government. The rebel forces, led by the fascist General Francisco Franco, turned immediately to Germany and Italy for aid; in response, the Soviet Union began to supply the Loyalist Republican side. Afraid that the conflict might spread, the British and French embarked on a policy of nonintervention, enlisting the support of all the major European powers—including Germany, Italy, and the Soviet Union—in an arms embargo against both sides. Despite flagrant contravention of the nonintervention agreement by Berlin, Rome, and Moscow, the British and French remained steadfast, denying the democratically elected Republican government of Spain much-needed supplies, and thereby collaborating in the triumph of fascism over democracy in Spain.

The American government was equally complicit. Although the Neutrality Act contained no provision for civil wars, the Roosevelt administration declared a moral embargo against exports to either side in the conflict. This policy pleased both isolationists (who believed it would insulate the United States from any danger of involvement) and internationalists (who saw it as cooperation with European collective security measures). Only the left wing in the United States opposed the administration's stance, seeing the war as a contest between fascism and democracy.

At this point, it seems appropriate to point out that women internationalists and experts on foreign policy were not confined to women's organizations. Some of them can be found in the pages of the nation's newspapers and journals. One such was Freda Kirchwey, owner and editor of the left-wing weekly *The Nation*. Historian Frank Warren has described Kirchwey as a "Russian sympathizer"[17]—a liberal whose commitment to the economic democracy supposedly being created in Russia was such that she overlooked, rationalized, and apologized for the political repression that accompanied the economic change. However, it was Kirchwey's fundamental antifascism that was the key to her attitude toward the Soviet Union and American foreign policy as a whole.[18] Kirchwey's commitment to the cause of antifascism led her to mute her criticism of the Soviet Union, even in the face of the purges of the late 1930s, so as to preserve a united front among the Left.[19] That she was not simply a fellow traveler is clear from her unequivocal criticism of the Nazi-Soviet Pact of August 1939. When American Communists and fellow travelers abandoned Popular Front rhetoric for isolationism after the announcement of the pact, Kirchwey remained an ardent advocate of collective security and, once the war had begun, of aid to the Allies.[20] In the early years of the twentieth century, she had been a peace activist and a member of WILPF. When she joined *The Nation* in August 1918, the magazine had a strong tradition of pacifism. Her left-wing leanings, however, led her to react with great hostility to the threat of fascism, and she never had any doubt that fascism must be resisted.[21] This would lead eventually to a break with *The Nation*'s former editor and columnist, Oswald Garrison Villard.

In 1936, under Kirchwey's guidance, *The Nation* indicted the administration's policy in Spain, arguing that the outcome of the struggle there was of vital concern to Americans: "While the success of the Spanish rebels would not immediately affect our national interest, who can say that the triumph of fascism in Europe would not intimately affect the life of every American? Thus in a very real sense the Spanish workers are battling for American liberties at the same time that they struggle for their own." This is not to say, however, that *The Nation* advocated an interventionist policy at this point. Indeed, the editorial continued, "Interference in the affairs of another nation can bring only woe, but it is at least possible to avoid a policy which plays into the hands of the anti-democratic forces." Moreover, it made a prescient prediction: "Neutrality would be of little avail in a world dominated by fascist doctrines."[22]

Such views had little impact on American policy, however. Indeed, there were elements of American opinion that sympathized strongly with Franco's fascists. The Republican government of Spain contained Communist members and was supported by the Soviet Union. Communists had long been hostile to the church, and the feeling was distinctly mutual. Thus American Catholics saw Franco as a liberator of Spain and a protector of the church against communism, greatly complicating the situation for American policy makers. Chief among Roosevelt's motives for supporting the embargo, however, was his desire to promote the collective action sponsored by Britain and France to avoid a European-wide war.[23] As a result, in January 1937, he backed a congressional resolution imposing an impartial arms embargo in the civil war.

The Nation was quick to point out the practical impact of this policy: "With Hitler openly aiding the insurgents, a general embargo by the United States, like the European non-intervention agreement, would be denying the government the resources of which the rebels are actually availing themselves."[24] Moreover, *The Nation* denounced the whole concept of mandatory neutrality legislation, characterizing it as a positive encouragement for fascist nations to embark on aggressive wars: "We have already moved past the point where neutrality can be considered in terms of a hypothetical next war. The next war is upon us, and it is almost certain that it will be a war of aggression precipitated by Hitler with or without the aid of Mussolini. Ranged against the fascist powers will be France, the Soviet Union, and almost as surely England. It happens that England and France are much more dependent on supplies from the United States than Germany. Any announcement by the United States that it will not under any circumstances furnish the belligerent countries with the sinews of war is an open invitation to Hitler to launch his attack."[25] The reality was that, in a world where nations occupied different geographic positions, had access to different raw materials, possessed different levels of industrial capacity, and relied to varying extents on foreign trade, no policy that treated all alike would actually have a neutral impact.

The Nation's doubts were shared by another important female commentator, Dorothy Thompson—undoubtedly the most influential woman political journalist of the day, with a readership numbering in the millions and a weekly radio show on NBC. She began to write "On the Record" for the *New York Herald Tribune* in 1936 at the request of Helen Rogers Reid, wife of the paper's publisher and a vice president of the board, who wanted "a column about politics, wars, and domestic and international problems written so that women could easily understand it and would not always have to be seeking information from their husbands."[26] Through syndication, Thompson's column reached an audience of some eight to ten million readers across the nation in the late 1930s,[27] and when the *Tribune* dropped "On the Record," it was picked up by the Bell Syndicate and run in more than two hundred newspapers throughout the United States, actually increasing its audience.[28]

Thompson was a staunch conservative on domestic issues, a vigorous critic of the New Deal, and an opponent of Roosevelt until October 1940. She regarded the Neutrality Act as misguided in the extreme. It was, she argued, "indicative of this country's determination to keep out, not only of entangling alliances, but out of any kind of political relations with Europe. This column believes that this is an ostrichlike attitude."[29] In Thompson's view, only a policy of "economic nationalism" akin to Nazi plans for autarky could disentangle the United States from the rest of the world, and few Americans supported such a plan. Indeed, as the expiration date of the second Neutrality Act approached in 1937, the question of preserving American trade took center stage.

The neutrality policy had been designed to ensure that the United States would not be drawn into any new European squabbles by prohibiting the kind of economic ties that many people blamed for U.S. involvement in the last war. However, refusing to trade with nations at war could be costly for the American economy—a sensitive issue in the midst of the Great Depression. The question was, Could American neutrality be protected without sacrificing American economic interests? Bernard Baruch, who had led the War Industries Board during the Great War, believed that it could. He argued that the threat to American neutrality came partly from American merchant ships being sunk; the answer to this danger, he said, was to ban American shipping from war zones. Neutrality was also compromised by the loans and credits that were part of the everyday business of exports and imports, since a defeated nation would be likely to default, tempting American creditors to promote intervention. The 1934 Johnson Act, which forbade private American loans to nations that were in default on their war debt, and the existing Neutrality Act, which made loans to belligerents illegal, dealt with much of this problem. To prevent belligerent nations buying on credit, thereby creating a similar vested interest in their survival, Baruch suggested that they be obliged to pay cash for everything they bought from the United States.

These two elements of the cash-and-carry policy were the most significant additions to the 1937 Neutrality Act. In the event of war, belligerent nations could purchase from the United States raw materials and manufactured goods, other than arms and munitions, only if they paid cash and took the stuff away in their own ships. Thus, no debts owed by belligerent nations could tempt the United States to intervene, nor would attacks on American ships threaten to whip up a war fever among the American people. American neutrality would be safe—and so would the economy. Roosevelt favored the plan, recognizing that in any European war it would give the advantage to Britain and France over Germany because of their greater naval power. (Unfortunately, it also favored Japan over China for the same reason.) However, most internationalists opposed cash-and-carry because it failed to make any distinction between aggressor and victim. And Dorothy Thompson described it contemptuously as a plan to make the United States into a "national Piggly-Wiggly."[30]

The bill had to be flown out to President Roosevelt on May 1—he was on a fishing vacation at the time—so that he could sign it before the previous act expired. Dorothy Thompson derided this urgency in her column about the new act, commenting sarcastically, "Lucky, we might have gotten into war in the fifteen minutes in between."[31] Nor was she much more impressed by the chances that the Neutrality Act would serve the purposes it alleged. "The cruel probability is that if the world went to war we could not more keep out of it than we could out of any of the other world wars since this country was founded. The Atlantic and Pacific oceans do not separate us from Europe and Asia, they connect us."[32]

The 1937 Neutrality Act also exposed the developing schism in *The Nation*'s editorial policy, as the main editorial line diverged from the journal's traditional pacifism, represented by Oswald Garrison Villard, former editor and still a weekly contributor. Villard's argument had two primary elements. One was a fear of the domestic implications of war—basically the belief that the total war of the modern age could not be successfully conducted by a democratic government and that therefore democracy would be sacrificed to the war effort: "If we do get into the next war, it will mean the disappearance of our democracy." The second part of Villard's argument revolved around what would be a frequent isolationist concern—that the democracies of Britain and France were so tainted by their imperialism and their past that they were not much better than the dictatorships and could not be counted upon to be more worthy recipients of American aid than the dictatorships in any war that might develop. "Save the democracies? What editor . . . can know whether the democracies may not be the aggressors for their own selfish ends?" The United States, Villard argued, should focus on preserving democracy at home. "The way to save democracy for us is to keep it intact in the United States, prevent our democracy from turning into a war-time dictatorship, conserve its resources for the benefit not only of our own people but of all peoples after hostilities have ceased. I want the United States to remain a great reservoir of means and strength, especially moral strength, available to put the world on its feet after the next holy war."[33]

The editors of *The Nation* were clearly not convinced by Villard's position, commenting, "We agree with Mr. Villard that our participation in another world war would mean the end of democracy in this country; and we feel that this is the strongest argument for *preventing* such a war. Mr. Villard believes that the neutrality bill guarantees that we will not get into war. We feel, on the contrary, that it offers no real protection to the United States, and that its inconsistency with the principle of collective security greatly increases the likelihood of war abroad. Moreover, any action by the United States at this time declaring a general embargo on war materials would be an open invitation to Hitler to launch an attack, since the latter knows full well the dependence of Britain and France on American supplies."[34] Here was a clear expression of the internationalist conviction that the Neutrality Acts increased the likelihood of war by preventing the United States from playing a role in collective security measures—indeed, even encouraging aggression by rewarding it with an embargo against the victims.

The problem with the mandatory provisions of the Neutrality Act became abundantly clear when the Sino-Japanese War broke out in July 1937. In some ways, this can be seen as the start of the Second World War, since it marked the beginning of the Pacific half of that conflict. On July 7, Japan attacked China north of Beijing, trying to extend its domination of China's economy. The Japanese hoped to create an economic sphere of influence for themselves in east Asia, which they likened to American domination of the Western Hemisphere.

American opinion was deeply divided. Friends of China, like former secretary of state Henry Stimson, called for a boycott of Japanese goods; but American diplomats in Tokyo, led by Ambassador Joseph C. Grew, argued that American criticism of Japan would only exacerbate the situation. Technically speaking, with a war going on in China, Roosevelt should have invoked the Neutrality Act and imposed an arms and loans embargo on both sides, establishing cash-and-carry procedures for all other trade. Unfortunately, this would have hurt the Chinese much more than the Japanese in the circumstances of 1937, since the Japanese navy dominated the Pacific, and its industries were better equipped than China's to support a war effort.

However, since neither the Japanese nor the Chinese had issued a formal declaration of war, Roosevelt adopted a wait-and-see approach and did not invoke the Neutrality Act. The Chinese turned to the League of Nations for relief in mid-September. As the League Assembly considered the issue, Roosevelt stepped up with an intriguing idea, outlined in a speech on October 5 in Chicago. "The present reign of terror and international lawlessness began a few years ago . . . and has now reached a stage where the very foundations of civilization are threatened," he explained. In a world of "international anarchy and instability," he argued, "there is no escape through mere isolation or neutrality." Instead, Roosevelt suggested an approach derived from the medical world: "The epidemic of world lawlessness is spreading.

When an epidemic of physical disease starts to spread, the community approves and joins in a quarantine of the patients in order to protect the health of the community against the spread of the disease." However, Roosevelt failed to elaborate on this idea, ending his speech simply with a declaration of his determination to pursue peace: "There must be positive endeavors to preserve peace. America hates war. America hopes for peace. Therefore, America actively engages in the search for peace."[35] The following day, the League of Nations resolved that Japan was in violation of the Nine Power Pact and the Kellogg-Briand Pact and called on the signatories of those treaties to meet in conference to consider what action to take. For a while at least, it seemed as if the international community might finally be willing to take some meaningful action against aggression.

The problem was that Roosevelt did not actually have any concrete idea in mind when he talked of a quarantine; and neither the British nor the French were willing to take the lead in confronting Japan without assurances of American cooperation. As a result, the conference, which opened in Brussels in early November 1937, failed to agree on any measures to punish the Japanese or assist the Chinese in their resistance. And the Japanese continued their campaign unfettered.

Roosevelt's speech contributed to growing tension between the National Board of the U.S. Section of WILPF and the International Executive chairmen over the question of sanctions, which were precluded by the Neutrality Acts—which the U.S. Section endorsed—but supported by many other national sections of WILPF. Shortly after the so-called quarantine address, the International Executive chairmen wrote to President Roosevelt to congratulate him for the idea, while the U.S. Section roundly condemned him for indulging in empty rhetoric more likely to provoke war than prevent it. Furthermore, the U.S. Section called upon the president to invoke the Neutrality Act in the China incident "as the only 'protective quarantine' for the American people in this crisis and as a first step toward a constructive and peaceful solution to differences."[36] It is scarcely surprising that many international members of WILPF were unimpressed by the idea of a "'protective quarantine' for the American people" as an alternative to a quarantine of aggressor nations.

The Far Eastern crisis raised some very important questions for other internationalist women's organizations as they considered the operation of the Neutrality Act. The decision of many of the major peace groups to demand that the Roosevelt administration invoke the act in regard to the "China Incident" prompted some women's organizations to end their membership. In August 1937, Frederick Libby, secretary of the National Council for the Prevention of War, sent a letter to friends of the cause, asking them to write to the president demanding that he apply the Neutrality Act to the Sino-Japanese conflict.[37] In response, he found that his organization had fewer friends than he imagined. Margaret Stone, assistant legislative representative for the WTUL, wrote back that it was her "firm conviction that if there is to be ultimate peace in the world there must be some sort of punishment for an aggressor nation. Certainly aggression must never be condoned if we hope eventually to wipe out war. Everyone agrees, including yourself, that invoking the neutrality law of the United States would tend to help Japan, the obvious aggressor in the present conflict. I can not believe, therefore, that it is the right thing to do in the circumstances."[38] Stone's rebuke, however, was mild in comparison with the reaction of Carrie Chapman Catt, honorary chairman of the National Committee on the Cause and Cure of War. In December, she wrote a curt letter to Libby asking him to remove her name from the council's letterhead. In it she declared, "I certainly am not on your side. I never did believe in neutrality as it was finally adopted, and I do not believe in its enforcement."[39]

In May 1938, the Executive Committee of the AAUW approved the International Relations Committee's recommendation that they withdraw from the National Council because of its "increasingly isolationist attitude . . . which was strongly at variance with the line of foreign policy which the AAUW is supporting."[40] In her report to the National Board in November, Esther Brunauer noted that the YWCA, the NCJW, the WTUL, and the National Council of Church Women had also withdrawn from the National Council over the past few years.[41] The WTUL withdrew explicitly because of the council's "support of mandatory neutrality."[42]

These organizations clearly understood that an impartial embargo would work directly counter to American interests in the Far East. As LWV National Board member Jeannette Cheek pointed out, invoking the act "would under present circumstances favor Japan over China, both from the point of view of munitions and merchant marine to cash and carry."[43] Moreover, she argued, "Although it is not either the League's business nor the concern of the Neutrality Act to take sides in a given issue, is it improper to point out the aggressor (if the word has any meaning) would be the gainer, and more important from the

State Department's legitimate view of American interest, we would be helping to strengthen the position of the one country in the Far East with whom our interests come in commercial and strategic conflict."[44] From the start of the war in Asia it was clear, at least to some women, that U.S. interests were vitally affected by developments in Asia and that it was neither moral, nor appropriate for American interests, for the United States to attempt to remain neutral, whether by invoking the Neutrality Acts or by taking no action beyond verbal condemnation.

In early March 1938, American attention was abruptly shifted back to Europe by Hitler's absorption of neighboring Austria into a greater Germany. This union, called the Anschluss, represented the first major revision of the Versailles settlement. Unlike German rearmament and the remilitarization of the Rhineland, it was not restoring a past reality—Germany and Austria had never been united. However, it was accepted in Europe under the rubric of German self-determination, and in the United States it provoked no response other than tacit recognition with the withdrawal of the American representative in Vienna.

At this time, preparations were under way for the LWV's biennial convention, to be held in St. Louis in April 1938. Louise Wright, chairman of the Department of Government and Foreign Policy, submitted to the National Board a proposed program item that would give the League explicit convention authorization to support discretionary neutrality legislation. Wright, after beginning her career as an interior decorator, had become a writer and lecturer on foreign policy issues. She was the author of several studies of foreign policy, including a treatise devoted specifically to American neutrality policy published in 1936.[45] Her husband, Quincy Wright, was a professor of political science at the University of Chicago, an early proponent of studies in international law, and a committed internationalist in his own right. However, the board rejected Wright's proposal, passing instead an item that cut out the endorsement of discretion and substituted a desire that the president should consult with other nations.[46] If the National Board was a little timid, however, the membership was rather less so. By mid-1938, indeed, the membership in general seems to have caught up with the thinking of the foreign policy department, although, as one would expect in an organization the size of the League, there remained some disagreement about this issue. But the 1938–40 program, adopted by the convention, endorsed a revised version of item 4 that combined support for executive discretion with international consultation: "Amendment of the Neutrality Act of 1937 to provide, at the discretion of the President, for embargoes on essential war materials and to provide for the application of all embargoes in co-operation with other signatories against those belligerent nations which have violated treaties to which the United States is also a signatory."[47] Here was a clear statement of League members' concern that the United States pursue a collaborative foreign policy that discriminated against aggressor nations. Discretionary embargoes would, the League believed, allow the United States to discriminate against aggressor nations and thus exert a positive influence for peace on the international scene.

Other women's organizations shared the League's concern that the mandatory character of neutrality legislation forestalled any hope of effective international cooperation, although they were not all as explicit in their pronouncements. Early in 1938, the AAUW's Committee on International Relations developed a statement of principle intended to act as a guide for determining which bills the organization should support. It was a study in vagueness: "The Committee on International Relations in discussing the present international situation and the legislative program of the AAUW restates its policy of support of the tendency toward international cooperation for peace rather than those measures which are based on a policy of isolation."[48] Thus, without specifically mentioning either the Neutrality Act or the mechanisms of "international cooperation for peace" that it had in mind, the AAUW aligned itself with internationalism.

In May 1938, Margaret Stone and Elizabeth Christman noted in a letter to the president of the Women's International Conference at Marseilles that the WTUL had been working over the past year for the revision of the neutrality laws "so as to conform with the implied obligations of the United States as a signatory of the Kellogg-Briand Pact."[49] In June 1938, Anne Hartwell Johnstone of the LWV wrote to Secretary of State Cordell Hull, providing him with a copy of the resolutions in favor of neutrality revision passed by five major women's organizations—the AAUW, the National Board of the YWCA, the NCJW, the National LWV, and the WTUL.[50]

In contrast, the U.S. Section of WILPF endorsed the Neutrality Act, but this position did not suit all its members. Indeed, some believed that neutrality in the face of fascism was morally indefensible. In 1938, the Bronx branch withdrew from the organization, declaring, "We believe that taking neither side in a conflict is analogous to helping the stronger side, namely the aggressor." Moreover, they argued that there could be no peace until the Nazi threat had been "eliminated or at least checked."[51] Thus, as early as 1938, some members of WILPF had already confronted the contradictions in their organization's philosophy that had been created by fascism and had chosen to put the cause of freedom before that of peace.

In August 1938, Hitler again expanded his demands and required that the Germans living in the Sudetenland of Czechoslovakia be given self-determination, allowing annexation by the Reich. As the tension built in August and September, Americans were divided—some fearing war and thus clinging more tightly to the imagined protections of neutrality; others advocating major changes in that policy, perhaps to prevent war, but certainly to prevent a repeat of the situations in Spain and China, whereby American policy encouraged and supported aggression. *The Nation* declared on September 17, 1938, "The Neutrality Act adopted in 1936 specifically prevents the shipment of arms and ammunition to belligerents, regardless of whether they are fighting to destroy international law and order or to preserve it, of whether they are aggressors or the victims of aggression."[52] Reacting to German pressure on Czechoslovakia, the editorial recommended trade discrimination against Germany. It also called on Congress to repeal both the Neutrality Act and the Johnson Act as its first order of business. "Neither law has served or can serve the purpose for which it was intended. Both stand in the way of help to possible victims of aggression. Repeal would in no way injure Germany or any other state. But it would serve warning that the United States does not propose to continue to encourage aggression by specifically outlawing aid to the victims of such aggression."[53]

Hitler, British prime minister Neville Chamberlain, French Premier Édouard Daladier and Mussolini met in Munich to discuss German demands. The Czechs were not invited and were essentially sold out by the British and French in these negotiations. Czechoslovakia became a sacrificial lamb in the cause of peace. The end result was that Germany attained the Sudetenland and Chamberlain, who took a leading role in this surrender, returned to England, declaring famously that he had secured "peace in our time."

The United States played no direct role in these negotiations. Although Roosevelt had sent telegrams to all the participants, appealing for a peaceful resolution of the issue, he had also made it quite clear that America would neither take part nor undertake any obligations in defense of any settlement that might be reached. Not all Americans were particularly impressed with the position taken by their government—*The Nation* indicted the administration for its role, for standing by while Chamberlain organized his "shameful sell-out."[54] Munich, however, marked the end of appeasement—during the negotiations, Hitler had repeatedly increased his demands, and this finally set off some warning signals. In October, both Britain and the United States undertook rearmament programs, with Roosevelt asking Congress to appropriate $300 million for national defense.

Internationalist American women regarded events in Europe with concern but hoped that neutrality revision—giving the president discretion in imposing embargoes—might prevent the outbreak of war there. In the Far East, however, conflict was already under way, and since the Neutrality Act had not been invoked, the United States continued to trade freely with Japan, a situation that made many Americans very uneasy. One solution to this problem was separate legislation enacting an embargo against Japan. The supporters of the Japanese embargo staked out their objectives by dubbing themselves the American Committee for Non-Participation in Japanese Aggression. Although the committee was organized before the fashion for cute acronyms, what its name lacked in elegance, it made up for in pointedness. And then to underscore their objections to American policy, they issued a pamphlet in late 1939 entitled "America Supports Japanese Aggression."[55]

Many women internationalists supported the committee's view of the situation. In October 1938, the National Committee on the Cause and Cure of War recommended to its member organizations that they promote legislation to impose an embargo on the sale of war materials to Japan. The recommendation noted that increased U.S. exports of certain goods, such as petroleum and scrap iron, were being used to fuel the Japanese war machine and declared: "At least we may refuse to sell our goods to nations who spurn peaceful settlement but fly to arms. We want no profits from such trade. We want no partnership in such policies."[56] This kind of moral repugnance at being party to and profiting from the war in the Far East was central to the arguments made in support of a Japanese embargo.

The recommendations of the National Committee on the Cause and Cure of War met with a generally positive reaction. The AAUW Board of Directors added a Japanese embargo to the association's legislative program early in 1939. The *AAUW Journal* noted, in explanation of this decision, that "because of the large amount of material being shipped to Japan, the United States is placed in the position of directly aiding Japan to a greater extent than any other nation, while at the same time protesting the aggression."[57] The NCJW also adopted the Japanese embargo as one of three planks in its program of "peace legislation" for the new year, alongside revision of the Neutrality Act and lifting the arms embargo on the democratic government of Spain.[58] The administration, however, failed to act.

The cash-and-carry provisions of the Neutrality Act were set to expire in May 1939, offering yet another opportunity for the nation to consider the wisdom of its neutrality policy. Roosevelt suggested his interest in neutrality revision in his annual message to Congress in January 1939. He opened the address by describing the dangers of the international situation and warning that law-abiding nations could not safely stand by while others defied international law and violated treaties. "They cannot forever let pass, without effective protest, acts of aggression against sister nations—acts which automatically undermine all of us." Roosevelt was clear, however, that he did not envision armed resistance. "The mere fact that we rightly decline to intervene with arms to prevent acts of aggression, does not mean that we must act as if there were no aggression at all. Words may be futile, but war is not the only means of commanding a decent respect for the opinions of mankind. There are many methods short of war, but stronger and more effective than mere words, of bringing home to aggressor governments the aggregate sentiments of our own people."[59] Unfortunately, Roosevelt was not any more specific about what he meant by "methods short of war." But he did indicate that he thought revision of the Neutrality Act was overdue: "We have learned that when we deliberately try to legislate neutrality, our neutrality laws may operate unevenly and unfairly—may actually give aid to an aggressor and deny it to the victim. The instinct of self-preservation should warn us that we ought not let that happen any more."[60]

The Nation welcomed the speech enthusiastically, seeing in it the promise of a change in American policy toward Spain. "'At the very least,' he said, 'we can and should avoid any action, or any lack of action, which will encourage, assist, or build up an aggressor.' If words mean anything, this sentence stands as the strongest possible condemnation of our policy with regard to Spain. . . . He has the power in his hands to make his words effective by raising the Spanish embargo. Hesitation will reduce a magnificent speech to mere wind."[61] But "mere wind" it turned out to be. Roosevelt refused to act on the Spanish embargo; indeed, by this time it was too late to help the Loyalist government in Spain. On February 10, Franco's rebel forces took Catalonia, and little more than two weeks later, the British and French recognized the new Franco regime. The United States waited until the fall of Madrid, extending diplomatic recognition to Franco on April 3. Despite this failure, the notion of "methods short of war" caught the public imagination and would serve as the rallying cry of the interventionist movement during the first eighteen months of the war in Europe.

Before that, however, there was one more peacetime battle to be fought and lost over neutrality revision. In February 1939, Senator Elbert Thomas of Utah proposed two significant amendments to the existing legislation. One added war materials to the embargo; the other allowed the discriminatory use of these embargoes against nations acting in violation of treaties to which the United States was a party. The Thomas amendments embodied the principles of discretion and discrimination advocated by women's organizations and as a result became their most favored revision proposal. They were also endorsed by *The Nation* as the proposed amendments most likely "to give the Neutrality Act that flexibility which it requires if it is to become the instrument of a positive foreign policy."[62]

In the context of the national debate, and in response to a request from the Wisconsin State Branch, the U.S. Section of WILPF undertook a referendum of its membership on the issue of neutrality.[63] Since the national leadership was itself divided on the issue, position papers were drawn up for both sides by prominent members, including Emily Greene Balch, honorary national president (for discretionary neutrality) and Dorothy Detzer, national secretary (for mandatory neutrality).

As a result of Detzer's concern that the question of the Neutrality Act should not be voted on out of context, materials distributed to the membership asked them to debate and vote on two alternative patterns of policies for WILPF: the "international pattern" and the "proneutrality pattern"—commonly referred to as "collective security" versus "neutrality." There was, in fact, a good deal of common ground between the two patterns. Both groups agreed on four basic goals for WILPF, derived from their common moral principles of peace and freedom: "1) To help keep war out of the world; 2) To keep the United States out of war; 3) To preserve democracy; 4) To dethrone fascism."[64] In addition, on a policy level, both groups supported an arms embargo, which would function in peacetime as well as during war, and a foreign war referendum amendment to the Constitution, known as the Ludlow amendment. The "international pattern," however, focused on the first goal—keeping war out of the world—urging a vigorous support of international law: "It is repeatedly stated that the difference between the violence of the would-be empires of Germany, Italy and Japan is only a little greater than the violence of the already existing empires of France and Great Britain, and that therefore the United States should hold entirely aloof. . . . This viewpoint overlooks entirely the basic importance of establishing law as a prerequisite to justice. It puts ends above means. . . . That is a kind of international blackmail and the complete antithesis of establishing law."[65]

The advocates of the "international pattern" believed in an "evolving public conscience," which had already developed to the point of rejecting "imperialistic and aggressive wars." To argue that no distinction should be made between, for example, Czechoslovakia and Germany would be to "suppress . . . this growing social conscience . . . [and tend] to force [people] back into a narrower world with more stress upon expediency and self-interest, and national self-sufficiency."[66] As a result, while the proponents of this view still supported the Neutrality Act, they also favored the Thomas amendments, which would permit the victims of aggression to be exempted from the act's provisions on the approval of both president and Congress. However, they did wish to limit that exemption to nonmilitary materials.

The advocates of the "pro-neutrality pattern," by contrast, adopted the traditional isolationist argument that Britain and France were "empires first," and that the brewing conflict in Europe was an "age-old struggle of rival empires." They argued that the "real way the United States could help keep war out of the world would be by striving to organize a world government, . . . by trade agreements with other nations, and by helping in every constructive way possible to deal with the basic factors making for world chaos."[67] They did not reject the international cooperation for peace advocated by supporters of the "international pattern"; rather, their vision of such cooperation was more idealistic and less grounded in contemporary reality. Elements of isolationist arguments were also evident in their suggestions for keeping the United States out of war. It was, they argued, "a question primarily of will." American economic power, particularly if the whole Western Hemisphere could be kept out of war, was such that the United States could survive the loss of international trade with "only approximately $1\frac{1}{2}$ million people . . . affected directly and indirectly by the dislocation, . . . [and t]he United States could spend money in subsidies to those industries losing money by the dislocation instead of spending the money in war."[68]

Advocates of the "international pattern" were less sanguine about the chances of the United States remaining aloof from a European war, advocating the adoption of the Ludlow amendment for a war referendum and greater education about "the causes, methods, and results of war," but concluding that "there is no assurance of keeping the United States at peace except by keeping war out of the world."[69] This was all very well, but in the context of early 1939, as war in Europe looked increasingly likely, this basis for keeping the United States out of war was rather more idealistic and less grounded in contemporary reality than that of the "pro-neutrality" advocates.

Thus, while the specific policy differences involved in the debate seemed to boil down to the mandatory or discretionary implementation of embargoes, the split among WILPF members reflected a deeper difference of moral perspective, with some members looking at the world from a global viewpoint from which the highest priority appeared to be preventing *any* wars through collective action by the international community, and others adopting a more American-centered perspective, from which keeping the United States out of war seemed to be the first order of the day. The advocates of the "international pattern," or collective security, would show much greater sympathy and support for the Roosevelt administration's foreign policy toward Europe than the proponents of the "pro-neutrality pattern," who would increasingly find themselves in an uncomfortable alliance with the isolationists.

The results of the poll showed a clear majority—75 percent of those voting—in favor of the "pro-neutrality pattern," and this decision was endorsed at the 1939 annual meeting by a vote of 95 to 10.[70] The "pro-neutrality pattern," and thus the policy of the U.S. Section, while paying sincere lip service to international cooperation and plans for world government, was clearly focused on keeping the United States out of war and was, therefore, a more meaningful stance for the U.S. Section of WILPF once war actually broke out in Europe in September 1939. It did, however, make it increasingly difficult for the U.S. Section to maintain the moral high ground as the issue of war or peace was muddied by the moral implications of the growing destruction in Europe.

Meanwhile, the 1939 Conference on the Cause and Cure of War came to a different conclusion. The delegates there launched a damning attack on the Neutrality Act, which served as the first strike in a major campaign for neutrality revision involving six national women's organizations. The conference issued a "Call to Action," which declared: "The Neutrality Act has failed of its purpose. It was designed to keep the United States out of war and to prevent war. It has brought the United States nearer to involvement in war. It has served to give aid to treaty-breakers and war-makers."[71] The delegates requested member organizations to push for revisions that would add war materials to the embargo and allow for discriminatory application of embargoes to aggressor nations. They also called upon these organizations to demonstrate to Congress the extent of public support for such revisions. Moreover, the "Call to Action" pointed to the Far Eastern crisis and the Spanish civil war as issues that required immediate attention, calling for an end to the embargo on Spain and suggesting specific legislation aimed at embargoing Japan as possible alternatives, though not preferred, to general revision of the Neutrality Act.

On March 15, 1939, the appeasement mentality was finally shattered, at least in European nations, when Hitler sent German troops into the rump of Czechoslovakia, occupying Prague. Germany had no conceivable claim there—no self-determination defense to offer. The appeasers had acquiesced in his one-sided revisions of the Versailles treaty on the basis that the postwar settlement had been excessively harsh and his demands were only understandable attempts to produce a more equitable result. The seizure of Czechoslovakia, however, finally demonstrated that Hitler's ambitions could not be satisfied by revising Versailles. Rather, he sought to overturn the settlement completely, creating a new European order dominated by Germany. His next target seemed likely to be Poland—specifically the Polish corridor that divided the German nation; and the old German city of Danzig that Versailles had designated a free city under League of Nations' supervision. So, on March 31, 1939, Britain and France guaranteed Polish independence against German attack.

The seizure of Czechoslovakia also had a chilling effect on opinion in the United States, adding considerable urgency to the debate over neutrality that once again occupied Congress as the expiration of the cash-and-carry provisions of the 1937 act drew near. Isolationists, scenting the approaching war, were more determined than ever to protect the fundamentals of the legislation. Senator Burton Wheeler of Montana, a Democrat, expressed the basic isolationist instinct when he insisted that Americans "mind our own business."[72] In the context of this crisis, Freda Kirchwey began to sign her own editorials in the pages of *The Nation.* In response to Wheeler, in mid-April 1939, Kirchwey attempted to define what America's business was: "To me it seems obvious that it is our business to prevent freedom from perishing from the earth. . . . our statesmen should turn directly to the job of finding where democracy still shows a determination to survive and there to lend it aid." The aid she had in mind was a boycott of the Axis nations. In a striking foreshadowing of Roosevelt's famous description of the United States as the "great arsenal of democracy," Kirchwey declared, "Today the United States is the grand arsenal for triumphant fascism. . . . It is our business to stop providing these three great aggressors with arms and the goods necessary to the manufacture of arms and the conduct of war."[73]

Where Kirchwey and internationalist women's organizations advocated revision of the Neutrality Act, Dorothy Thompson supported outright repeal, which would leave the nation free to respond to international developments in whatever way seemed most likely to promote American interests. The most important thing, in her view, was for the United States to retain its "freedom of action" in the international arena. "Therefore," she argued, "we ought to repeal the neutrality bill. . . . We ought to repeal it because through it we restrict our own actions, in a world where we cannot possibly know what is going to happen from one day to the next."[74] Thompson could also take a pragmatic view, however, and in June she backed Secretary of State Cordell Hull's proposals for revision (no loans, no American travel, no American ships in war zones, and transfer of the title for all exports before they left the United States) as the best available alternative to the existing legislation, which she described as "lamentable." In particular, Thompson rejected the arms embargo: "An embargo on arms to all belligerents, as provided for in the present neutrality act, puts us in the position of adopting a rigid policy regardless of what the national interests may or may not be. It cuts off the industrial resources of the United States from those countries which are weakest, which have no great arms industries of their own, which are most unlikely to attack anyone, and most likely to be attacked. It is inconsistent, even in this, for it does not make it mandatory to forbid the sale of all essential war materials, and thus is discriminatory against our own industries."[75] But Hull's proposals lacked the key idea of discretion—all belligerents would be treated alike. So most internationalist women continued to favor the Thomas amendments.

The Thomas amendments were also promoted by the renamed American Union for Concerted Peace Efforts (AUCPE), which designated the week of April 26 to May 3 "National Security Week" to publicize the amendments and build public support for revision. An AUCPE flyer demanded, "Protect Our National Security, No More Aid for Aggressors!"[76] and asked people to write to their congressmen in support of the amendments.

Six national women's organizations cooperated in the publication of a similar pamphlet, which declared, "Under the Neutrality Act as now written we must either retreat before aggression and violence in a crisis or resort to war. There is no middle road. There is no room for positive measures short of war."[77] The idea of "positive measures short of war" foreshadowed the position of women's organizations in the early months of the war when they favored aid to the Allies, but still with limitations. The same six organizations also combined to submit joint testimony to the Senate Foreign Relations Committee hearings on neutrality. On April 7, representatives of the AAUW, the General Federation of Women's Clubs, the National Board of the YWCA, the NCJW, the National LWV, and the WTUL met to discuss what Louise Wright, their chosen representative, should say to the Senate committee on April 13.[78]

Her testimony, Wright declared, embodied the conclusions of years of study and discussion within these organizations. She affirmed their belief that peace could best be secured by encouraging respect for international law and that this required some kind of penalty for those who violated their treaty obligations. The Neutrality Act, she argued, failed to achieve this end and, thus,

> in the present form thwarts the desire of the American people for peace and security. . . . Three times the principles of the neutrality act have been tried and found wanting. Three times the United States has unexpectedly found itself a silent partner of the aggressor. The organizations I [represent] believe that the American interests of peace and security are served by having a foreign policy which contributes to respect for law rather than arbitrary use of force in international affairs. As one means of achieving this end they advocate discrimination against treaty violators. . . . Furthermore, we are convinced that those who violate treaties should not be given assurance in advance by Congress that they may commit aggression with impunity so far as the United States is concerned.[79]

This indictment combined a moral rejection of neutrality as a policy that undermined international law and order and encouraged aggression with the pragmatic criticism that the law as it stood had not in practice been neutral at all but had served the interests of aggressor nations. Wright continued by considering the various amendments before the committee, rejecting outright repeal, since that would eliminate the Munitions Control Board, which all six organizations endorsed. She also discarded Senator Pittman's proposal to repeal the arms embargo in favor of a cash-and-carry provision, since it did not incorporate the idea of discrimination against aggressors, and, although it would favor Britain and France in Europe, it would also favor Japan in the Far East.[80]

Instead, Wright endorsed the Thomas amendments as best representing the views of the organizations she represented—extending the embargo on arms to include war materials and establishing the principle of discrimination.[81] Thus, six major national women's organizations expressed their support in April 1939 for the principle that would, once the war had started, lead them to support increasing measures of intervention. By the time the United States entered the war, most of them had endorsed all-out material aid for the Allies, some had advocated convoying, and one had accepted the idea of direct military involvement. However, in 1939, they endorsed the principle of discrimination because it seemed the most likely way to secure peace.

In this view, they were joined by Freda Kirchwey, who nevertheless had a more daring and proactive approach in mind. She not only supported revision of the Neutrality Act to allow the president to discriminate against aggressors, but also called for a policy of economic sanctions against Germany, Japan, and Italy.[82] The Tariff Acts of 1930 and 1934 gave the president authority to retaliate against nations that imposed restrictions on American imports. Kirchwey argued that "both Germany and Japan, the chief treaty-breaking states, have gone so far in high-handed action against American trade that the President could legally ban their imports completely. . . . In view of the economic weakness of the aggressor states, it is possible that a sweeping embargo on American economic assistance might turn the tide of world events. Japan certainly cannot go on without American aid. Germany and Italy are not quite so dependent on the United States, but they might well hesitate to plunge the world into war if they were denied American scrap iron and other materials essential for war making."[83] Kirchwey still hoped that an effective display of solidarity on the part of the antifascist states might preempt fascist aggression—the best way to avoid American involvement in a war was to prevent the outbreak of that war in the first place. Both the advocates of collective security in WILPF and the other internationalist women's organizations shared this basic conviction. In a world at war, American peace would be almost impossible to preserve. Thus, to keep the United States out of war, war had to be prevented everywhere.

Louise Wright's claim to represent the members of the six women's organizations did not go unchallenged. On May 1, 1939, the *New York Times* published a letter from Edith Abbott, dean of the Graduate School of Social Service Administration at the University of Chicago. Abbott, a charter member of the LWV and longtime member of the AAUW, charged that the officers of these organizations "clearly have no evidence that the members of their organizations share the opinions of [Wright]. On the contrary, the women of these organizations, like other women in America, hope and believe that the Neutrality Act will be extended and strengthened, as the only way at the present time that will make it possible for America to remain outside the battle lines of Europe."[84] Given that Abbott also claimed that the members had had no opportunity to express their opinions on the subject, her assumption that they actually agreed with her rather than Wright is interesting and perhaps reflects the belief, very common at the time, that women would naturally advocate whatever course was most likely to ensure peace above any other consideration, and that that course was undisputed and quite clear to any observer.

Significantly, other LWV members did not share Abbott's belief that she really represented League opinion. As Anne Talbot Donaldson, state president of the New York LWV pointed out to her in a letter on May 8, the 1938–40 program of the League endorsed such amendments to the Neutrality Act, and of the some four hundred delegates at the 1938 convention only about twenty voted against that item of the program. Moreover, Donaldson noted that at the recent General Council meeting in April 1939 in Washington, D.C., she had been quite alone in supporting an extension rather than the repeal of the embargo provisions of the Neutrality Act. She concluded that "if there is a majority or even a fair minority of members who agree with my pacifist point of view, they are singularly inarticulate."[85] Similarly, the AAUW Committee on International Relations reported to the Board of Directors at the end of May 1939 that some 215 branches had been active in support of the Thomas amendments.[86]

The General Council meeting that Donaldson referred to had endorsed a significant shift in the League's neutrality policy by abandoning the requirement for international consultation in the application of discriminatory embargoes. In some ways this was a move away from the collective security principles which the League endorsed. But it was also a vital step toward an interventionist position because it authorized the League to support *unilateral* action by the United States. Once the war in Europe had begun, the United States would be the only power in a position to provide meaningful aid to the Allies that was not already in some way involved in the conflict.

The requirement of international consultation adopted at the 1938 convention had caused the Board of the Directors and the Department of Government and Foreign Policy some problems in shaping League activities on the neutrality question. In November 1938, they had decided that this requirement of the program precluded League support for a Japanese embargo.[87] Early in 1939, when the Thomas amendments were under consideration, Marguerite Wells had acknowledged that these measures did not provide for the consultation required under the program but had explained League endorsement nonetheless on the basis that the determination of treaty violation was generally an international question, and, therefore, such consultation was implied by the embargo amendment.[88] League leaders, however, were conscious that this was a bit of a stretch. As a result of these problems and the nature of the developments in the international situation, the Board of Directors decided, in April, to present the General Council with a revised version of the embargo item of the League's program.[89] The new program items authorized discriminatory embargoes without the need for international consultation. This would give the League a free hand to advocate aid to Britain and France once the war in Europe had begun. Moreover, more immediately, it meant that the League could endorse the Thomas amendments unreservedly.[90]

However, the Thomas amendments were not the only revisions under consideration. Senator Pittman suggested the repeal of the arms embargo and the extension of cash-and-carry to all exports, including arms. However, Pittman's procrastination and unreliable leadership in the Senate eventually persuaded the administration to turn to Representative Sol Bloom, acting chairman of the House Committee on Foreign Relations, as a sponsor for revision. The bill that Bloom introduced into the House of Representatives on May 29, 1939, amounted to a sort of discretionary cash-and-carry: it repealed the arms embargo and instituted cash-and-carry trade with belligerents, but it gave the president discretion as to whether to invoke the act, to designate combat zones, outside of which the "carry" restriction would not be operative, and to determine what kind of goods would be so restricted.

The Bloom bill was not as good a match with the principles of the women's organizations pursuing revision as the Thomas amendments, but given that the latter apparently had no chance of passage, it seemed the best possible result. Although it did not embrace the idea of discriminating against aggressive nations explicitly, it gave the president a good deal of discretion; in the European context it would operate to the advantage of Britain and France over the Axis, and this seemed, in mid-1939, to be the best hope of forestalling further Axis aggression. The LWV noted that the bill "in no way recognizes the principle of discriminatory action against treaty violators [but i]t is a practical solution of the problems created by our present Neutrality Act, and is probably the only proposal that has a chance of being passed by Congress."[91] Similarly, the NCJW acknowledged that the bill did not make the distinction between aggressor and victim that the council wanted but argued that it would help Britain and France in Europe and that separate legislation should also be pursued to deal with the situation in the Far East, specifically the Pittman-Schwellenbach resolutions calling for an arms embargo on nations in violation of the Nine-Power Treaty regarding China.[92]

However, isolationists in the House, led by John Vorys of Ohio, succeeded in sabotaging the Bloom bill on June 29 by adding an amendment that restored the mandatory arms embargo. When the Senate Foreign Relations Committee met on July 11 to consider the cash-and-carry provisions, it instead voted to postpone consideration of neutrality until the next session of Congress began in 1940 and the campaign for neutrality revision collapsed. This left the United States with, in Freda Kirchwey's view, "two foreign policies, an Executive policy and a Congressional policy. . . . One is based on the assumption that the United States can best protect its interests by withdrawing as completely as possible from foreign commitments in case of war. The other is based on the assumption that a general war may easily involve the United States and that the best hope of peace lies in strengthening the anti-aggression forces in Europe with the promise of arms and other war materials."[93]

Despite the failure of the campaign for neutrality revision in mid-1939, the women's organizations involved hoped that attempts in the next session would be more successful, and the LWV optimistically noted an apparent swing in favor of discretionary legislation across the nation.[94] Moreover, while internationalists did not get the embargo against Japan that many of them were hoping for, the administration did announce, on July 26, 1939, that it did not intend to renew the trade treaty that existed between the United States and Japan. This would allow the United States to wield economic weapons against Japan, which many internationalists hoped would force the Japanese to reconsider their expansionist agenda. From the start, Louise Wright had been optimistic that Japanese expansion could be curbed with a little flexing of American economic muscle. In October 1937, Wright had commented to Marguerite Wells on the subject of possible economic penalties for Japanese conduct: "If these follow the line of the sanctions imposed against Italy there would be prohibition of imports and some exports and no financial assistance. Such a policy if carried out with vigor ought to have a crippling effect upon Japan."[95] While not exactly constituting punishment of aggression, the abrogation of the 1911 trade treaty with Japan at least opened the door for some kind of punitive action by the United States.

Before any such action could be taken against Japan, however, the international situation would be turned upside down by the outbreak of war in Europe. On August 22, 1939, the Germans and Soviets finalized the terms of the Nazi-Soviet Pact, a nonaggression pact that freed Hitler to embark on the conquest of Poland, without fear of facing a two-front war. The implications of the pact were not lost on American observers. *The Nation* described it as a "colossal diplomatic victory" for Germany and condemned the Soviet Union—"it has timed this rapprochement with Nazism for the moment when Hitler will derive the greatest possible benefit from it."[96] The agreement effectively sealed Poland's fate. As Anne O'Hare McCormick commented, "The Nazi-Soviet alliance is a merger of the forces of destruction."[97]

McCormick is the last of the women journalists considered here. She was born in England, but her family emigrated to the United States when she was still very young. She began her career as a journalist in Cleveland and Dayton before landing a job writing freelance for the *New York Times* in 1921. She traveled widely in Europe with her husband and sent numerous dispatches back to New York, thereby establishing her position with the *Times*. However, it was not until 1935 that *Times* publisher, Arthur Hays Sulzberger, asked her to join the editorial board, declaring: "You are to be the 'freedom' editor. It will be your job to stand up and shout whenever freedom is interfered with in any part of the world."[98] Her thrice-weekly column began on February 1, 1937. In the same year, she won a Pulitzer Prize for journalism for her "distinguished foreign correspondences."[99] Her interventionist views were generally implicit rather than explicit, her columns descriptive rather than prescriptive.

McCormick's politics are rather difficult to determine, especially given her descriptive style. Reporter James "Scotty" Reston, in an introduction to a collection of her columns published in 1956, commented: "I remember her showing up at the 1952 Republican convention wearing a lovely white silk dress with tiny Democratic donkeys on it, and appearing the following week at the Democratic convention in another white silk dress with small blue Republican elephants."[100] However, while her party politics may have been in doubt, her conviction that international developments were of vital importance for the United States was very clear.

At the end of August 1939, Europe stood on the brink of war. American foreign policy remained a prisoner of neutrality legislation designed to deal with an earlier conflict. Women internationalists had fought hard, but in vain, to modify the Neutrality Act to allow the United States to play a meaningful role in preventing war by promising to throw its weight behind the victims of aggression. When the depth of their failure became clear in early September 1939 with the outbreak of war in Europe, they reoriented themselves to the new situation. Now, before they could hope to secure a lasting peace through collective security measures and respect for international law, the aggressor nations, which had shown such contempt for that law, had to be defeated. So most American women internationalists worked to promote aid to the Allies at the start of the European war.

3

Rethinking Neutrality

"Until yesterday the crisis had the quality of a nightmare. . . . it was like . . . a projection in a dark room of the horror that has now taken shape and stalks the earth as a living thing."[1] Thus, Anne O'Hare McCormick responded to the outbreak of war in Europe. On September 1, 1939, at 4:45 A.M., German forces had invaded Poland. The Luftwaffe took the Polish air force largely by surprise, destroying most of its planes before they could get airborne. Before the end of the first day, the Germans had undisputed control of the air. Progress on the ground was equally rapid. Reaction in the United States was somber. Freda Kirchwey believed that the German assault on Poland had finally laid to rest any idea of negotiating with Hitler: "For back in the mind of almost every listener is the cold realization that no peace can be made with Adolf Hitler. . . . War would be preferable to another deal with Hitler."[2] And war was what the world got. On the morning of September 3, the ultimatums issued by Britain and France in accordance with their guarantee of Polish independence expired, and Britain and France declared war on Germany.

On the night of September 3, Americans sat down in front of their radios to hear what their president had to say about the crisis. Roosevelt's speech was carefully designed to appeal to Americans' inclination toward the Allied side, without exacerbating their fear of war. "Let no man or woman thoughtlessly or falsely talk of America sending its armies to European fields. . . . This nation will remain a neutral nation, but I cannot ask that every American remain neutral in thought as well. Even a neutral has a right to take account of facts. Even a neutral cannot be asked to close his mind or close his conscience. . . . I hope the United States will keep out of this war. I believe that it will. And I give you assurance and reassurance that every effort of your government will be directed toward that end. As long as it remains within my power to prevent, there will be no blackout of peace in the United States."[3] Two days later, Roosevelt invoked the Neutrality Act, bringing into effect an embargo on arms and loans to the belligerents in Europe.

With the outbreak of war, internationalist American women's organizations looked to the future, emphasizing the crucial role that the United States would play in the creation of a more lasting peace when the conflict was over. As Marguerite Wells declared in a statement to LWV state presidents: "War has come to Europe. At its end will come America's opportunity to help. Whatever way war ends, the United States should be prepared to help with peace plans that include a workable system of collective security against more war."[4] Similarly, the NCJW's Committee on International Relations and Peace issued a statement of policy in the first weeks of the war declaring, "Preparation for our new efforts for world organization—this is a major part of our peace work now."[5] A fundamental part of any hopes for the postwar world, however, was the need for an Allied victory, and interested women's organizations would soon have more immediate goals to pursue.

On September 13, Roosevelt summoned a special emergency session of Congress to consider the question of neutrality revision, specifically, repeal of the arms embargo. In response, congressional isolationists, calling themselves the "peace bloc," began a concerted campaign to prevent significant changes in the legislation.[6] The first step was a nationwide radio address by Senator William E. Borah on September 14, broadcast by NBC. The speech set out first of all to challenge the idea that the United States could not realistically hope to remain isolated from the conflict in Europe. "Though we seek no people's territory, nevertheless, because Europe is 'near,' we must sacrifice the savings of our people and the sons of our mothers in this endless imperialistic strife. . . . What a fateful doctrine to propose! Let us renounce it and make the effort at least to establish freedom from the European system."[7] Borah further sought to cast the debate as one over military intervention in the war, appealing to the solid majority of the public who opposed such intervention. This would become a standard isolationist device, as they resisted each administration measure to assist the Allies. With it, they played to their one great strength—the tremendous reluctance of the American people to become directly, and militarily, involved in the war. Borah demanded of the advocates of repeal: "Is it not your main purpose in securing repeal to enable us to furnish arms, munitions and implements of war to one group of nations and to deny them to another group of nations, which groups are now in mortal combat? Is not this laying the foundation for intervention—in fact, is it not intervention—in the present European war? . . . I feel we are really considering in this debate the broad question of whether we are justified as a people in intervening in this conflict and meet the issues as they are being presented upon the battle fields of Europe, for we cannot escape that destination if we move along the lines now proposed."[8]

Advocates of revision attempted to counter such tactics both by focusing on what they saw as the larger issues at stake in the war and by rejecting the assertion that repeal of the arms embargo would effectively bring an end to neutrality. Dorothy Thompson, always among the most forthright of interventionists, subjected Borah's speech to a searing attack in her column. In particular, Thompson highlighted the great weakness of the arms embargo as an international peace policy. While at peace, potential aggressor nations were free to prepare themselves for war by buying anything they needed from the United States; then once they were ready and launched their attack, they could relax in the knowledge that their victims would not have the same access to the productive resources of the United States as they struggled to defend themselves. As Thompson put it: "Britain and France have not poured the entire energies of their people for five long years into nothing else than building a war machine. For that we are to penalize them! . . . The Senator and the so-called peace bloc are doing this country and its peace a great disservice when they spread at home and abroad the idea that to repeal the embargo on arms constitutes a violation of neutrality. They are arguing that a return to the traditional practices of international law is an act of war. . . . To be a neutral nation in this war does not mean that we bury our wills and our conscience for its duration or keep legislation to aid aggression, oppression and revolution."[9]

Thompson also rejected Borah's failure to recognize that the new war was significantly different from the last. "Senator Borah, throughout his Thursday speech, was talking not about the war, but about 20 years ago. . . . The frontiers of reason and justice, Senator, are on the Rhine. Whether or not they were there in 1917 is no longer pertinent. That is where they are today."[10] This, however, was by no means apparent to the isolationists, who typically characterized the conflict as one in a long line of power struggles within Europe.

On September 15, the "peace bloc" deployed one of its most prominent supporters, when Colonel Charles Lindbergh entered the debate with a radio broadcast appealing for isolation from the European war. In this, his first speech on foreign policy, he made no explicit reference to the issue of neutrality revision, focusing instead on the broader question of the importance of the war to the United States. "This is simply one more of those age-old struggles within our family of nations—a quarrel arising from the errors of the last war—from the failure of the victors of that war to follow a consistent policy either of fairness or of force."[11]

Interventionists, naturally enough, disagreed. The day after Lindbergh's speech, Anne O'Hare McCormick noted in her column, "Already it is clear that this war is on a different plane and in a different dimension from the last war."[12] Freda Kirchwey considered the comparison important enough to devote a whole editorial to debunking it. "The new war has old causes," she acknowledged. "It has roots in the age-long desire of Germany to become a world power equal to Britain; it has fresher roots in the Versailles treaty. . . . But its nearer causes lie in the Nazi doctrine of corrupt and despotic force."[13] Similarly, Thompson argued that the war was not a power struggle but a struggle of civilizations: "This is not . . . a war of rival imperialisms. It is a revolutionary war. Its object is not to effect reasonable adjustments which will give greater justice to nations suffering from a lack of raw materials and commercial outlets. Its object is to change the whole structure of human society, to destroy all existing Western forms of political and economic organization and to substitute for them a new model which will not retain a remnant of what since Greece and Rome has been known as Western civilization."[14]

Thompson, indeed, was just at the beginning of a lengthy campaign against isolationist leaders at whom she leveled frequent personal attacks. Lindbergh was a favorite target. In this first speech, he had called upon Americans to be wary of propagandists and their motives: "We must learn to look behind every article we read and every speech we hear. We must not only inquire about the writer and the speaker—about his personal interests and his nationality—but we must ask who owns and who influences the newspaper, the news picture and the radio station."[15] Predictably, Thompson exploited the opportunity thus created to inquire about Lindbergh's background in a column entitled "Col. Lindbergh and Propaganda." She noted his long sojourn in Europe during the 1930s, the medal he had received from the German government less than a year before, and his admiration for the Nazi air force, commenting that "Col. Lindbergh's inclination toward fascism is well known to his friends."[16] Such ad hominem attacks would become increasingly common from both sides over the next two years.

As the debate gathered pace, interested women's organizations considered how best to respond. On September 19, the NCJW declared its commitment both to keeping the United States out of the conflict and to revising the Neutrality Act: "Another major part of our program will be support of such revisions of the neutrality legislation as will minimize the danger of our country being involved in war and withhold aid to nations that are resorting to war in violation of their pledged word, and attempting to settle grievances by forceful means."[17] Indeed, those women's organizations which had advocated neutrality revision in mid-1939 continued to do so in the fall. However, they did so with a significant difference. In the spring, they had demanded revisions that would allow the president discretion to apply the embargo provisions of the act against aggressor nations and not against their victims. In the fall, the cause of discretion was sacrificed to practical considerations—how best to secure changes that would help Britain and France, given the climate of American public opinion—and a natural desire to keep out of the conflict. Discretionary legislation had been rejected, but American policy might still be formulated to benefit Britain and France rather than Germany. The LWV announced on September 19 that it would support "revision of the Neutrality Act by repeal of the present embargo section and substitution of provisions for the control of all trade under restrictions of 'cash-and-carry' or some similar proposal for trade under conditions that tend to safeguard the United States."[18]

A few days earlier, Marguerite Wells had sent out a long letter to the members of the League's National Board asking for their views on neutrality revision. The letter outlined two possible interpretations of the League program and how each might be reflected in a policy on neutrality. The first interpretation emphasized the League's commitment to "international cooperation to prevent war."[19] It would allow support for repeal of the arms embargo on the basis that it would, in effect, discriminate against the aggressor in the European war and therefore serve to promote respect for international law. Cash-and-carry could be supported on the same basis, but not "taking the program logically and literally, merely for the purpose of making more certain that our war trade does not risk getting the United States into war."[20] The second interpretation noted the changed conditions brought on by the outbreak of war and emphasized the importance of keeping the United States out of the war. Under this interpretation, Wells noted, the League could support cash-and-carry as a policy designed to reduce the danger of "incidents" that might draw the United States into the war, with the added bonus that it favored the Allies, whose victory would make a return to international order more likely.

The point at issue here was not the policy that the League would support—there was no question that it would back repeal of the arms embargo—but rather *the basis upon which the League would argue for that policy.* Would the League prioritize discrimination against aggressor nations or keeping the United States out of the war? The vote was very close. Six board members favored the first interpretation, and eight chose the second.

Significantly, those who preferred the first interpretation also advocated outright repeal of the arms embargo rather than the substitution of cash-and-carry, clearly showing their adherence to the principle of discriminating against aggressors. Jeannette Cheek declared herself "immediately for raising the arms embargo. Further, if it were governed in choice only by logic and honesty, against cash and carry, i.e., we would participate to that extent too, carry the pig to market."[21] Thus, Cheek expressed unequivocal support for the Allied cause, advocating not merely the sale of arms to Britain and France but also American involvement in the delivery of those arms. Since this would expose American ships to attack by German U-boats, and thus open the United States up to the possibility of direct military involvement in the war, Cheek had clearly already abandoned any desire for American neutrality. However, she also recognized that the American public was not yet ready to go this far and suggested that it "might be wise for the League to support cash and carry if that is the price of raising the embargo."[22]

Clearly some members of the National Board were much more intimidated than others by the possibility of American involvement in the war. Cash-and-carry was a theoretically neutral policy, which, because of Allied naval power, would operate in the European context in favor of Britain and France; but it was not the policy of discriminatory embargoes that the League had advocated earlier in the year and that now seemed to eight members of the board much more dangerous—too dangerous even. These board members feared that a discriminatory embargo might lead to U.S. entry into the war, either by provoking a German declaration of war or by exposing American shipping in the Atlantic to attacks, which might create public support in the United States for war.

As a result of the board's decision, Marguerite Wells wrote to state League presidents on September 19, asking for their support for repeal of the arms embargo and the adoption of cash-and-carry "or some similar proposal for trade under conditions that tend to safeguard the United States."[23] Thus, the primary reason offered by the LWV for supporting cash-and-carry was that it would reduce the danger of U.S. entry into the war. However, the knowledge that this policy would also aid Britain and France made things much easier for the National Board. Indeed, given the strong support among board members for discriminating against aggression, it is possible, even likely, that had cash-and-carry not served the dual purpose of aiding the Allies and protecting the United States from dangerous incidents at sea, the board would have voted simply for repeal.[24] As it was, some board members were concerned that the cash-and-carry policy would also favor Japan in the Far Eastern conflict, but, in a striking indication of the greater importance attached to the European war by League leaders, the board argued that separate legislation should be developed to deal with that problem.[25] When it came to neutrality revision, the interests of the European democracies were deemed more important than those of China.

When Congress reassembled for the special session on September 21, President Roosevelt addressed the gathering to ask for the repeal of the arms embargo and the reinstitution of cash-and-carry, this time for all trade. In his speech, the president attempted to counter the isolationist tactic of characterizing the issue as one of war or peace: "Let no man or group in any walk of life assume exclusive protectorate over the future well-being of America—because I conceive that regardless of party or section the mantle of peace and of patriotism is wide enough to cover us all. Let no group assume the exclusive label of the peace 'bloc.' We all belong to it."[26] Roosevelt couched his arguments for the changes carefully, to emphasize that they would rationalize America's neutrality policy and provide greater protection than the current law against being drawn into war. What he notably did not do was acknowledge that repeal of the arms embargo and the sale of arms under cash-and-carry would have the practical effect of assisting the Allies, since they dominated the Atlantic Ocean.

Supporters of repeal outside the administration were a good deal less reticent. Indeed, for them, this was precisely why repeal was so important. A LWV press release commented, "It is commonly assumed that opening our trade in a way that obviously discriminates in favor of one set of belligerents will result in an overwhelming urge to go to war on their side. It is possible that the contrary is true. A vast majority of our people are known to favor the English-French belligerents, both out of sympathy and out of convictions about what is best for civilization. It is possible that if we persist in depriving them of necessary commodities, feelings of frustration or regret might, if the situation becomes desperate, bring about just what it sought to avoid."[27] This reasoning combined two of the three most prominent arguments made by the advocates of repeal—that it would, in fact, make war less, not more, likely, and that it would help the nations with whom most Americans sympathized. The third—an administration favorite—was that repeal made American law *more* neutral and *more* in line with traditional international law than the arms embargo.

Many advocates of repeal, however, were impatient with this administration charade. As Freda Kirchwey argued in an editorial in *The Nation* on September 23: "What a majority of the American people want is to be as unneutral as possible without getting into war. . . . The embargo must be ended not to make the United States neutral but to enable it to sell to the Western powers the goods which may save them from defeat by the Germans."[28] She also argued vigorously against isolationist charges that the administration's proposals would make American involvement in the war more likely: "Under the present law, we are sending them [the Allies] every sort of war supply except guns, explosives, poison gases, and airplanes. The materials we are shipping are considered contraband by every warring nation. To add munitions to the list is to increase the danger by only an insignificant degree. . . . What does endanger the peace of the United States is the present use of American boats for shipping war supplies. The cash-and-carry provision advocated by the Administration group would eliminate the danger to our peace that lurks in every submarine patrolling the Atlantic." More than that, Kirchwey believed that "our chance of staying out of the war depends in great part on the amount of equipment we can ship to Britain and France and the speed with which we can get them [*sic*] there. The more guns we send and the sooner we send them, the better the chance that we shall not have to send men as well." And this was the essence of the interventionist position—that helping Britain and France was the best way to keep out of the war. As early as September 1939, Kirchwey was convinced that the American public would support war to prevent an Allied defeat: "If England and France faced defeat by Germany, the United States would almost certainly decide to go to war . . . because their survival is fatally bound up with the hope of freedom on our continent as in the whole world."[29] Thus, Kirchwey enunciated the two fundamental tenets of interventionism—that aid to the Allies was the best hope of keeping the United States at peace; and that the war was a conflict of ideas and values, the result of which would have a profound impact on the future of all Americans.

Dorothy Thompson emphasized similar arguments. As the swiftness and overwhelming nature of Polish defeat became increasingly apparent in late September, Thompson commented that "the lesson of Poland is that modern war is not primarily a war between men but between machines. . . . This is the essential and crucial issue of the embargo. It is not whether England and France can draw upon the man power of this country. It is not whether we shall 'send our sons to be slaughtered.' It is whether the Allies, and particularly England, can purchase machine power in this country."[30] The Germans, as Thompson noted, had pursued a policy of autarky—economic self-sufficiency—for years before the war. "The embargo is a justification of their policy. And this is the real issue of the debate! It is whether nations that trust in freedom and have built their philosophies of life and their democratic systems on the concept of free intercourse between friendly nations are going to have the advantages of that policy or whether they are going to be penalized for it."[31] The arms embargo punished nations that had not prepared for war and was thus an incitement to aggressors. But the United States could help to redress the balance by providing arms to the Allies—and this was the best hope of keeping American soldiers safely at home.

Both Kirchwey and Thompson expressed their disbelief over the attitudes of isolationist congressmen. At the end of September, Kirchwey wondered aloud what isolationists imagined the world would look like after the war: "When Senator Borah talks about a 'phony' war and contemplates with democratic disgust the intrenched [*sic*] power of the British Empire, does he also consider the sort of Nazi empire that will succeed it if the British are defeated? . . . When he considers, if he ever does, the results of a possible Nazi victory, does he imagine that the United States can insulate itself against the influence of a Western world dominated by Nazi ideas and Nazi force?"[32] A few days later, Thompson asked a similar series of loaded questions in her column: "What will happen to the United States if the Germans and Russians, with their separate or merged ideologies and practices, win the war? . . . Would we like to see the British Navy in Nazi hands? Do we think that a victorious Naziism and Communism would interfere with our internal affairs? . . . Are we indifferent—thinking solely in terms of the welfare of the United States? . . . Neutrality does not mean indifference to the national welfare."[33] The war, for both Kirchwey and Thompson, was a conflict of monumental importance, not just for Europe, but for the future safety and prosperity of the United States.

On October 2, the debate over repeal began in the Senate. Senator Key Pittman, chairman of the Senate Foreign Relations Committee, presented the arguments for the legislation, focusing, as the president had done, on the question of consistency and portraying cash-and-carry as a means designed to keep the United States out of the war. "The embargo list . . . purports to include instruments of war, and yet it does not include oil that propels the battleship and the submarine, or gasoline that makes it possible for the airship to fly. . . . it does not include scrap-iron, steel, iron, lead, zinc, or any other raw material used in the manufacture of those things in the list of arms, ammunition, and implements of war."[34] It made no sense, then, to supply these materials but to draw the line at selling arms. Repealing the embargo would simply rationalize American policy.

In response, Senator Borah tried to refocus the question on the underlying motive for repeal—helping the Allies. He also challenged interventionist characterizations of the war: "I look upon the present war in Europe as nothing more than another chapter in the bloody volume of European power politics." The Allies were acting not in defense of ideals and values shared by the United States but only in defense of their own power and influence in Europe: "Was the cruel and brutal and revolting creed of Naziism any different at Munich than it was at Warsaw? Was the civilization of the democracies any less under challenge when Czecho-Slovakia fell at the hands of the combined assassins than when Poland was threatened?" He also made a compelling argument that repeal of the embargo was but the first step on the slippery slope toward military intervention in the war:

> Our law is being changed and our policy modified and our arms and munitions and implements of war are being sent to the Allies because it is claimed, and no doubt by many believed, that the democracies of Europe are in peril and must be saved, because civilization in Europe is being threatened and must be maintained. . . .

> Let us accept this thesis. And suppose the war goes on a year, or years . . . and the tide runs heavily against the Allies, what then? . . . Will we say: We can do nothing for you without the cash? . . . Hitler may reign supreme, as you verily declare he is on the verge of doing. But the extent of our sacrifice, our contribution, is measured by cash. No, you will do no such thing. You are Americans. If you believe what is now being preached throughout this country and indirectly supported by this measure you will send munitions without pay and you will send your boys back to the slaughter pens of Europe.[35]

Thus Borah anticipated the inexorable logic of intervention. If Americans truly embraced the Allied cause, in the end they would stop at nothing to ensure its victory. Freda Kirchwey had herself argued as much just a few days before.

The administration tactic of ignoring the underlying reason for repeal, combined with the isolationist opposition's attempt to make the issue one of war or peace, created a great deal of frustration among interventionist observers. At the end of September, Kirchwey complained about the "air of unreality" in the debate. The "real point of difference" between supporters and opponents of neutrality revision "is on the question of American support, by all measures short of war, for the armies of the Western powers. This issue will emerge now and then from under the legalisms and the oratory. But I wish it could be made the focus of debate."[36]

Thompson also expressed some impatience with the tenor of the debate: "The objection that this column has to the arguments advanced by both sides is that both are promising the American public more security than it is wise for Americans to think they can have. Not a single people in the world today is safe."[37] Whatever policy the United States pursued, Thompson believed, the nation could not isolate itself from the war or guarantee that it would avoid involvement.

Thompson, although in some ways less forthright than Kirchwey about the role that the United States should play in the war, nevertheless went further in advocating repeal—she called for repeal not only of the arms embargo but of the entire Neutrality Act. She was consistently critical of the isolationists' version of neutrality that seemed to her to be derived from fear of war and to advertise weakness. "A curious and dangerous concept of neutrality is growing up which is quite unique. . . . It is the concept that neutrality means the relinquishment in time of war of all rights of nations that are at peace. . . . Neutrality is a policy adopted for the purpose of defending the integrity, independence, welfare and institutions of a nation. It is not capitulation." Neutrality of this kind, she argued, was an invitation to aggressors. "If the United States wants to maintain its safety and neutrality the worst possible thing it can do today is to announce that under no circumstances will it go to war. . . . If there is one lesson we can learn from other nations during the last five years it is that weakness and preventive capitulation did not bring peace. This column believes that we ought to repeal the neutrality act in toto" and take back the initiative in foreign and defense policy.[38]

Some of the leaders of interested women's organizations were similarly disgusted with some aspects of the debate in Congress, although they generally kept such views out of the public forum. Martha Gellhorn, National Board member of the LWV, was particularly trenchant in a letter to Marguerite Wells in late September: "I heard that hatchet faced dope Nye speaking in the movie news reel and wanted to throw up . . . I cannot understand anyone anymore; either the Isolationists are crooks or they are slow in the head; either the Cash-and-Carry Clique is too ignorant to know their own points or they need a proper press agent. . . . Seeing Congress and the Senate these days gives one the gravest doubts about democracy. Those dopes: and we the people elected them. . . . We cannot be as bad as what we have selected."[39] Neither side in the debate, in Gellhorn's view, was addressing the issues at stake clearly and honestly.

But then, Gellhorn was unusually hawkish for a LWV board member in 1939, commenting, "But the main point of all this is: the Allies must win. . . . [W]e must make it possible for England and France to obtain the materials they need from us. They have money (providing we control the profiteers here and sell them what they need close to cost). So let's sell. And if at some future time we find it necessary to give, let us give (NOT loan). It will be a very cheap price to pay to keep Americans from dying and to keep us from being involved in the ghastly moral and mental and economic retrogression which is war."[40]

In public, however, the LWV pursued its standard approach of attempting to educate the voters about the issues, trying to appear as objective as possible while still presenting its favored policy in the best light. While the NCJW and the WTUL urged their members to write to their congressmen,[41] local branches of the LWV worked to get airtime on local radio stations and favorable editorial coverage in local newspapers.[42] The National LWV issued a release to its members entitled "A Plea for Calm," which encouraged members to help their friends and neighbors focus clearly on the issues. "Let us not say one word to add to the panic irresponsible people are inciting. Let us not say 'vote yes (or no) and we are lost. Vote no (or yes) and we are saved.'" The release attempted to present the issues clearly and simply, arguing that the revision of the Neutrality Act being sought by the administration would both prevent the United States from being drawn into the war and help Britain and France.[43] These ideas were also presented to the public at large in a League flyer entitled "You Can Help While Congress Debates."[44] This flyer presented a series of questions and answers carefully designed to lead the reader toward the conclusion that cash-and-carry was the best policy for the United States at this time by asserting that it would make U.S. involvement in the war less likely *while at the same time* helping Britain and France.[45] Some 250,000 of these flyers were printed, and at the end of November, Florence Kirlin, the National League's congressional secretary, reported that only seventeen thousand had not been used.[46]

Marguerite Wells emphasized the importance of League efforts from the start of the campaign. In a letter to state presidents on September 19, 1939, Wells suggested: "It may be that communications from women will be more influential than usual as being a reassurance to congressmen that women will understand a thoughtful vote at this time."[47] While one might expect the president of an organization to assert the importance of that organization's activities, the implications of this statement are significant. It was, apparently, assumed that women would oppose repeal of the arms embargo, presumably on the basis that it was a warlike action and women were naturally inclined to peace. As a result, the LWV could play a vital role by reassuring politicians that a vote for repeal would not arouse the wrath of women.

Other internationalist women's organizations pursued a similar approach in supporting the administration's bill. On October 10, the National Committee on the Cause and Cure of War met in New York and adopted a statement supporting neutrality revision, which it sent to the president, the secretary of state, and every member of Congress, "in the belief that this expression of the considered opinion of a group of women, conversant with foreign affairs for the past fifteen years, will be of definite significance to you."[48] The statement declared, "We believe that the United States should be kept out of war. . . . We believe that our country's course of action is not limited to a choice of retreat before aggression or resort to war, but that there exists a wide area of positive measures short of war which should be immediately employed." This language incorporated ideas from Louise Wright's testimony to the Senate Foreign Relations Committee in May 1939 with President Roosevelt's phrase "methods short of war." "We reaffirm our belief in provision for the adoption of financial and economic measures designed to withhold aid from treaty-breaking nations. We believe that the present Neutrality Act has failed of its purpose. It was designed to keep the United States out of war, but it has served to give aid to treaty-breakers and war-makers." Instead, the committee declared, the administration's bill "more nearly conforms to the recommendations of the past three Conferences on the Cause and Cure of War than the existing legislation."[49]

The NCJW similarly committed itself to working for changes in the law. On October 10, Fanny Brin, the national chairman of the Committee on International Relations and Peace, wrote to local committee chairmen, declaring, "The NCJW must do its part in the great effort to secure peace through revision of the Neutrality Law. We believe that such revision lessens danger of American involvement. We believe also that such a revision would not aid Hitlerism to the disadvantage of the Democracies."[50] Brin was born in Romania, but her parents had emigrated to the United States when she was just three months old. Educated at the University of Minnesota, she played a leading role in the NCJW and was a member of numerous other women's organizations, including the LWV and WILPF.[51]

Early in October, concerned by the vocal criticisms of the isolationist bloc, the administration approached William Allen White, a Republican editor from Kansas, to organize public support for revision of the Neutrality Act. The group he formed called itself the Non-Partisan Committee for Peace Through Revision of the Neutrality Law. This new committee built on the foundation of the American Union for Concerted Peace Efforts, with which many internationalist women's organizations had been working earlier in the year. It embraced the same rhetorical approach employed by internationalist women's organizations, characterizing repeal of the embargo and the substitution of cash-and-carry as the best way to keep the United States out of war, while helping the cause of freedom and democracy in the world. White invited various prominent women to join the group, including Esther Brunauer of the AAUW and Elizabeth Morrow, mother-in-law of Charles Lindbergh.

On October 13, Lindbergh gave his second radio address, this time specifically entering the debate over neutrality revision. His proposals differed in some respects from those of many of the congressional opponents of revision, who wished to maintain the Neutrality Act unchanged. Lindbergh, in contrast, advocated selling "defensive" weapons to European nations. But he embraced many of the assumptions of other isolationists about the nature of the war in Europe: "I do not believe that repealing the arms embargo would assist democracy in Europe, because I do not believe that this is a war for democracy. This is a war over the balance of power in Europe. . . . If we repeal the arms embargo with the idea of assisting one of the warring sides to overcome the other, then why mislead ourselves by talk of neutrality? Those who advance this argument should admit openly that repeal is a step toward war."[52] Lindbergh suggested that the outcome of the war was not of great importance to the United States and that Americans should fight only to defend the Western Hemisphere, which he dubbed "Our domain." "We must protect our sister American nations from foreign invasion, both for their own welfare and our own. But, in turn, they have a duty to us. They should not place us in the position of having to defend them in America while they engage in wars abroad. . . . We desire the utmost friendship with the people of Canada. . . . But have they the right to draw this hemisphere into a European war simply because they prefer the Crown of England to American independence?"[53] The implicit challenge to Canadian sovereignty here was bound to draw fire—and it did.

If Lindbergh's speech can be seen as a challenge to interventionist opinion, Dorothy Thompson took great delight in taking up the gauntlet. Following this speech, Thompson devoted three columns to deconstructing its message and portraying Lindbergh as a Nazi sympathizer at best. In one she wrote, "The important thing about Col. Lindbergh's speech is that he advocates openly and clearly that the United States should desert all the ideals of world order which have historically linked her to the western powers and advocate the new Germanic concept."[54] She also challenged Lindbergh's confidence in American security: "The prophets who indulge in the comforting, if gruesome, thought that after this war Europe will be finished, that no one can win the war, and that Europe will be economically bankrupt and thereby no longer a menace, seem unable to make deductions from even the most recent and obvious facts. The most threatening people in the world are not the most prosperous, the so-called 'haves,' but the most economically weak, the so-called 'have-nots.'. . . A bankrupted Europe in which the Nazi state was dominant would be looking for markets and raw materials, and both are on this hemisphere—with only half the population of Europe to defend them."[55] The United States would not be safe in a Nazi-dominated world, she argued; it would merely be alone.

As the vote drew near toward the end of October, the administration was confident of securing a majority in the Senate, but the outcome in the House was less certain, and women's organizations redoubled their efforts. Marguerite Wells wrote to state League presidents on October 25, suggesting some arguments to counter the opposition. "The basic error seems to me to be the assumption that if we admit that it is best for us that Germany should [not] win the war, we ought to go to war, but we don't want to go to war, so we must not admit that it is to our interest that England and France should prevail. Most arguments seem to me to be mere rationalizing of this feeling."[56]

Toward the end of October, the Executive Committee and department chairmen of the General Federation of Women's Clubs held a three-day conference to consider the crisis and develop a statement on neutrality and peace. The statement noted that the federation's program had in the past emphasized a commitment to international cooperation as the best way to ensure peace. The outbreak of war presented two specific problems. First, how to keep the United States at peace; second, how to bolster "the forces of Democracy . . . in the world." The statement concluded with a series of assertions, including the following:

> We believe that the welfare of humanity depends upon the recognition of the sanctity of treaty obligations. . . . We are convinced that a wise and constructive foreign policy is an important part of national defense and believe that legislation should not hamper diplomatic strategy in advance. The neutrality act of 1937 while it is technically and legally neutral, actually intervenes in the present war by destroying the normal balance of power. The proposed law, also technically neutral, would restore the balance of power and bring our concept of neutrality in line with that accepted by other nations. . . . Quite definitely, the proposed law . . . is more within the spirit of the resolutions adopted by the General Federation than the present law, and would seem to provide more safe-guards against the possibility of involvement.[57]

On October 26, 1939, Margaret Stone sent out a letter to individual members and donors to the WTUL asking them to write to their representatives advocating the repeal of the arms embargo: "To me it is not just a question of how to keep the United States out of war. The question is, or should be: What measures can we take to keep the United States out of war and at the same time look forward to the possibility of a world based on law and order after the European war is over? If we are honest with ourselves in answering this question we say that there will be a better chance of having such a world if the countries whose whole regime is based on force do not win. Why, then, penalize the countries whose foreign policy is based on cooperation and not on war?"[58] Such arguments eventually proved persuasive.

On October 27, 1939, the Senate voted 63 to 30 to repeal the arms embargo and place all American trade on a cash-and-carry basis. On November 2, the House concurred by a vote of 243 to 181. President Roosevelt signed the bill into law the following day. Looking back on the campaign, Marguerite Wells was confident that the LWV had played an important role, writing to state League presidents that the organization had "been a major influence in the final result because the fact that an organization of women such as the League was not afraid of repeal of the arms embargo gave confidence to those who wished to vote for repeal, but were afraid of public reaction."[59]

Wells's perception echoed an editorial in the *St. Louis Globe Democrat* on October 7, 1939: "No espousal of the revised neutrality act can mean as much as that by the LWV. In placing the stamp of their approval on the 'cash-and-carry' plan, the women have pledged themselves, and their earnest desire for peace, to this plan. If it fails to keep us out of war they are the sufferers, for they are the mothers to whom war is most terrifying."[60] Women in their role as mothers were thus assumed, at least by this editorialist, to have the greatest interest in the preservation of peace. Therefore, their support for a foreign policy measure that many saw as increasing the risks of war was a potent weapon in the campaign for the passage of that measure. However, these women supported revision as a means to keep the nation out of the war, explicitly rejecting the isolationist contention to the contrary. In supporting cash-and-carry, these women's organizations temporarily abandoned their commitment to the principle of discrimination in favor of a measure that looked like the best hope of keeping the United States out of the war. They were able to surrender the *principle* partly because, in Europe at least, the measure was, in *practice,* discriminatory.

Not all internationalist women's organizations participated equally in promoting revision, however. The AAUW's policy-making machinery proved to be too slow to respond effectively to the sudden renewal of the neutrality debate. The International Relations Committee recommended that the Board of Directors support cash-and-carry, but the board was reluctant to do so in a context so different from the peacetime circumstances in which the program had been adopted. The directors argued that since there was not enough time to consult the membership, it was better that the association take no position. However, individual members were able to take action, and Dr. Esther Brunauer, associate for international education, joined William Allen White's Non-Partisan Committee for Peace Through Revision of the Neutrality Law on October 13, 1939, establishing a working relationship between the interventionist movement and the AAUW that lasted right up to the attack on Pearl Harbor. The board's reluctance to act established a pattern for AAUW inactivity between the outbreak of war and the biennial convention in May 1941. In general, the Board of Directors voted against the association taking any public stand on the very controversial issue of intervention and aid to the Allies, but individual members, especially the foreign policy leadership, were very active in other organizations specifically created to lobby for aid, and the *AAUW Journal* carried interventionist articles and editorials urging support for Britain and attacking isolationism.

If the AAUW was unwilling to take a stand, the U.S. Section of WILPF positively opposed revision, fearing that it would lead to U.S. participation in the war and would undermine any possibility of American mediation of a peace agreement. This stand exacerbated tensions with other national sections of WILPF considerably. In October 1939, the Swiss Section wrote to the U.S. Section, describing its dilemma as a fellow neutral and expressing doubts about the Americans' plan to resist the repeal of the arms embargo. "As pacifists," the Swiss wrote, "we can hardly demand for the abolition of the embargo . . . yet, we cannot but see a great danger in the campaign against the abolition of the embargo. We are afraid that such a campaign is an indirect support of the Nazi system and wrongs the Western Democracies. Does the embargo not render the situation of the Western Powers more difficult and give easier play to the Third Reich? We are far from wishing to set you right or to meddle in your politics, but as a section belonging to a neutral State and as we feel solidarity through our work with all our co-workers we cannot but express our doubts on account of the campaign which you plan."[61] Dorothy Detzer's reply, however, rejected any comparison between the positions of the United States and Switzerland as ill conceived, suggesting that "because of the natural imperialistic designs of any great industrial country, our peace movement must consider the temptations which lie before our great industrialists both in Latin America and the Far East. May we point out that whatever action we take in regard to Government policy, it must consider those two problems, even before the question of Europe."[62] Thus, Detzer avoided the moral quagmire of whether the embargo aided the Nazis, preferring to dwell on the more American-centered concern of relations with Latin America and the Far East and the power of American industrialists.

The growing gulf between the U.S. Section and the International Executive was further illustrated by Detzer's report to the National Board meeting in early 1940 on her trip to Geneva. Here one of the key planks of the U.S. Section's response to the war—mediation—came under fire. In October 1939, the National Board had "urge[d] the President of the U.S. to call immediately upon all neutral nations to send representative men and women as delegates to a conference which shall sit continuously offering mediation to the warring nations."[63] The idea was reiterated in 1940 and 1941. This advocacy of mediation was an essential part of the U.S. Section's belief in the importance of American neutrality. Detzer argued in a radio speech in October 1939 that the United States would "forfeit the role of mediator and impartial judge at the conference table should we enter the war on one side or the other."[64] For her, neutrality was not supposed to isolate the United States from the European war; rather, it held the promise that some kind of peace might be negotiated with the aid of a genuinely impartial mediator. However, as she reported, in Geneva: "My situation was very difficult. I took the position that we should ask for mediation at all costs . . . [b]ut the majority of the Executive insisted that mediation merely to stop the war was futile, and took the position that any offers of mediation must be based on certain specific agreements. For example, one member of the Executive said that unless the Germans agreed to get out of Poland and Czechoslovakia, there could be no basis for mediation. . . . Gertrud Baer stated that if peace were made at the present moment it would mean 'the domination of the monster lying in the center of Europe over all the rest.'"[65]

Clearly, the European perspective on the war was quite different from Detzer's. European members evidently placed the cause of freedom above that of immediate peace, but apparently Detzer did not for a moment doubt the wisdom of the U.S. Section's position. Moreover, she did not even attempt to engage their argument. Instead, she concluded, rather smugly, that American "distance and safety permitted a certain perspective and perhaps a little more objectivity than was humanly possible when one is so close to the evil of fascism," and, therefore, that it was important to ensure whenever possible that the American position was represented at meetings of the International Executive.[66]

In November, the phony war began to take on an unreal quality, as observers waited for the next step. On November 20, Thompson even speculated that the reason there had been so little fighting was that nations could not, in fact, afford to conduct a modern, total war.

> The first and most impressive thing about this war and the thing that furnishes the greatest cause for optimism is that no one fights it. . . . [T]otalitarian war is, perhaps, the *reductio ad absurdum* of war. Perhaps it cannot be waged between nations at all, but only by an overwhelmingly strong nation against a weak and isolated one. . . . Given an approximately equal number of bombing planes on both sides, and war by wholesale bombing is almost certain not to occur at all. Germany could afford to bomb Warsaw because she put the inferior Polish air force out of commission at the very outset of the war. . . . Now this may really mean the beginning of the end of war.[67]

Such hopes were dashed by renewed fighting when the Soviets attacked Finland at the end of November. Russian forces had occupied eastern Poland in mid-September as provided for under the Nazi-Soviet pact, and Stalin had then turned his attention to the Baltic states of Latvia, Lithuania, and Estonia. Under intense diplomatic pressure, these nations had agreed to allow Stalin to station troops within their borders, a concession that led to their absorption into the Soviet Union in 1940. Stalin then turned on Finland, demanding territorial concessions on the Karelian Isthmus, close to Leningrad, and access to key strategic naval bases. The U.S. government saw these moves as preparations for defense against Germany. Convinced that the Nazi-Soviet relationship was fragile and vulnerable, Roosevelt wanted to avoid any response that might push the Russians into closer alliance with Germany. As a result, he did not invoke the Neutrality Act against the Soviet Union after its invasion of Poland in September, nor make any protest against Russian domination of the Baltic States.

The attack on Finland created considerable difficulties for this policy, however. American public reaction was sharp and hostile. Dorothy Thompson commented, "I think there is no question that the country is more perturbed and more outraged than it has been at any point thus far in the European war."[68] Indeed, the brave resistance of the Finns, who gave the Russians a great deal of trouble before being overwhelmed by greater numbers in March 1940, won tremendous sympathy in the United States. Even some leading isolationists expressed a desire to help. Former president Herbert Hoover, an isolationist, organized the Finnish Relief Fund, although the Finns were greatly chagrined by his unwillingness to permit these funds to be spent on arms.[69] The Roosevelt administration, however, was aware that public support for significant aid was brittle and so left the issue up to Congress. As Congress stalled in early January, Thompson indicted it for its failures: "The action of the United States Congress in the matter of the loan to Finland is simply incredible. . . . the world's greatest neutral has slapped Finland's face in the most ostentatious way and in view of the whole earth."[70] Others were more philosophical. Freda Kirchwey suggested that the Finns needed to understand American sympathies in the larger context of American politics. Such sympathies, she argued, were "not going to be translated directly into anti-aircraft guns or pursuit planes, because they are only part of a much more complex emotional compound made up of such other ingredients as isolationist sentiment, timidity, pacifism, and suspicion of the British."[71] And she was right. By the time Congress voted for a nominal $20 million loan to Finland in March 1940, the Russians had finally broken Finnish resistance; on March 12, the Finns signed a peace treaty conceding to Soviet demands.

Having embraced cash-and-carry to support the European allies, women's organizations increased the pressure to secure other legislation to deal with Japan and aid China. One fear expressed by Josephine Schain, chairman of the National Conference on the Cause and Cure of War, was that the European war might encourage Britain to appease Japan, creating "a 'Munich settlement' of the Far Eastern situation. There is a dread that Great Britain will throw her influence along with Japan for a 'peace' conference in the immediate future—which would leave Japan in control of China."[72] Such a denouement of the Far Eastern crisis would completely undermine the principle that aggression should not pay that was central to women's organizations' faith in international law and collective security. As a result, they pursued a policy of discriminatory measures aimed at persuading the Japanese to withdraw.

In particular, these women's organizations were anxious that no new trade treaty with Japan be negotiated, so that when the 1911 treaty lapsed in January 1940, trade with Japan would no longer be protected. Indeed, they had called for the abrogation of the trade treaty in order to allow the United States to wield economic weapons against Japan. There was considerable optimism that such pressure would force the Japanese to reconsider.

The reaction of Japan to the U.S. decision to abrogate the 1911 treaty was encouraging. In the League's January 1940 "Foreign Policy Problem"—a monthly educational publication—Louise Wright discussed "American Far Eastern Policy." She noted, "The perturbation caused in Japan by this action of the United States and the resulting, if tardy, attempts to placate the United States by announcing that they would open the Yangtze and Pearl rivers to foreign shipping have indicated the bargaining possibilities of a positive policy."[73] In early January 1940, the question of trade relations with Japan was also a high priority for the NCJW's International Relations Committee.[74]

However, abrogating the 1911 trade treaty was not enough, since trade continued on an ad hoc basis, so even after the U.S. decision had been made public in July 1939, leading figures in women's organizations had continued to criticize the irrationality of American policy in the Far East. On November 21, 1939, Josephine Schain argued in a radio address: "We are bound by treaty [the Nine Power Pact] to defend the integrity of China. Now Japan has invaded China. We in the United States are supplying Japan with the materials which make it possible for her to carry on this devastation. Without our help Japan would be severely crippled. Japan has challenged American interests in China, bombing hospitals and colleges that we have established there. We are supplying her with the means for wrecking the very institutions we have given our efforts to establish. Does this make sense?"[75] Here Schain illuminated the central paradox of American policy. Throughout the twentieth century, the United States had pursued a close relationship with China, with many nongovernmental organizations, such as the YWCA to which Schain belonged, hoping to Christianize and civilize the Chinese and open up the China market to American business. Now the United States was providing the Japanese with the raw materials necessary to ensure the failure of those goals, undermining decades of effort.[76] Few women foreign policy experts could accept the inherent contradiction in U.S. policy.

When the AAUW International Relations Committee discussed the embargo in December 1939, some of its members expressed concern that such an embargo might make war with Japan more likely, but this was outweighed by their moral abhorrence for aiding the Japanese war effort: "It was emphasized that the United States by continuing to sell oil, scrap iron, etc., to Japan was participating in Japan's aggression and for the sake of our moral position we should stop it."[77] This comment foreshadowed the conclusion many organizational women reached during 1940–41—that there were worse things than war, and that some risks were worth taking.

However, women's organizations did not simply advocate increased pressure on Japan; they seem also to have hoped for a compromise settlement in the Far East. Alongside the support for embargoes on Japan, they discussed possible rewards for Japanese withdrawal. Early in 1940, when the National Committee on the Cause and Cure of War's Commission on the Far East recommended that the United States not renew the 1911 trade treaty, it further recommended an "embargo on oil, scrap-iron, munitions and war materials, loans and credits" as the "most expedient" policy.[78] At the same time, however, it outlined concessions that should be made to Japan in the event of its withdrawal from China, including the repeal of the Japanese Exclusion Act and the handling of Japanese immigration in accordance with the quota system; reciprocal trade agreements with Japan and China; and a conference of the Nine Powers plus the Soviet Union "for a consideration of Japan's economic needs."[79] None of these women's organizations ever suggested that the United States make concessions to Germany or even seem to have conceived of the possibility of voluntary German retreat. Thus they had hopes of Japanese withdrawal that they never had with Germany.

The National LWV also favored what it called face-saving concessions to Japan, but it remained hesitant about embargoes. In a letter to the League's state presidents on January 22, 1940, Marguerite Wells laid out the options. There was little question that the American people wanted to secure peace in the Far East and preserve China from Japanese aggression, she declared. The issue was how best to achieve those ends. One possibility was an immediate embargo on exports to Japan. However, Wells believed that there were disadvantages to this approach. It would probably have little immediate effect; it might create economic problems within the United States; it would likely be considered a hostile act by the Japanese; and, if it should fail to have the desired effect, there would be nothing left but to fight or to abandon China to its fate. The strategy Wells favored was what she called "gradual or progressive pressure." The administration had already begun to exert such pressure, she pointed out, by refusing to negotiate a new trade agreement with Japan. Further pressure might be applied by gradually increasing tariffs on imports and then by cutting off imports altogether. The United States could also increase loans to China and offer concessions similar to those envisaged by the National Committee on the Cause and Cure of War.[80] Thus, Wells envisaged a range of diplomatic options other than embargoes, shying away from their provocative nature.

In March 1940, Wells clarified her concerns to the state presidents: "League members favor United States action of some sort to restrain Japan in her depredations upon China in violation of treaty agreements. The League program authorizes us to support such a policy. Our problem is to find a way to express our position without urging immediate specific action whose effect the League is not in a position to judge."[81] In other words, Wells feared that an embargo might precipitate war rather than forcing Japanese retreat. Moreover, League rhetoric lacked the moral element apparent in the attitude taken by the AAUW and the leaders of the National Committee on the Cause and Cure of War. While these organizations argued that it was hypocritical for the United States to supply the means for a Japanese aggression that it simultaneously condemned, the League did not. Wells even sought to disavow any League association with the American Committee for Non-Participation in Japanese Aggression, which by its very name established this as the central argument for embargoes on Japan.[82] In contrast, the AAUW supported legislation to permit an embargo on the sale of war materials to Japan explicitly to achieve its goal of "halting American economic support of a war of aggression."[83]

As the major European combatants dug in for the winter, American observers had leisure to contemplate the larger meaning of the war and its implications for the United States. Dorothy Thompson described the war in global terms, as a struggle for more than just the European continent. At stake were the ideals of Western civilization —freedom, democracy, and individual human rights. In January 1940, she framed the issues in this way: "The question is whether we are to have a totalitarian world—a world dominated by one race or an association of master-races controlling through absolute governments the lives and work of their citizens and their helots—or whether we are to give new, twentieth-century meanings to the words 'freedom' and 'democracy' and develop a cooperative world in which nations and persons can enjoy freedom . . . and in which the eternal struggle of western man for freedom and equality will again be vindicated."[84] Thompson then reflected specifically on the comments of Dr. Robert Ley, head of the German Labor Front, who dismissed the notion of human rights as "twaddle." She responded, "The same liberal twaddle, however, happens to be in the line along which the Western World has moved since Greece. And if Western civilization means anything it means the constant vindication of this 'twaddle.'"[85] For Thompson, the war was a struggle between Western civilization and a Nazi "barbarism . . . which baffles analogy."[86]

She also began to develop the theme of Christianity as the hope of the world, arguing that the "Germans followed National Socialism . . . because they had to follow something, and there was nothing else on their horizon that offered to fill a despairing heart. That almost the only people who withstood the seduction were the deeply religious must be taken into account as a fact of great social significance."[87] Thus, she depicted National Socialism as the product of a religious vacuum and a collapse of traditional values. Salvation could be found only in a renewed commitment to Christian values: "In the Judao-Christian faith and philosophy alone, for the Western world at least, it is possible to discern the outlines of that synthesis between discipline and freedom, between nationalism and internationalism, between equality and differentiation, between service and self-expression, between tradition and change, which is obviously what the world is seeking and which it calls 'peace' and 'democracy.'"[88]

Freda Kirchwey was a good deal more skeptical than Thompson—about the virtues of Western civilization, but not about the horrors of National Socialism. Kirchwey's commitment to the struggle was deeply rooted in her understanding of the nature of fascism. Although she had little time for the imperialist character of Britain and France, she saw it as quite definitely the lesser of two evils, never wavering in her conviction that "Hitler's struggle for power must be thwarted. The qualified blessings of old-fashioned imperialism must be preserved as a bulwark against the spread of fascist domination. And democracy—even that "pluto-democracy" so derided by Hitler—must be defended against a despotism that would crush all attempts to make democracy real."[89] For Kirchwey, the war was a struggle for the *potential* of democracy against the *certain* tyranny of National Socialism. And the outcome of this struggle was of vital importance to the United States. "The sort of settlement reached after the war will determine the course of American trade, the size of our navy, our relations with every country in the world, and in the end our political and economic institutions here at home. The war in Europe may not be 'our war,' but the peace will be our peace even if we neither fight for it nor help negotiate it."[90]

Early in 1940, President Roosevelt authorized an extremely controversial trip to Europe by Sumner Welles. Publicly, the administration claimed it was purely a fact-finding mission; but Welles's task was, in fact, to determine the attitudes of the governments in Berlin, Rome, Paris, and London toward the possibility of a long-term peaceful solution to the conflict. Nor was this unclear to commentators in the United States. As Dorothy Thompson put it dryly, "The 'secret mission' . . . is about as secret as a Hollywood divorce."[91] The mission was a delicate one—it ran the risk of provoking charges of appeasement from one side in the United States and of interventionism from the other. On the other hand, if the president could successfully mediate a satisfactory end to the war, it would increase his political capital immeasurably.

Both Dorothy Thompson and Freda Kirchwey understood the Welles mission in the context of the domestic politics of the United States. As Kirchwey put it, "Europeans would save themselves a lot of useless speculation if they would repeat to themselves every morning, 'This is a Presidential year in the United States. Everything that happens there must be judged in the context of the campaign.'"[92] Perhaps inevitably the Welles mission came to naught. The Allies had publicly committed themselves to the destruction of National Socialism, and there were few incentives for Hitler to make any concessions.

Many Americans, however, continued to hope that the United States could play a crucial role in the war while maintaining its neutral status. Indeed, they believed that it could play the most important role *by* maintaining its neutrality. Anne O'Hare McCormick rarely made the sort of overt policy recommendations that littered the columns of Thompson and Kirchwey, but she did suggest that the United States had a crucial role to play as a neutral—not as a nation isolated from the war but as a key player in the international situation: "The neutral can play an active part, especially the neutral that gives the lead to others."[93] McCormick never saw the world as one in which the United States could insulate itself from events beyond the Western Hemisphere. The United States was a part of the world—an important and influential part—and would inevitably be affected by developments in Europe.

Moreover, McCormick believed that all the neutrals shared vital interests in the war, and this view is central for understanding her subsequent interventionism. In November 1939, she argued that "all the noncombatants are beginning to feel that they have interests and aims in common. If one is attacked, all are attacked."[94] Thus, Germany's attacks on Norway, Holland, and Belgium in the spring of 1940 would have very serious implications for the United States, at least from McCormick's perspective.

Thompson also saw a potentially crucial role for neutral nations and called for the creation of a neutral bloc. "The neutrals must be dynamic. They must not be passive and disinterested observers, but an active force, working for the only kind of future world that will have any stability at all—a peaceful world whose policies are based upon reason, intelligence, realism and humanity."[95] Thompson was very clear that neutrality must be a positive position, an active stance. "If neutrality turns out to be an invitation to aggression, a self-imposed blockade, a position of impotence, a relinquishment of rights, a registration of panic and general paralysis, there will finally be no neutral nations. For the weak ones will be drawn into war by assault, and even those that are now strong will eventually fall prey to the combination of economic strangulation, fomented internal disintegration, and, finally, intolerable provocation which are the political weapons of the modern war-makers."[96] The United States had, she believed, a tremendous opportunity in the war to establish a lasting and meaningful peace *and* a leading role for itself in the international community: "This is as much our critical moment in history as it is the critical moment of the belligerents. How we act will determine whether, in the future, we shall enjoy the respect of ourselves and of others, or whether we shall take a back seat in history."[97]

Thompson's idea of neutrality, however, would doubtless have made a typical isolationist's blood run cold: "I think that without any alliance with anyone, we should demonstrate our solidarity with these nations [the weaker neutrals especially in western Europe and Scandinavia]—*demonstrate* it; not say it . . . we should aid them and in a grandiose way, economically, financially and in the fortification of their defenses."[98] Moreover, those neutrals should be exempt from the provisions of the Neutrality Act should they, by attack, find themselves involved in the war. This was surely a prescription for rapid involvement in the war, if it spread at all. Less belligerently, in February 1940, she called for a "neutrality benevolent in the economic field to the northern neutrals and to the Allies" as "wholly in the interests of the United States."[99] And this at least was an honest representation of her own very partial version of neutrality.

An important key to understanding these sorts of grandiose prescriptions for America's role as a neutral and for assessing the sincerity of the interventionist position in the first six months of the war lies in the widespread belief that France and Britain would turn back any German assault to the west. Dorothy Thompson was particularly optimistic, repeatedly expressing her confidence that the Allies would win the war and that there was very little danger that any American expeditionary force would be sent to Europe. On November 10, Thompson speculated: "How can they [the Germans] engage in a mass attack in the west? It is possible that the Maginot Line can be broken, but only at a prodigious cost in materials and men. It is a question whether any nation in the world today is strong enough to undertake this kind of totalitarian warfare. . . . The only other way westward is through the neutral countries. But an attack on Holland or Belgium would be politically disastrous. It would make Nazi Germany the worst aggressor, solidify the opinion of the world against Hitler and remove his own best propaganda."[100] Less than a week later, Thompson went even further, arguing that Hitler was a "bad chess player" who had "checkmated" himself by attacking Poland: "For at that moment he called into being a genuine collective security which the League of Nations had been unable to create—a collective security which extends to the neutrals as well as the belligerents. . . . [N]ow if he attacks Holland he has got to deal with Belgium, and if Belgium asks French protection he has got to deal with France—with that enormous French army—on a battlefield advantageous to the French."[101] In February 1940, she went further still, arguing: "Hitler cannot, this column believes, conquer the west. He cannot seek a decision on the field of battle. He cannot do so because he has not the material necessary for a 'real' war."[102] A week later she added the insight that "Germany hesitates to attack on a large scale because her generals and her economists know that she runs the serious risk of being beaten in the very first stage of an offensive. The morale of the people is indescribably low."[103] With hindsight, Thompson's underestimation of German strength and exaggeration of Allied power seems naive, but her optimism is an important indicator of the sincerity of interventionist claims that aid to the Allies was the best way to keep the United States out of the war. There was a genuine belief that, with access to American productive capacity through cash-and-carry, Britain and France could defeat Germany.

Anne O'Hare McCormick shared Thompson's optimism about the prospects for an Allied victory. In early April, she declared that the momentum of the war had shifted to the Allies because of German inactivity, noting in an April 6 column the "sudden revival of self-confidence in Britain." "Almost overnight they [the British] acquired the conviction that their economic power plus Allied military force after a six months' speed-up was more than a match for the armed might of Germany. . . . What has happened is that Britain and France feel the initiative has passed to them."[104]

Unfortunately, nobody explained this to Hitler. On April 9, he unleashed the next phase of the war, sending German forces into Denmark and Norway.

4

Blitzkrieg

On February 16, 1940, the British destroyer *Cossack* intercepted the German supply ship *Altmark* in Norwegian territorial waters, relieving it of some three hundred British prisoners of war. Hitler was furious, and this humiliation encouraged him to order the conquest and occupation of Norway to prevent any possible recurrence. The operation, launched on April 9, 1940, also included the seizure of Denmark. Thus began a new phase of the war. The Danes, quite unsuspecting and unprepared, surrendered on the first day. The Norwegians, however, although surprised, put up stalwart resistance, assisted by British and French troops who began to arrive on April 18. The most effective resistance came at Narvik, where Allied troops laid siege to German forces occupying the city, finally forcing the Germans to retreat toward the Swedish border. Only after British and French troops were withdrawn from Norway to bolster the collapsing front in France were the Norwegians finally defeated in June 1940.

With this dramatic end to the phony war, on April 20, Freda Kirchwey asked the readers of *The Nation* a basic question: "Can we stay neutral?" In her response she identified the fundamental issue—how developments in Europe were changing American perceptions about the war. The blitzkrieg of spring 1940 shattered Americans' easy confidence that Britain and France would prevail over Germany. "Until last week the possibility of Allied defeat was a distant threat even in the calculations of the Administration. Last week it pushed forward and demanded consideration."[1] Over the next three months, the horrifying prospect of German victory would push many Americans to support a much more vigorous policy of aid to the Allies, encompassing all possible material, financial, and moral aid, short of sending American troops to Europe. In such aid, these Americans believed, lay the only chance to avoid full American participation in the war. If Germany won the war in Europe, the United States would soon have to confront Hitler alone; but if Britain and France could overcome the onslaught, the United States might be spared. This was their hope. It was not, however, shared by all Americans, and one result of the blitzkrieg was to draw the lines between interventionist and isolationist positions much more starkly than before.

In the offices of *The Nation,* the split between Freda Kirchwey and Oswald Garrison Villard approached the breaking point. In late April, Villard submitted a column attacking Roosevelt's defense program, arguing "that the over-emphasis in Washington on the need for a stronger fleet and that Roosevelt's meeting-force-with-force speech are victories for Hitler because he can claim that this country has adopted his own point of view and policy."[2] Kirchwey rejected this line of thinking as based on an unrealistic assessment of Hitler: "Growing militarism can be attacked on its own grounds and I surely have no objection to your attacking it as strongly as you please. I do object to your assumption that American militarism makes other militarists rejoice. I am certain that the opposite is the case. However you and I may disapprove of a huge navy we must, I am afraid, assume that Hitler will feel the same way."[3] And for Kirchwey, anything that Hitler would dislike was probably a good thing. As the German campaign progressed further, she would become increasingly belligerent.

The National LWV, meeting at its biennial convention at the start of May 1940, confronted the latest developments in Europe. The key foreign policy item in the program was a revised version of the resolution on embargoes against treaty violators passed at the 1938 convention. It declared the League's commitment to "a foreign policy as a non-belligerent which permits discrimination against an aggressor and favors the victim of aggression."[4] While there was one impassioned speech against the resolution, much of the debate revolved around whether the designation "treaty violator" was preferable to "aggressor," and the item was passed comfortably with over the two-thirds majority required.[5] Thus, in full convention, as the phony war came to a dramatic end in Europe, the League clearly expressed its desire to aid the victims of aggression, with the caveat of "nonbelligerency"; delegates were not yet ready to question the policy of keeping the United States out of the war. Indeed, few Americans were, but the momentum for greater aid grew rapidly over the spring months.

The shift in American attitudes was apparent in the letters pages of the newspapers as early as the start of May. One woman, who signed herself "mother of sons," commented in the columns of *Washington*

Post on May 4, "This talk of our protecting the entire Western Hemisphere from future depredations with the power of the British fleet gone, etc., amazes me. How can we go on believing that it is not to our own self-interest to swing all the weight possible to the Allies? . . . My sons and my daughters' husbands are no less precious to me than those of the shortsighted parents who sentimentalize in blind ignorance that greater costs are paid by those peoples who can't face facts."[6] And as the month of May wore on, these facts became increasingly frightening.

Early in the morning of May 10, the German assault on western Europe began with attacks on Belgium, Holland, and Luxembourg. The Dutch fought valiantly but were quickly overwhelmed. Advancing German forces reached France on May 13. The crisis produced a change of leadership in Britain as Neville Chamberlain, architect of appeasement, resigned, and Winston Churchill took over on May 10. The speed and success of the blitzkrieg were stunning. By May 28, Belgian forces had been overwhelmed, and the British Expeditionary Force (BEF) was trapped in a rapidly shrinking zone around Dunkirk. Only a moment's caution on Hitler's part saved the BEF. Concerned that his panzer divisions were outstripping the infantry advance, leaving themselves vulnerable to attack, Hitler had ordered a halt in the advance on May 24. It was not until May 26 that German forces resumed their advance, and those two days proved invaluable in the organization of the Dunkirk evacuation, in which some 338,000 Allied troops escaped to England between May 24 and June 4. Of this total 110,000 were French soldiers who were quickly returned to the Continent to join the remaining French forces in the field in Normandy and Brittany.

In the face of German successes, concern that the Allies might be defeated grew. As Dorothy Thompson commented on May 15, "The gravity of this hour cannot possibly be overrated. It must be said bluntly that it is by no means certain that Britain and France will win this war."[7] Thompson's anxiety was such that she began to move openly toward supporting Roosevelt for a third term as president—a considerable shift on her part given her history of hostility to the New Deal. "The President's handling of the foreign affairs of the United States has been masterly. . . . Alone among all the leaders of the three great free nations, the President of the United States has from the first faced and grasped the whole bitter reality. . . . The greatest thing, it seems to me, that the Republican Party could do now for the Nation it has served so often and so magnificently would be to announce . . . that if the President will accept a third term it will offer no candidate in opposition to him, but will offer instead only a Vice Presidential candidate."[8]

The following day, May 16, Roosevelt asked Congress for new military appropriations in response to events in Europe. "No old defense is so strong that it requires no further strengthening," he declared, "and no attack is so unlikely or impossible that it may be ignored." To dramatize his concerns, Roosevelt gave the American people and Congress a simple geography lesson, noting the distances and times that separated the United States from parts of the world now controlled or threatened by the Axis powers. "We have the lesson before us," he went on, "over and over again—nations that were not ready and were unable to get ready found themselves overrun by the enemy." In conclusion, he asked Congress for nearly $1.2 billion to expand American defenses.

However, there was a danger here for interventionists—that American preparedness would take precedence over aiding the Allies. Roosevelt attempted to prevent this by specifically requesting that Congress not "take any action which would in any way hamper or delay the delivery of American-made planes to foreign nations which have ordered them or seek to purchase more planes. That, from the point of view of our own national defense, would be extremely shortsighted."[9] Isolationists, however, would be quick to ask why, if the United States was in such danger, valuable military supplies should be given away. And they had a point. On May 10, Roosevelt had received a report from the War Department indicating that the United States could put into the field only eighty thousand troops and had on hand the arms to equip fewer than half a million combat soldiers. Moreover, in May 1940, the United States had eighty-three fewer planes than the military thought necessary for American defense.[10]

Freda Kirchwey, however, had an answer—one that was central to the interventionist position. Only if the Allies could defeat Germany might Americans escape direct involvement in the war. "Consciously, as a matter of deliberate policy, we should do our best to save France and Britain and their invaded allies from defeat. And the only chance of doing it without ourselves going to war is through providing equipment in unstinted amounts at rates and on terms that will enable the Allies to hold out and to win."[11] Kirchwey, moreover, emphasized a vital underlying assumption of interventionists—that even American entry into the war was preferable to a German victory. "It would be foolish," she argued, "to make commitments even in the form of goods and money if we had not already decided that victorious fascism was worse than war. Once that decision is made, the material aid we send serves the opposite purpose; it offers the one chance of saving our stake without fighting for it."[12] Kirchwey also rejected the more extreme interventionist argument that the United States should enter the war immediately—for practical reasons: "Our troops are not now either wanted or needed on the anti-Nazi fronts. The raising and equipping of an expeditionary force would deflect the stream of military supplies into American arsenals, crippling the Allied armies for months or even years."[13]

If the progress of the Wehrmacht across the Continent frightened interventionists in the United States, isolationists were equally concerned, albeit for rather different reasons. The developments in Europe, and the administration's response, encouraged Charles Lindbergh to take to the airwaves again on May 19. In this speech he took issue, in particular, with Roosevelt's assessment of the impact of airpower on American security. "In fact, there is hardly a natural element contributing to air strength and impregnability that we do not now possess. . . . A foreign power could not conquer us by dropping bombs in this country unless the bombing were accompanied by an invading army. . . . No, the advantage lies with us, for great armies must still cross oceans by ship. . . . As long as American nations work together, as long as we maintain reasonable defense forces, there will be no invasion by foreign aircraft. And no foreign navy will dare to approach within bombing range of our coasts."[14]

Lindbergh also criticized American foreign policy, alleging that it represented the greatest danger to American security: "We are in danger of war today not because European people have attempted to interfere with the internal affairs of America, but because American people have attempted to interfere with the internal affairs of Europe. . . . [T]he course we have been following in recent months leads to neither strength nor friendship nor peace. It will leave us hated by victor and vanquished alike, regardless of which way the tide of battle turns. One side will claim that we aided its enemies; the other, that we did not help enough." Lindbergh also presented a conspiratorial view of interventionist activity, suggesting that the media and, through it, the American people were being manipulated by unnamed advocates of war: "The only reason we are in danger of becoming involved in this war is because there are powerful elements in America who desire us to take part. They represent a small minority of the American people, but they control much of the machinery of influence and propaganda. They seize every opportunity to push us closer to the edge."[15] For the moment, those "powerful forces" remained unnamed. This speech, more than those of 1939, would undermine Lindbergh's reputation among the northeastern elite class from which his wife, Anne, hailed. She noted in her diary that this was not so much because of what Charles had said but because of the changed perspective brought about by developments in Europe: "Not that [the speech] was more violent than the others but because *they* now feel more violently."[16] As pro-Allied Americans faced for the first time the very real prospect of German victory, their fear made them increasingly intolerant of the isolationist viewpoint.

Anne Lindbergh's diary suggests her own tremendous ambivalence, torn between her love for Europe, her horror at German tactics and successes, and the "logic" of her husband's views:[17] "When the Germans first moved into Holland and Belgium and I heard the news, I had, as always, that first terrible emotional shock that I always have with *all* acts of the Germans. 'This is too horrible, they *must* be stopped. Oh, why can't we stop them?' My first reaction is always 'French' or Allied, and it is the average reaction of normal people throughout America and, in fact, everywhere."[18] Anne also noted the impact of the blitzkrieg on American opinion: "People here are terribly shocked. Nobody really believed they [the Allies] could be beaten."[19] This assessment was borne out by the opinion polls. In September 1939, 82 percent of Americans polled expected the Allies to win the war. By mid-May in 1940, that number had dropped to 55 percent.[20]

The shocking news from Europe led Dorothy Thompson to call for the United States to "revise [its] concepts." "More than untold hundreds of men have died in the last ten days, in Norway, in Holland, in Belgium and France. A world has died. The formulae and cliches by which we have been limping along have proved themselves tragically false. We must revise our thought and action. . . . Neutrality is a myth. It presumes the universal rule of international law, and this presumes the power to enforce it by nations stronger individually or collectively than any potential aggressor."[21] Neutrality was no longer a sustainable policy, she believed.

That view was shared by a group of interventionists who, under the leadership of William Allen White and encouraged by the Roosevelt administration, organized the Committee to Defend America by Aiding the Allies in mid-May. The committee's initial statement declared that "as one democracy after another crumbles under the mechanized columns of the dictators, it becomes evident that the future of western civilization is being decided upon the battlefields of Europe. Here is a life and death struggle for every principle we cherish in America, for freedom of speech, of religion, of the ballot—every freedom that upholds the dignity of the human spirit." Great were the stakes in the conflict, and great the responsibility of Americans. "Terrible as it may seem, the people of our country cannot avoid the consequences of Hitler's victory and of those who are or may be allied with him. A totalitarian victory would wipe out hope for a just and lasting peace. The time has come when the United States should throw its economic and moral weight on the side of the nations of Western Europe, great and small, that are struggling in battle for a civilized way of life; that constitute our first line of defense."[22] This was an unambiguous call for the abandonment of neutrality. The United States was not, and could not be, neutral, the Committee to Defend America proclaimed. Instead, it should openly align itself with the Allied cause and provide all aid, short of war, to Britain and France.

Correspondents of the *Washington Post* expressed similar opinions. One mother declared: "There must be thousands of other mothers who have sons who are afraid that if this war lasts we can't keep out of it. Everyone knows that if Hitler is successful and conquers England and France and takes over their possessions, we will have to fight to preserve our country from this terrible beast."[23] Mary Donnally declared, "People must be made to realize that our very existence demands all the help America can give the Allies—and quickly."[24]

How many women with these attitudes joined the Committee to Defend America by Aiding the Allies is difficult to determine in the absence of any careful, national record keeping. People from all parts of the country joined the national committee; many others established or joined local branches. At the national level, it is clear that there were women involved from the start but that they never amounted to a substantial presence in the lists of members. By May 29, 1940, the committee had attracted 354 sponsors, only 47 (13 percent) of whom were women. A list of national committee members, dated January 17, 1941, shows 95 women out of a total 603 (16 percent).[25] The earliest committee press releases indicate that a number of prominent women joined the organization at its inception, including Freda Kirchwey and Esther Caukin Brunauer of the AAUW.[26]

As the Committee to Defend America began to take shape, a number of women's organizations considered the question of American foreign policy in the crisis. On May 22, the General Federation of Women's Clubs met in council in Milwaukee. The delegates voted unanimously to adopt a resolution calling for "a modernized and forward-looking program of national defense."[27] They also debated a resolution presented by the Illinois delegation that would have declared the federation "unalterably opposed to military participation by the United States in any foreign war."[28] However, the Illinois delegation was not wholeheartedly isolationist but rather opted to advocate a role for the United States as a "'non-belligerent' because we could not use the term 'neutral,' since everybody realizes that we are not neutral—that our sympathies and our help have been and are for the Allies."[29] The debate included opposition to the resolution from the federation's chairman of international relations, Mrs. Frederick Beggs, who argued that the group's call for "adequate national defense" was in conflict with support for "non-participation in foreign wars."[30] This is a striking argument because it clearly assumed that the result of the war in Europe was of immediate significance for American security. The result of the debate was a resounding defeat of the Illinois resolution, 202 votes to 74.

On the same day, the national board of the YWCA prepared a message to send to President Roosevelt. Significantly, the wording it used bore a close resemblance to the appeal made by the Committee to Defend America just days earlier. The board called on the administration to "throw its economic and moral weight on the side of nations, great and small, that are struggling in battle for a civilized way of life. We in America," the board concluded, "must aid with our supplies of every kind nations that are now fighting to stem the tide of aggression."[31]

On May 23, the WTUL also took action, issuing its "Statement of Policy in the Field of International Relations," which declared: "There is no choice left for this country except to equip herself as quickly as is humanly possible to meet any emergency. . . . [T]he League pledges its full support to the President in his expressed intention of giving material aid to the victims of aggression in Europe and of preparing our own country to defend to the uttermost its democratic form of government."[32]

This statement emphasized the WTUL's commitment to resisting aggression by aiding the victims and its conviction that the United States could not isolate itself from the war and its implications. Of the nine members of the WTUL National Board, seven gave their full support to the statement—Rose Schneiderman, Mary Dreier, Elisabeth Christman, Marion Burns, Pauline Newman, Mollie Dowd, and Mary Winslow. Margaret Dreier Robins expressed conditional support, emphasizing in particular the last paragraph of the statement, which declined to commit the League to support any specific piece of legislation. A note in the League's records indicates that she opposed the League's neutrality policy.

Agnes Nestor also expressed some concerns, notably that the statement might commit the WTUL to supporting U.S. entry into the war: "We all feel that we must defend our own country in case of attack but I hope that none of this language means that we are going to become involved in the war in Europe unless our own country is attacked."[33] Nestor was, however, clearly in the minority, as Margaret Stone pointed out in her reply on June 23: "I do not favor sending men to Europe, and do not feel that sending all possible material aid to what is left of the allies would lead to sending men. I do earnestly believe that by sending material aid as quickly as possible we are extending the time which we have for preparing for the final showdown with Hitler here in this hemisphere. And sending aid to the allies has already been approved by the Board in its actions of 1938 and 1939 in favor of 'discrimination against treaty violators.'"[34] The board hoped, as did most interventionists, that aid would reduce rather than increase the likelihood of American involvement.

However, not all American women looked to the Allies for defense. On May 22, some fifty members of the right-wing, isolationist National Legion of Mothers of America met in New York City and organized themselves as an "anti-parachute rifle corps." According to the *New York Times,* Edna Johnston, the group's leader, explained that "she felt that if the housewives of Europe had been armed and trained, the story might have been a very different one there. As it was, she said, the men, all at the front, were not in a position to cope with such aerial attacks."[35] Not all Legion members were supportive of this effort, however. A few days later, four national officers resigned from the organization, arguing that the creation of the rifle corps was antithetical to the Legion's purpose, "the first wedge in breaking down the mothers' resistance to the United States entering the European war."[36]

Nor were they alone in their doubts. The day after the story of the rifle corps appeared in the papers, Dorothy Thompson heaped scorn on the venture and questioned the motives and influences behind the Legion of Mothers' activities. "This is no time for panic—for the organization of American mothers to receive parachutists! The Nazis won't come to America in parachutes—not for a long time, anyway, and probably never. But they have already been among us for some time, agitating American mothers not to permit us to be drawn into war by sending aid to the Allies. What we need are not minute ladies with rifles, but a council of national defense with full powers to plan the organization and speeding up of our industries for the most rapid delivery of weapons to England and France—and the delivery of what we have now."[37]

Although such a council was not forthcoming, neither Congress nor the president was sitting idly by. In the two weeks following Roosevelt's appropriations request, Congress approved $1.5 billion in defense spending, over $300 million more than the president had asked for. Additionally, on May 22, Roosevelt declared an assortment of World War I vintage arms surplus to American needs and instructed his advisers to find a way around the legal restrictions of the Neutrality Act, which prevented the transfer of these weapons to the Allies.[38]

As the news from Europe got worse in the last week of May, commentators began to speculate about the possible consequences of a German victory. Freda Kirchwey commented that a "grim game has become popular these days. It consists of thinking of all the things that will happen if Hitler wins the war. . . . What will happen to the United States if Hitler wins? people ask. And then they talk about Greenland and the West Indies and the Guianas. Or about navies and the possibility of long-distance invasion. Or about autarchy and foreign trade. Or about political freedom."[39] She went on to contemplate the fate of Europe, in particular France and England, and finally that of the Jews: "I think about the Jews of Britain and France, and of all Europe. . . . But the game at last becomes unbearable. It is not possible for the sane mind long to contemplate the end of sanity. These things must not happen. That they can happen and indeed may happen is not an answer that we know how to tolerate."[40] Such concerns reflected the internationalist conviction that the United States was vitally affected by developments around the world and could not hope to continue blithely unaffected by a global conflagration that threatened completely to overturn the international balance of power.

Thompson engaged in similar speculation in a column entitled "If the Allies Lose." "If the Allies lose this war it will prove to be the worst catastrophe for the United States in our whole history," she declared.[41] Thompson focused on the economic repercussions of a German victory, suggesting that the United States could not provide adequate markets for South American surpluses and that, as a result, South America would be drawn into the Nazi orbit, putting even more pressure on the American economy. The fifth column would also be at work, she predicted, turning Americans against each other, creating another Spanish civil war. Her solution was all-out aid to the Allies: "We should send aid to the Allies, now, today. Every airplane that can be shipped, every gun that can be crated, in every ship that can be floated and convoyed, while there is a toehold in Europe where they can be landed and while there are still men alive offering their bodies to be broken. We should send aid regardless of all mistakes which all the Allied governments have made: for their mistakes are our own mistakes—the errors of incredulity and complacency. They—and we—have been giving away our world, inch by inch and position by position, retreating to the last stand in the last trench. The last trench is a trap."[42]

Elizabeth Morrow shared this anguished concern, and Anne Lindbergh described both her mother's horror and her own ambivalence in her diary: "Mother . . . is terribly worked up about the way the war has turned and at the appalling spectacle of suffering, which has only just begun. Everyone feels like her. . . . But not everyone feels her terrible sense of shame and even guilt for America not helping more. 'How they will *hate* us—oh, how they will *hate* us.' . . . Aubrey [Anne's British brother-in-law] says that England will *never* give in; even if invaded, she will 'go down fighting.' Mother thinks this is wonderful (spirit) and right and all they can do—to hand on to their children the heritage of having fought and died for what they know is right."[43] Morrow's concerns would shortly lead her to take a public stand in support of more aid to the Allies. On May 28, she sent a telegram to the *New York Times* supporting aid to Britain and France,[44] and at the end of May, she aligned herself with the Committee to Defend America, informing William Allen White: "I and friends have telegraphed to President Roosevelt . . . upholding the Committee to Defend America by Aiding the Allies. I feel strongly that every effort should be made to arouse the rank and file voter to take similar action."[45]

As the month of May drew to an end, some members of the LWV expressed their impatience with the lack of action by their organization. After adopting the resolution in favor of aid to victims of aggression at the start of the month, nothing further had been done. On May 31, Ophelia Demaree, of the Missouri LWV, wrote to Louise Wright, demanding, "When does the League start 'aiding the victims of aggression'? After the victim is masticated and digested until he no longer has enough entity to be recognizable as a victim?"[46] In the absence of satisfactory action by the League, Demaree had joined the Committee to Defend America by Aiding the Allies. However, the League's record on foreign policy issues shows that it rarely took the initiative in pressing for legislative enactment of its principles; rather, those principles served as a guide for deciding how the League should respond to measures initiated by others, so the League's inactivity was unremarkable, if frustrating for some of its members.

On May 31, 1940, Dorothy Thompson explored the economic consequences of German victory in more depth:

> Germany's plan is to make a customs union of Europe with complete financial and economic control centered in Berlin. This will create at once the largest free-trade area and the largest planned economy in the world. . . . As far as the United States is concerned, the planners of the World Germanica laugh off the idea of any armed invasion. They say that it will be completely unnecessary to take military action against the United States in order to force it to play ball with this system. They point out that there will be no other foreign markets for the raw materials and agricultural products of the United States, since these can hardly be sold in the Western Hemisphere. . . . The United States will become an economic colony, for its economic independence will be lost.[47]

Invasion would be unnecessary; the American economy would be crippled if the United States did not cooperate with the German bloc. Thus, Thompson laid out a bleak future for the United States if the Allies were defeated. Americans needed to understand, so interventionists such as Thompson believed, that the Nazi threat was not just, or even primarily, a military threat. One did not have to imagine German paratroopers raining from the skies, like the Legion of American mothers, to believe that the Nazis imperiled American security and prosperity. Members of Congress were also clearly alarmed. When Roosevelt requested an additional $1 billion for the military on May 31, it took less than four weeks for the legislature to appropriate a further $1.7 billion to add to the $1.5 billion it had approved during May. This, however, was money for American national defense, not appropriations for the aid to the Allies that so many interventionists were demanding with generally increasing support from the American public.

The drama of events in Europe—the seemingly irresistible force of the blitzkrieg—propelled a shift in American public opinion away from isolationism and toward support for greater aid. As Freda Kirchwey commented, "Slowly American isolationism crumbles in the heat of the struggle in France and Belgium. Understanding is coming to take the place of complacency and detachment. . . . America had to wake up. Even now it is stirring itself too slowly to be of much use in helping to prevent immeasurable catastrophe in Europe. But the new mood of awareness is growing, and the Administration should take advantage of it. What can we do to help the Allies resist Hitler?" Kirchwey had a straightforward prescription: "We can send planes and guns and even ships—but planes most of all. We can provide credit for their purchase, or we can give them away if the Allies come short of funds or hesitate to place orders. We can offer some of our own equipment, as Senator Pepper proposed, if our factories are unable to turn out new machines fast enough. We can provide ships if Allied ships are insufficient to get the goods over there in quantities and in time. We can do all this, and we should—now."[48] Here, Kirchwey anticipated the most significant issues of 1941—lend-lease and convoys. She had already begun to move ahead of the interventionist pack.

In the same issue of *The Nation,* however, Oswald Garrison Villard challenged Roosevelt's characterization of the threat to the United States, in particular, "the actual danger of an invasion from overseas," in his May 16 address to Congress. But, in fact, few interventionists made much of the threat of invasion. As Thompson declared on June 3, "I am not among those who think that we are threatened with an imminent invasion, either from Mars or from the Nazis. It is something quite different with which we are threatened—the complete collapse of the world of which we are an integral part, and the redistribution and reorganization of that world, socially, economically, politically, financially and spiritually, in such a manner as will menace our institutions, our way of life and our possibility of independent survival."[49] The war was not just a military conflict but a clash of ideologies with global repercussions.

On June 4, Elizabeth Morrow gave her first public broadcast on behalf of the Committee to Defend America, entreating Americans to "earn" the "miracle" of German defeat by providing all possible aid, short of war, to the Allies.[50] She tried to reassure her daughter that the speech was not intended as an attack on Charles Lindbergh, but, as Anne commented in her diary, "of course it will be used and publicized in that light."[51] After the broadcast, Anne wrote to her mother, and the letter resonates with her anguish and confusion: "It was a beautiful speech and courageous and very much you, with some of that wisdom about living in it that is especially yours. . . . There was a fundamental spiritual truth in it that I agree with. . . . And the text itself my heart and feelings go along with, though not my judgment. I wish so much they could pull together, but at the moment they are poles apart."[52] Fortunately for Anne, this political divide did not translate into a personal one. Elizabeth Morrow visited her daughter a few days later, and she consulted Charles about her new publishing contract. Anne commented, perhaps with some relief, "That is nice. They can meet and talk without trouble."[53]

As Morrow gave her speech, the "miracle" of Dunkirk drew to a close, leaving a bleak outlook for Allied forces on the Continent. And still the Roosevelt administration struggled to find a legal way to provide aid to the Allies. The cash-and-carry provisions of the Neutrality Act prohibited the U.S. government from selling arms to belligerents, although private companies were permitted to do so. On June 3, the administration's legal advisers proposed, as a way to circumvent this restriction, that the government could sell surplus weapons to private American firms, which could then sell them on to the Allies. Isolationists in Congress, however, opposed such maneuvers, and on June 5, the Senate Foreign Relations Committee blocked the sale of modern warplanes and ships to Britain and France. So the administration could sell only some 140 obsolete planes to the Allies, although when this sale was announced to the public on June 8, the president commented that these days "a plane can get out of date darned fast."[54]

None of this, however, was sufficient to satisfy interventionist advocates. On June 5, Dorothy Thompson addressed her column to Congress, demanding immediate and expanded aid for Britain and France: "Gentlemen: Four billion dollars appropriated for armaments and defense or ten billion will be useless to protect America or American democracy unless you act and act now. . . . The choice of the United States is independence or war. . . . [I]f you are determined that the black cross of the Nazi flag shall not wave over the world, nor we live as its subjects; if you are determined that the ideals of the Declaration and 'The Federalist' and of Lincoln shall not perish from this earth, then you should go to war and go now." The belligerence of this declaration was moderated greatly, however, by her next words: "How you may go, whether merely to say for the time being that we are *not neutral* and that in our own good time we shall no longer be non-belligerent is unimportant. But you must declare that America will not accept a world settlement that leaves her out and that we shall stand with Britain and France to achieve a new world compatible with our interests, our freedom and our faith. That amounts to a declaration of war." Thompson almost sounded more like an isolationist here, apparently making just the argument that most interventionists were vigorously resisting—that aid meant, in effect, entry into the war. But her goal was to cast aside the brittle shield of the rhetoric of neutrality and embrace the Allied cause openly and wholeheartedly. "Today we have an Atlantic Navy, if we wish to share it. Today we have a heroic Army in France, if we wish to hearten and supply it. They are not our first line of defense. They are our last line of defense."[55]

On June 8, 1940, Freda Kirchwey made a similar argument: "We all know that a Nazi victory will mean either American submission to German domination of world trade or a stubborn, solitary resistance, backed by economic and military weapons as mighty and ruthless as those of triumphant fascism. Neither prospect pleases, but no one doubts we shall choose the second. In fact we have already chosen. We shall resist. We will not be *gleichgeschaltet* [nazified] without a struggle, and we have the resources for a mighty struggle." The Allies' cause was America's cause, in Kirchwey's view, and their military fate was of tremendous importance for American security. Once Americans accepted that their interests were fatally bound up in events in Europe, the Allied front line became America's front line. There was only one rational response: "The first step is to prevent a Nazi victory if it is still possible. At this moment France and Britain are defending a line that is, in a sense both actual and immediate, our own front line. . . . We are frightened enough to scramble toward a state of preparedness in this country. But isn't it obvious, and shouldn't it be understood, that the present front line against fascism is now held by France and Britain with the support of their empires?"[56]

One striking thing about the arguments made by Thompson and Kirchwey is that they rarely, if ever, addressed women directly or specifically. And, indeed, few interventionists, male or female, targeted American women in 1940—which is one reason that Morrow's June 4 speech was so unusual. Even more exceptional, however, was a speech made by Judge Dorothy Kenyon, a member of the League of Nations Commission on the Status of Women, which appealed to women not on the grounds of their maternal interests but on the basis of their own self-interest. Kenyon, delivering her speech under the auspices of the Committee to Defend America, argued that the Nazis were attacking the American way of life:

> Particularly is this true of women. In our democratic society women have come into their own; . . . they have come to share equally in the democratic blessings, life, liberty, and the pursuit of happiness. In Hitler's world, as we all know, women are enslaved and degraded. Hitler wants only soldiers, and more soldiers, cannon-fodder for his insatiable ambition. Every other attribute of women is to be sacrificed to that one end, to supply more and more cannon-fodder for more and more wars. . . . Women of America, emancipated women of this democratic world of ours, this is our battle. As free women in a free world we must lead the vanguard in the fight for human liberty.[57]

This was a very unusual kind of appeal to American women. Kenyon spoke to women's self-interest—under the Nazis, the freedom and equality that American women enjoyed would be lost. She also argued that women's maternal role would be a means for their exploitation, yet that was not really Kenyon's point. She was not suggesting that women should resist Nazism to defend the purity of their maternal roles but that they should do so, so they might explore other possible roles—for example, a professional career like Kenyon's. However, this was a rare approach for the Committee to Defend America. Women speakers, on the few occasions when they appealed specifically to women, tended to focus on maternal rhetoric as the key to winning women's support.

On June 10, the French government withdrew from Paris, and on June 14 the Germans entered the city. As the French retreated, the Committee to Defend America launched a major advertising campaign focused around a full-page advertisement, which ran in newspapers across the nation, with the headline "Stop Hitler Now!" The text below declared, "If Hitler wins in Europe—if the strength of the British and French armies and navies is forever broken—the United States will find itself alone in a barbaric world—a world ruled by Nazis, with 'spheres of influence' assigned to their totalitarian allies."[58] The advertisement dismissed any immediate concern about invasion of the United States but raised the specter of the fifth column and called for "a vast program of national defense." However, the Nazis would not wait until American defenses were ready, and the advertisement denounced anyone who thought they would as "either an imbecile or a traitor." Civility was an early American casualty of the blitzkrieg.

Meanwhile, Mussolini, anxious not to miss out on the spoils of victory, declared war on France on June 10, although his twenty-eight divisions made little headway against the four French divisions they faced. On the same day, President Roosevelt gave the commencement address at the University of Virginia, declaring that "the hand that held the dagger has struck it into the back of its neighbor." More significantly, perhaps, Roosevelt dismissed as a "delusion" any notion that Americans could "safely permit the United States to become a lone island, a lone island in a world dominated by the philosophy of force," and proclaimed that the United States would "extend to the opponents of force the material resources of this nation and, at the same time, . . . harness and speed up the use of those resources in order that we ourselves in the Americas may have equipment and training equal to the task of any emergency and every defense."[59] It was not that easy for Roosevelt to deliver on such promises, however. On June 11, Churchill requested "thirty or forty old destroyers" to try to combat possible Italian naval incursions into the Atlantic,[60] but American navy chiefs refused to agree that these vessels were surplus to American defense needs, thereby tying Roosevelt's hands.

Nor would such measures have satisfied all interventionists. One group of those who sought greater action, who would be known as the Century Group after the gentlemen's club in which they congregated, came together at the start of June after a meeting at the home of Francis and Helen Hill Miller in Fairfax, Virginia. Both the Millers were professionally engaged in the foreign policy field—he worked for Council on Foreign Relations, she for the National Policy Committee. As a result of this meeting, a statement was issued on Monday, June 10, entitled "A Summons to Speak Out." It called for "all disposable air, naval, military and material resources of the United States [to be] made available at once to help maintain our common front."[61] An unambiguous call for American entry into the war, it was, particularly in June 1940, an extreme position. Among the thirty signers of the "Summons," Helen Hill Miller was the only woman, but the male war hawks would not be alone for long.

Indeed, the letters pages of the newspapers contain, along with a good mix of isolationist and moderate interventionist views, the occasional hawkish statement from American housewives and mothers. For example, Janis Vassalla of Hollywood wrote to the *New York*

Times on May 11 recommending, "Rather than wait for Hitler to cross the Atlantic and bring us to our knees, we had better fight now for our principles and our liberty and so forestall the contingency of being forced to defend them a few months hence."[62] Such belligerence, however, remained the exception at this time.

As the Italians entered the war, the clash between Kirchwey and Villard came to a head over the issue of universal military service. In a June 15 editorial, Kirchwey declared her support for conscription: "The first requisite for a democratic program of defense is universal military training."[63] She was the first to acknowledge that this was a major shift for her: "This is a hard prescription for me to write, and it will be an unpalatable dose for many readers to swallow. Universal service, in the lexicon of liberals, has meant just one thing—state coercion of the individual. But new conditions demand the fresh examination of old dogmas. A small army could safely be a volunteer army. A large army must be based on the training and service of all citizens if it is to avoid military and class discrimination."[64]

Villard could not accept this rationalization, and in an exceptionally acrimonious resignation letter, he accused Kirchwey of adopting an "insane course" that was "a complete and absolute break with all the traditions of *The Nation,* of which there is nothing left now but the name." She had, he declared, "struck hands with all the forces of reaction" and "prostituted *The Nation,*" and he hoped "that it will die very soon or fall into other hands." For such opinions as *The Nation* was now propagating, he argued, one might as well read Walter Lippmann or Dorothy Thompson.[65] Kirchwey's response was rather more moderate. She expressed her distress at the "bitter, vindictive tone of [his] letter" but could not resist the temptation to take a shot at him in return: "It is exactly as if I should accuse you of 'striking hands with reaction' because you advocate exactly the policy for America that the Nazi propaganda in this country supports."[66]

A final public exchange on the issue took place in the June 29, 1940, issue of *The Nation.* In his "Valedictory," Villard declared that his "retirement has been precipitated at this time by the editors' abandonment of *The Nation's* steadfast opposition to all preparations for war, to universal military service, to a great navy, and to *all* war, for this in my judgment has been the chief glory of its great and honorable past. . . . I believe, too, that the present editors will some day awake to a realization that the course they are now proposing will inevitably end all social and political progress, lower still further the standard of living, enslave labor, and, if persisted in, impose a dictatorship and turn us into a totalitarian state."[67] Kirchwey responded in her own editorial: "When I read an article like Mr. Villard's Valedictory in this week's *Nation* I feel as if I had been transported into a dream world. . . . It frightens me to read such articles. They represent, to my mind, a danger more present than fascism. They represent a retreat from the grimmest reality that has confronted our nation in many generations, a reality so plain that one would hesitate to state it were it not for the fact that so many good people refuse to admit it. The reality is that a system of highly organized tyranny has now established its control over the continent of Europe and is attempting to impose itself on the world."[68] It was not possible to hide from this reality. Indeed, American hopes for the future required that it be confronted openly and courageously. "What is necessary, if Britain is to continue the struggle against present overwhelming odds, is an assurance that the United States will send planes and guns—and later food as well—in increasing amounts as production rises in response to wartime demands. A beleaguered country can resist only if it has hope of ultimate rescue. . . . If Britain is defeated, its fleet may be sunk or surrendered to Hitler. Should Hitler take over the French and British fleets, his sea power, together with Japan's, would be three times that of the United States."[69]

With the French almost on their knees, the Committee to Defend America continued its campaign for aid. On June 12, the committee presented a radio address by Dean Virginia Gildersleeve of Barnard College, who advocated a broad-ranging program, including revision or repeal of the Neutrality Acts and the provision to the Allies not just of obsolete American planes but of the latest technology and money to help refugees in France and England.[70] The following day, the biennial conference of the North Atlantic Section of the AAUW met at Barnard, and the gathering was dominated by discussion of the war. Although the AAUW's National Board felt unable to endorse an interventionist policy in the absence of a conference vote by the whole organization, the North Atlantic Section discussed the recommendations of the Committee to Defend America and voted more than two to one to support aid to the Allies.[71]

On June 15, Charles Lindbergh once again took to the airwaves to criticize the Roosevelt administration's foreign and defense policy. In a speech entitled "Our Drift Toward War," Lindbergh declared that Americans "must not confuse the question of national defense with the question of entering a European war."[72] The former was "compatible with normal life, commerce and culture," he said. The latter would require the complete regimentation of American life, "probably for the next several generations." This was a common conception—that total war could only be fought by totalitarian nations. Democracy, many believed, could not survive the rigors of modern war. Lindbergh asserted that the foreign policy being pursued by Roosevelt would soon lead to war and noted that some Americans were already calling for war. In particular, he warned against "men . . . of less honesty who advocate stepping closer and closer to war, knowing well that a point exists beyond which there can be no turning back. They have baited the trap of war with requests for modest assistance." Once again, Lindbergh alluded to a covert interventionist conspiracy to trick the American people.

The following day, the French premier, Paul Reynaud, was replaced by Marshal Henri Pétain, who declared his intention to seek an armistice. As French resistance crumbled, Roosevelt did what little he could to shore up the British. Any as yet unfulfilled French arms contracts were given over to the British, and on June 19 Roosevelt brought two prominent interventionists, both Republicans, into key cabinet positions: Frank Knox as secretary of the navy and Henry Stimson as secretary of war. These appointments signaled not only an attempt to reassure the British but also Roosevelt's determination to build bipartisan support for aid to Britain and lay the groundwork for a successful re-election campaign later that year.

At the same time, the ranks of the Committee to Defend America grew. Clark Eichelberger, executive director of the organization, estimated that some 250 chapters had collected between 1.5 and 2 million signatures to petitions in support of "material, financial and moral aid to the Allies. . . . The volume of signatures and correspondence reaching the President . . . indicates beyond doubt the extent to which the belief is held in this country that common sense demands we give all possible support to the Allies, short of war, in their fight to halt the totalitarian hordes and their anti-democratic ideology. Not the Rhine, but the English Channel now is our frontier, and with France's efforts crippled, it is more than ever up to us to support the British Commonwealth of Nations to the fullest, while at the same time strengthening our own defenses."[73]

Even the National LWV reviewed the agenda of the Committee to Defend America, but it determined that no action was necessary either because a specific aim had already been fulfilled or because the program did not authorize the League to act on such a proposal.[74] However, the board did decide to move up the publication of the next Foreign Policy Problem, a series of guides for discussion of major foreign policy issues. The traditional summer break was abandoned, and a study guide focusing on the likely impact on the United States of a Nazi-dominated Europe was sent out in July.[75]

As the German campaign in France came to a successful conclusion, Freda Kirchwey called on Americans to learn from European mistakes: "We should recognize certain basic facts and build on them our opinions and our policies. The first fact is that *the United States is at war with Germany and has been for years*. . . . The war was forced upon us by the very nature of fascism; and while we have tried to avoid the full implications of our involvement we have been driven further and further into the struggle. . . . Today the chance and the time for pretense are gone. We have openly sided with France and Britain. We shall not by any last-minute repentance be able to dodge the consequences of that alliance. We should not, therefore, repent." Americans must accept an active role in the war. However, Kirchwey did not agree with the Century Group's call for military participation by the United States. Such a proposal, she feared, would lead to a tremendous struggle with the isolationists on the home front, which they might even win. And even if they did not, the preparation of American military forces for war would divert resources and supplies urgently required by the Allies. Finally, Kirchwey declared her support for Roosevelt's reelection in the fall: "Until very recent weeks I have doubted the wisdom of putting Mr. Roosevelt in office for a third term. Today his reelection seems to me vitally important. No other candidate in either camp represents a vigorous resistance to the double danger of fascism working through reactionary forces inside the country and through pressure or attack from outside."[76] The wartime emergency would propel Roosevelt into an unprecedented third term in office.

Although Charles de Gaulle, broadcasting from London on June 18, called on the French people to continue their resistance, an act for which he was court-martialed by the Pétain government, formal French opposition to the German invasion came to an end a few days later. The armistice was signed on June 22, 1940, leaving Germany in occupation of northern and western France. As Churchill had commented in Parliament a few days earlier, "The Battle of France is over. I expect that the Battle of Britain is about to begin."[77]

5

Fifty Ships and a Third Term

With the likelihood that British defeat might follow hard upon the French collapse, there was a powerful argument against providing further aid to England in late June 1940. Such aid might simply end up in the hands of the enemy, possibly to be used against the United States at a later date, while at the same time reducing American defensive readiness. As a result, on June 24, Roosevelt accepted advice that the United States should agree to sell to the British "only if the situation should indicate that Great Britain displayed an ability to withstand German assault, and that the release of such equipment as we could . . . spare would exercise an important effect in enabling Great Britain to resist until the first of the year."[1] A few days later, on June 28, Congress prohibited the sale of military supplies unless service chiefs declared them surplus to American national defense requirements. Nevertheless, the Roosevelt administration remained anxious to contribute to Britain's survival, and the activities of interventionist organizations in the United States expanded in the summer and fall of 1940, as advocates of aid sought to rally American opinion behind a more vigorous policy. Behind every domestic development, however, lay the prospect of the 1940 presidential election, and the administration had to assess every foreign policy move in terms of how it might affect the outcome of that electoral contest.

In July 1940, the Committee to Defend America by Aiding the Allies decided to add a Woman's Division to mobilize American women in the cause of intervention. Early in August, William Allen White appointed Jean Rushmore Patterson to lead the division and put together a National Advisory Committee. This committee, according to Patterson, "represent[ed] a true cross-section of American women,"[2] and, indeed, it boasted among its members Mary Vail Andress, recently of the Chase National Bank of New York; Dr. Esther Caukin Brunauer, associate in international education and board member of the AAUW;

Margaret Forsyth, National Board member of the YWCA; Elizabeth Christman, secretary-treasurer of the WTUL; and Candace Stimson, sister of Secretary of War Henry Stimson.[3]

Despite the impressive credentials of its sponsors, the position of the Woman's Division within the committee as a whole was uncertain. The male leaders of the committee shared the stereotyped assumptions of the era, which placed women firmly in the home and interpreted their interests in terms of their families. Clark Eichelberger, executive director of the Committee to Defend America, appealed to American women to support interventionist policies by focusing on the threat that National Socialist doctrines posed to women's traditional sphere: "Because Naziism considers no home sacred, no family sacrosanct, the women of America have a right and a duty to work for any contributing cause of Naziism's defeat."[4] Thus, he located women's interventionism clearly in the context of their nurturing protective roles and their interest in the home and the family.

Furthermore, despite the need to appeal to women as a constituency, the Committee to Defend America tended to marginalize women's contribution at the national level. In April 1941, the Executive Committee considered whether to invite Ellin Berlin, wife of composer Irving Berlin, to serve on the national committee, but "it was suggested that Mrs. Berlin might more appropriately be asked to serve on the committee of the Woman's Division and that Mr. Berlin himself should be placed on the National Committee." This was the motion that passed.[5] In the view of the Executive Committee, apparently, women belonged in a separate sphere. Moreover, the director of the Woman's Division was a man, A. R. Crawford, and although his functions were wholly administrative, rather than public, this is suggestive of rather a condescending attitude on the part of the male leaders of the organization.

This limitation of women's influence at the highest levels of the national committee presents a striking contrast to the activities of the women in the organization as a whole. A significant amount of the publicity produced on behalf of the committee's goals was due to the activities of women, particularly on a local level.[6] Furthermore, a statement issued by Clark Eichelberger in early September 1940 noted that "more than half of our 650 local chapters throughout the country are headed by women."[7] This may not have been wholly satisfactory to the male-dominated organization, however. Within a week of this statement, A. R. Crawford wrote to Claire Franklin, a resident of

Santa Maria, California, asking her whether she would "be willing to take steps towards organizing a local chapter of this Committee in Santa Maria and to head the Woman's Division of the chapter."[8] Although Crawford hoped Franklin would take the lead in putting together a local Committee to Defend America, he apparently assumed that someone else would lead the organization once it had been established, and that Franklin would happily accept the subordinate role of chair of the Woman's Division. The Committee to Defend America hoped to harness the power of women—as organizers and voters—in the promotion of its cause but nevertheless tended to segregate and relegate their activities to a peripheral position in the organization.

The Woman's Division was intended to "act as a clearing house for individual women and groups of women to aid Great Britain . . . [and] to dramatize to women the emergency that the country faces."[9] Every local chapter would, it was hoped, have its own women's branch. The activities of the Woman's Division were not, however, very often directed specifically at women, and many activists at the local level remained unconvinced that a separate women's committee was necessary. Harold Weston, county chairman of the Committee to Defend America, in Essex, New York, wrote to the national Woman's Division on August 12, 1940, declaring his belief that most of the small community chapters could do without, and that only Lake Placid and Saranac were large enough centers of population to merit separate women's divisions.[10] In fact, many of the most significant publicity campaigns sponsored by the national Woman's Division were not aimed particularly at women, and local chapters were called upon to participate whether or not they had special women's divisions.

For example, the Woman's Division launched the "Stop Hitler Now" poster contest at the start of October 1940. This was intended not to promote any special woman's agenda but rather to "crystallize and unify the thinking of all local chapters . . . [and] to secure publicity for the Committee."[11] The nation was carved up into nine zones, each of which would hold a regional contest, the winners of which would go on to a final round of judging by a national "Jury of Awards." The Society of Illustrators and the Artists' Guild endorsed the competition, and the Woman's Division appointed painter Elisabeth Worthington as chairman of the poster committee. She recruited leading artists to serve on the panel of judges, including sculptor Gutzon Borglum, then working on Mount Rushmore.[12] The winner was announced at the end of November, and the finalists were exhibited in New York.

In addition to such publicity campaigns, the Woman's Division exploited private social networks among women to spread their message and recruit new members. Many of the letters sent out from headquarters began in the following way: "Dear Miss _____, Mrs. _____ has suggested that you might be willing to help us in your locality."[13] The division also tried to tap into the existing public networks of women within women's organizations, asking Committee to Defend America members who also belonged to large women's organizations to obtain membership lists for mailing purposes and to arrange forums in which the committee's message could be presented.[14]

Neither these activities nor the poster contest, however, really required a separate women's division, and this made the promotion of the Woman's Division at the local level problematic. In February 1941, Frances Thomas, who organized and coordinated the local chapters, wrote to Jean Patterson that she was "a little disappointed" with the "rather meager list of special activities for a Woman's Division. The Retail Store campaign is fine and is something which a woman's group could do best, but teas are not a new idea and the poster exhibition, I should think, could be handled by any chapter head as well as by a special Woman's Division. In other words, I think we have to put up a more convincing argument than this for a Woman's Division." Thomas further argued that the list of ideas should be circulated as a standard memorandum from headquarters rather than a personal letter from the chair of the Woman's Division "because our chapters would naturally expect you to urge a woman's division."[15] Clearly, local committees did not always think that a woman's division was necessary. Indeed, the idea of a separate arena for women reflected contemporary assumptions about women's activities rather than any real organizational need. Within the Committee to Defend America, the national Executive Committee, composed largely though not exclusively of men, debated the issues and made policy, while the Woman's Division organized publicity and raised money, as women's auxiliaries so often did. Activities like the poster contest did not have to be aimed particularly at women; rather, they fell naturally into what was assumed to be women's sphere.

New York City was home both to the national headquarters of the Committee to Defend America and to a bustling and vigorous local chapter. Within that context, a separate sphere within which women could organize and lead was probably the only way committed women could wield the authority and influence they desired. The proximity of local and national women's divisions also produced a series of jurisdictional conflicts in New York, suggestive of the personal importance these women attached to their roles. In September 1940, William Loeb, director of the New York chapter of the Committee to Defend America, went to bat for his Woman's Division, writing to Jean Patterson that "the New York Chapter has complete jurisdiction over all women's activities within this area and is well organized to handle the situation in connection with all phases of women's activities in this city. I am sure this simple definition of our jurisdiction will clear up this matter once and for all."[16] By December, however, the tables had turned, and it was the national Woman's Division complaining to executive secretary, Roger Greene, about a national appeal for support for aid to Britain issued by the New York Woman's Division as well as a national fund-raising mailing.[17] These problems were eventually defused when the New York chapter of the Committee to Defend America, which had consistently taken a more aggressive stance than the National Committee, merged with the Fight for Freedom Committee in August 1941 to become the Fight for Freedom Committee to Defend America. In the already somewhat marginalized context of the women's divisions, these sorts of turf battles were, perhaps, predictable as interventionist women sought to play a meaningful role in the campaign for greater aid to Britain.

The New York chapter of the Woman's Division had, in fact, conceived one of the more inventive publicity schemes developed by the Committee to Defend America and one of the few that was clearly and explicitly directed at women. Known as the Minute Americans, this campaign focused on recruiting and harnessing the power of American women's opinions. The idea was to create a core of volunteers who would spring into action, in the event of an emergency, to rally public opinion behind whatever measure the Committee to Defend America advocated.[18] These volunteers would function as a general publicity machine—"organizing mass rallies, luncheons, parades, etc. designed to stimulate public sentiment for the cause of defeating Hitler's aims in the Western Hemisphere"[19]—as well as operating in legislative emergencies to bring pressure to bear on their representatives. The Minute Americans hoped to exploit the relatively widespread use of the telephone to propagate their message, embarking in the autumn of 1940 on an ambitious campaign to contact personally every private telephone subscriber in the city of New York. Since these numbered over half a million, this was quite an undertaking.[20]

The campaign was intended both to recruit new volunteers and to establish a path of communication that could be retraced in an emergency. Each volunteer would have a given set of telephone numbers that she would call in order to urge the woman of the house to back whatever aid measure was before Congress.

At the end of August 1940, Grace Allen Bangs, chairman of the Woman's Division of the New York chapter, issued a call for 500 volunteers from each of the five boroughs in New York to enroll as campaign workers. Each volunteer would receive a page of the telephone directory. They would then call every private home listed, targeting the woman of the house, to explain the Committee to Defend America's reasons for advocating aid to Britain and to persuade the subscriber to volunteer herself as a Minute American who would then recruit others. The campaign was inaugurated on Tuesday, September 24, 1940, at the Bell System Exhibit at the New York World's Fair, with a call from Broadway actress Glenda Farrell to Hollywood movie star Constance Bennett to enroll her as the first Minute American on the West Coast. Although the campaign began with only 1500 volunteers, rather than the hoped for 2,500, by Thursday night the Woman's Division estimated that some 75,000 calls had been made, and on October 1, the Woman's Division announced the addition of another 500 volunteers.

The Minute Americans were born partly from a desire to increase support for aid to Britain but also from a conviction that a silent majority of Americans already supported the cause. Mrs. H. V. Milligan, chairman of the Manhattan borough Woman's Division, claimed, rather disingenuously perhaps, "we 'Minute Americans' are not out to propagandize. . . . We just want to help make articulate the great number of housewives who are already in favor of defending America by aiding the Allies."[21] The campaign was apparently very successful. The Woman's Division claimed approximately 80 percent of responses were favorable, although their "typical" example—"a young Manhattan matron"—had a success rate of just over 68 percent: of 48 assigned numbers, 41 calls were completed, 28 responded very positively, 11 "were too occupied elsewhere or too unconcerned to take any stand at all, and two were outright hostile."[22] These numbers reflected, very closely, opinion poll figures for the summer of 1940; *Public Opinion Quarterly* reported 73 percent of those polled on July 20, 1940, supported doing everything possible to aid Britain short of direct involvement in the war.[23] Thus, the Woman's Division could certainly claim success for its aim of giving voice to the silent majority: its campaign publicized the opinions of thousands of housewives who had few avenues through which to express their views. It also recruited more than 4,500 new women members in New York as a result of its efforts. Similar telephone campaigns followed in other cities, and in 1941 the national Woman's Division adapted the idea, creating the American Minute Women—a group intended primarily for fund-raising purposes.[24]

As the Woman's Division got going, the main problem facing interventionists was how to secure sufficient aid for Britain so that it might survive the anticipated cross-Channel invasion by the Germans. On July 16, 1940, Hitler ordered the Luftwaffe to prepare the way for the invasion of England, code-named Operation Sealion. Führer Directive number 16 instructed that the Luftwaffe should "'prevent all air attacks,' engage 'approaching naval vessels,' and 'destroy coastal defenses . . . break the initial resistance of the enemy land forces and annihilate reserves behind the front.'"[25] The conflict over the skies of Britain that followed in the late summer of 1940 constituted a crucial moment in the war. Having failed to compel British surrender, Hitler would, in 1941, turn his armies eastward. But in the summer of 1940, in the wake of the French collapse, the focus of the war and the attention of Americans was firmly fixed on the British Isles.

Interventionists campaigned vigorously for continued aid, emphasizing the vital importance of the events taking place across the Atlantic. As Dorothy Thompson argued in early July, "If Britain falls, it is preposterous for us to think that we can defend the Western Hemisphere. We shall have our hands more than full defending North America. . . . Now is the time either to accept Nazi domination and know what it will mean to American independence and American institutions, or to show such clarity of vision and such generosity that it includes everything for Britain except active military support."[26] And, indeed, the British sorely needed all the help they could get as the Nazis launched their aerial onslaught to pave the way for invasion.

From mid-July to early August, the Luftwaffe concentrated its fire on the Channel coast, targeting the towns of Plymouth, Weymouth, Falmouth, Portsmouth, and Dover. In early August, German fighters and bombers shifted their attention to British squadrons, supply lines, and aircraft factories. But their losses ran much higher than those of the Royal Air Force (RAF), and British aircraft production outstripped that of the Germans in the summer of 1940.[27] Unfortunately, British shipbuilding was not in such a good position. New orders, placed at the outbreak of the war, would not be filled before the winter, and

Churchill feared that without American assistance in the shape of destroyers, the war might be lost. The prime minister had first broached the issue of destroyers with Roosevelt in early June and repeated his request on June 15, declaring, "We must ask therefore as a matter of life and death to be reinforced with these destroyers. We will carry out the struggle whatever the odds but it may well be beyond our resources unless we receive every reinforcement and particularly do we need this reinforcement on the sea."[28] By July, as the Battle of Britain got under way, the need had become extreme. "Destroyers," Churchill explained to Roosevelt, "are frightfully vulnerable to air bombing, and yet they must be held in the air bombing area to prevent seaborne invasion. We could not keep up the present rate of casualties for long, and if we cannot get a substantial reinforcement, the whole fate of the war may be decided by this minor and easily remediable factor."[29] Time was of the essence, as Churchill emphasized: "Mr. President, with great respect I must tell you that in the long history of the world, this is a thing to do now."[30]

American interventionists agreed. On July 30, the Committee to Defend America by Aiding the Allies took out a half-page advertisement in the New York papers. Under the headline "Between Us and Hitler Stands the *British* Fleet!" the committee called for aid to Britain and quoted both presidential candidates declaring their support for such aid. In particular, the advertisement addressed the issue of destroyers: "Destroyers convoy Britain's food and supplies through the submarine zones. Destroyers patrol the perilous, narrow waters between England and the Continent, and are thus the first line of defense against invasion. We have 162 over-age destroyers, most of which have lately been recommissioned. We could easily spare sixty of these. In the interests of our own defense—for the future security of our country, our homes, our lives—we should and can and must make available to the British navy the needed destroyers."[31]

Roosevelt's reluctance to transfer the destroyers sprang from two related sources. His primary concern was that isolationist reaction to any such aid to Britain might cost him the upcoming election. Moreover, he was not sure that the transfer could be accomplished legally, giving the isolationist opposition additional ammunition with which to blast him if he went forward.

The interventionist campaign for aid hoped to legalize such a transfer with new legislation. On August 11, the Committee to Defend America sponsored a rally at Manhattan Beach Stadium in New York.

Speakers at the "Stop Hitler Now" rally called on the audience to contact their congressional representatives to support changes in the law to allow greater aid. One of the speakers was Mrs. Kermit Roosevelt, wife of Theodore Roosevelt's grandson. Her husband was fighting in the British army, although, as she emphasized, he remained an American citizen. Her argument combined a standard interventionist idea—that the best way to stay out of the war was to ensure that Britain could win without direct U.S. involvement—with an appeal to women's maternal instincts, which were widely assumed to give the isolationist position a greater attraction for women. Roosevelt declared, "If Britain goes, as France has gone, let no one think we here in America will escape German aggression. The surest way to save American sons and husbands from the tragedy of war is to give Britain now the help she so desperately needs."[32] Mothers might fear war, but they were not all in agreement about the best way to avoid war.

While the Committee to Defend America worked publicly to increase pressure for the destroyers, the Century Group worked behind the scenes to promote the deal. On August 1, it came up with a plan, proposing that Britain might be asked to reciprocate with a promise that, in the event of a successful invasion of Britain, the fleet would withdraw to American waters and thus not fall into German hands. In addition, the British would be asked to provide access to military bases in British possessions in the Western Hemisphere, which would significantly increase American security.[33]

Seeking to protect himself as much as possible from the potential political fallout from the deal, Roosevelt sought assurances—from Churchill that the British fleet would not fall into German hands; and from his Republican opponent in the election, Wendell Willkie, that he would not use the issue against Roosevelt in the campaign. Churchill was willing to give such an assurance—privately: "None of us would ever buy peace by surrendering or scuttling the fleet."[34] A public declaration to this effect, however, might have a devastating impact on British morale, since it might allow an "impression to grow that we regard the conquest of the British Islands and its naval bases as any other than an impossible contingency."[35] Willkie was also, initially, reluctant to commit himself, but since he was also a strong advocate of aid to Britain, eventually he came around and promised not to make the destroyers a campaign issue.[36]

Interventionists in the press added their weight to the debate. On August 10, Freda Kirchwey called for action to provide the British with the destroyers they needed, expressing herself in uncompromising terms: "Today, more than ever, Britain is fighting our battle. We know that we shall face Nazi aggression if Britain is defeated. . . . Our active fighting forces are the troops on guard in England; our main Atlantic fleet is the British navy patrolling the coast of the Continent. We cannot afford to withhold supplies from these forces, even to equip our own future forces at home."[37] Kirchwey emphasized the urgent need for the destroyers in particular, advocating that "these vessels should be released promptly, by executive order if possible, by legislation if necessary."[38]

One final obstacle—Roosevelt's legal concern—was overcome by the navy chief's declaration that the destroyers were surplus to American defense needs. This reflected the belief that the acquisition of military bases in the Western Hemisphere significantly increased American security, thereby offsetting the loss of the ships. So, on August 13, Roosevelt offered Churchill fifty destroyers in exchange for leases on bases in the Western Hemisphere and a private assurance that the British fleet would not fall into German hands. Nevertheless, Roosevelt still feared public and, especially, congressional reaction to the deal. The administration's strategy was to present the exchange entirely as a way to augment American defensive capabilities, emphasizing the tremendous strategic value of the bases for protecting American national security while playing down the importance of the destroyers for British survival.

Even without the bases, however, the plan received considerable public support, undercutting the deal's usefulness to Roosevelt's political opponents. As early as August 17, several weeks before the deal was formally announced, an opinion poll showed some 61 percent of Americans approved of "selling fifty of our destroyers to England."[39] And this poll made no mention of the bases, which dramatically improved the deal from an American standpoint. Indeed, the relative value of the exchange was so unequal that Churchill was reluctant to accept it as a simple swap, fearing reaction in Britain. He hoped, too, to make the deal symbolic of a much greater American commitment to the British cause, just as Roosevelt hoped to make it less so.

In many ways, this sort of deal did not present great opportunities for action by women's organizations. Their modus operandi was designed to deal with ongoing policy problems, which could be studied and debated, and the passage of legislation, which, by virtue of being a longer process, was more subject to public influence and lobbying.

For issues such as the destroyers-for-bases deal, women's organizations were often limited to board statements in support of measures already taken, always assuming that they were in line with the national program of the group. Thus, the LWV, while it did not play an active role in pushing for the exchange, did express its support for the deal, once it had been organized. On August 29, Anne Johnstone contacted Marguerite Wells and Louise Wright to ask "whether the LWV should have something to say when the expected announcement of the transfer of the U.S. warships (destroyers) to England is made."[40] Wright telegraphed the following day: "Eager to have League urge sending destroyers to England. Program authorizes it."[41]

Moreover, interventionist members of some women's organizations volunteered to work with lobbying groups, like the Committee to Defend America by Aiding the Allies, sometimes even openly associating their organizations with those lobbying groups in the campaign for aid to Britain. For example, as the destroyers-for-bases deal loomed in late August, Elisabeth Christman, secretary-treasurer of the WTUL, gave a radio speech addressing the British people. Christman had begun her working life in a Chicago glove factory, which she helped to unionize in 1903. The broadcast was part of a series, entitled *Hands Across the Sea,* organized by the Committee to Defend America by Aiding the Allies, partly to reassure the British of American interest in, and support for, their cause and partly to propagandize that cause in the United States. "Only the blind and foolish among us," Christman declared, "can fail to understand what is at stake. In a word, it is simply whether the hard-won liberties and decent living standards which have been wrung from the past shall be sacrificed to the totalitarian monster that seeks to engulf us all. . . . We in this country . . . are coming to realize, with increasing unanimity, that your cause and ours are one."[42]

Thus, she affirmed the vital interest of the United States in the outcome of the war. Christman also pointed particularly to the fate of labor under totalitarianism, clearly casting the conflict in moral terms as a war between freedom and oppression. Moreover, when she argued that "ultimately, our superior resources must count," and talked of the "large supplies of materials for your defense" that were "flowing across the sea," her listeners, on both sides of the Atlantic, would have had the destroyer exchange in the forefront of their minds.[43]

The destroyer deal was finalized at the start of September 1940. A week later, the Committee to Defend America organized a bipartisan public statement of support with the aim of emphasizing the cross-party backing for the measure—thereby undermining its significance as an election issue. The statement read, "The undersigned citizens of this country, irrespective of their party affiliations or their views on domestic issues, join in unqualified endorsement of President Roosevelt's action in releasing fifty destroyers to Great Britain and the acquisition of vital strategic defense bases in this hemisphere."[44] The statement was signed by seventy Americans, representing both parties, including Elizabeth Morrow, the actress Helen Hayes, the novelist Dorothy Canfield Fisher, Mary Woolley, president of Mount Holyoke College, Carrie Chapman Catt, and Freda Kirchwey.

By that time, the Luftwaffe had begun to focus on British airfields, inflicting significant losses on the RAF. However, Hitler was also running out of time to launch an invasion before the arrival of winter. As a result, on September 7, the primary focus of German bombing activity shifted again—this time to the city of London, in an attempt to draw the full force of the RAF into the skies, where it could be dealt a lethal blow. In mid-September 1940, the Battle of Britain reached its climax, and although British losses were heavy, the Luftwaffe was unable to overwhelm the RAF. On September 15, a massive bomber force of some two hundred planes, with a large fighter escort, encountered stubborn British resistance east of London, and the scale of German losses—nearly sixty planes—convinced Hitler that he could not hope to launch an invasion in 1940. On September 17, he postponed Operation Sealion indefinitely.[45]

Pressure continued to mount, however, in the Far Eastern theater of the war. German victories in Europe had encouraged Japanese ambitions in Asia as European nations looked increasingly unable to defend their colonial possessions in that part of the world. The Japanese were particularly interested in the fate of the Dutch East Indies, a vital source of oil and other essential raw materials, and in ways to increase pressure on the Chinese. A defeated France quickly agreed to close the Indo-China border, cutting Chinese supply lines. With their hands full in Europe, moreover, the British were also unwilling to take on the Japanese without full American support. In July, Churchill agreed to close the Burma Road, a major supply route for the Chinese Nationalists, for three months.

Most of the internationalist women's organizations had announced their support for sanctions against Japan early in 1940. Only the LWV hesitated, largely because of Marguerite Wells's concern that sanctions might provoke the Japanese rather than encourage them to rethink their approach. The reluctance of Wells and the League to take a more active role in promoting embargo legislation was, however, a source of unhappiness for some of the organization's state foreign policy chairmen. In May 1940, six chairs of state foreign policy departments urged the National Board to take a more active role in promoting legislation that would give the president the authority to impose an embargo. "With this power to wield as a club," they argued, "the Executive could then apply diplomatic pressure, if desirable, (and with vastly more force than at present) to whatever extent it should prove to be effective."[46] Wells, however, declined to take the initiative.[47]

Shortly after this exchange, the passage of the National Defense Act at the start of July 1940 resolved the legislative issue. The act was designed primarily to prevent the United States from exporting materials that would be essential for its own national defense in the increasingly likely event of war. Indirectly it made possible embargoes on exports to Japan by executive order. As Louise Wright noted in a circular letter to League foreign policy chairmen: "While the provisions of this law are general in practice, licenses may be withheld from any nation for the shipping of a long list of finished munitions and essential war materials."[48]

Wells, however, remained reluctant to promote the imposition of embargoes made possible by the National Defense Act. After its passage, most League leaders chose instead to focus on the growing problem of supplying aid to Britain rather than encourage the president to exert his authority by imposing embargoes on Japan.[49] As Anne Johnstone, secretary of the Department of Government and International Cooperation, noted in a memorandum to Louise Wright in December 1940, "No legislation is required to implement this country's policy of aid to China and discrimination against Japan, while . . . legislation will undoubtedly be required to make possible significant financial aid to Britain when it becomes necessary."[50] Thus, League leaders felt the organization's efforts could be more usefully applied to other issues.

Roosevelt's advisers were divided over the best approach to dealing with the Japanese. Secretary of War Henry Stimson and Secretary of the Treasury Henry Morgenthau favored a firm stance; Cordell Hull and Sumner Welles, of the State Department, feared that this might provoke war and advocated a more moderate policy. On July 25, Roosevelt, influenced by Stimson and Morgenthau, announced a ban on the export of petroleum and scrap iron and steel. However, in response to State Department protest, the ban was modified the following day, limiting its extent to aviation-grade fuel and the highest-quality scrap. Nevertheless, this decision constituted a significant change in American foreign policy—for the first time since the earliest Japanese expansion into Manchuria in 1931, the United States had imposed an economic sanction to back up its verbal protests.[51] The move, however, did not deter the Japanese.

On August 1, they began to move into Indo-China, pressuring the helpless Vichy regime into allowing them to build airfields and station troops in northern Indo-China. These moves clearly foreshadowed a larger goal of dominating Southeast Asia, prompting the Roosevelt administration to consider expanding its sanctions. Even Joseph Grew, American ambassador in Tokyo and long an opponent of sanctions, reevaluated his position, warning in mid-September that Japan, intoxicated by the example of German victories, would seek to take advantage of the weakness of European powers in Asia to satisfy its own ambition. As a result, he now supported sanctions as a "show of force" designed to deter further Japanese aggression in Asia.[52]

On September 19, the administration decided to add all scrap metal to the list of materials that could not be exported, although, bowing to pressure from a concerned Hull, the prohibition on oil exports was not expanded. The new sanctions were announced on September 24, although they would not go into effect until October 16. Even with the continued export of oil, however, these measures were sufficient to push the Japanese toward the seizure of the Dutch East Indies, whose resources could make good their shortages, as well as providing for their oil needs, should the United States increase its sanctions.

American action was having a paradoxical effect. In order to curb Japanese aggression, the United States withheld vital war materials; in response, the Japanese sought to win control over territories that could supply them with those materials. Thus, American sanctions encouraged Japanese aggression, or at least accelerated the Japanese program of conquest. But Americans could console themselves with the thought that they were no longer fueling that conquest—in Louise Wright's words, they were, at least, no longer the "silent partner of the aggressor."[53]

United States' policy also encouraged Japan to embrace a closer relationship with Germany and Italy. On September 27, the three Axis nations signed the Tripartite Pact. Under the terms of this alliance, the signatories agreed "to assist one another with all political, economic and military means when one of the three contracting Parties is attacked by a power at present not involved in the European War or in the Sino-Japanese Conflict," although a separate provision explicitly excluding the Soviet Union from this obligation made it very clear that the United States was the intended target.[54]

Many interventionists interpreted the Tripartite Pact in the broadest possible terms, emphasizing its importance for the European war. In this way, it also served to increase the pressure for aid to Britain. Dorothy Thompson made the argument in the following way: "The German-Italian-Japanese Pact ought to make clear to Americans, if there are any who still need convincing, that this is no European war, but a world revolution for the redistribution of the entire planet."[55] The nature and scope of this revolution made it vital for the United States to make allies: "It is not and never has been a question of whether the British Empire needs us; it is a question of whether we need the British Empire. We do. We need very nation and every people that we can range up on our side."[56]

Louise Wright also understood the Tripartite Pact as a serious threat to the United States, especially in the context of ongoing Japanese expansion. In a letter to local foreign policy committee chairmen, she noted that "extension of the Japanese empire to the south confronts the United States with two grave problems—its responsibility for the status quo of the Philippine Islands and a change in the control of the strategic rubber and tin supplies upon which the United States relies."[57] Of National League leaders, in fact, only Wright clearly favored a more vigorous policy toward Japan. In a letter to Marguerite Wells on December 16, 1940, she welcomed the most recent restrictions on exports to Japan, commenting that "I have a feeling . . . that you think I take an attitude of vindictiveness toward Japan. . . . My attitude . . . is that of the average person who can't help thinking it is a little silly to condemn Japanese policy as we have done consistently since 1931 and then provide her the means with which to carry out that policy, and at the same time provide her victim with means of defense." Thus, Wright embraced the moral arguments of the AAUW and the National Committee on the Cause and Cure of War. Moreover, while Wright insisted on a close connection between the wars in Europe and Asia, she did not regard Japan as a serious military threat to the United States: "I have always thought that Japan had more reason to worry about our use of our power and influence than we have to fear an attack from Japan."[58]

The NCJW also noted the importance of the Far East for American trade: "Of eighteen strategic materials vitally needed for national defense, we are largely dependent on the Far East for four, to a lesser degree for seven more. Victory for Japan would mean dislocation and possible elimination of our trade."[59] Taking action against Japan was, thus, never simply a matter of taking a moral stand, although that was a central concern. Rather, the foreign policy experts in these women's organizations believed in the fundamental interdependence of the world and that Japanese expansion imperiled not only their hopes for long-term peace based on collective security but also more immediate American national security interests. Their concerns combined idealism with pragmatism to produce a sophisticated and multifaceted view of American foreign policy.

It was in the context of the destroyers-for-bases deal and the imposition of the first sanctions against Japan that leading isolationists organized the America First Committee on September 4, 1940. The group's purpose was explicitly to counter the efforts of the Committee to Defend America, which had been much too successful, in their view. America First was not a peace committee. Rather, it advocated that the United States focus on its own defensive needs, rejecting any suggestion that American security might be dependent on British survival or any particular outcome in the war. But there were also pacifists who backed America First or cooperated with it. Strikingly, given his criticism of Kirchwey for her advocacy of conscription, Oswald Garrison Villard was an early sponsor of the America First Committee.[60] Kirchwey challenged him specifically to justify his endorsement of an organization that demanded increased military preparedness as well as isolationism.[61] Villard defended himself, declaring that "in accepting membership in the America First Committee, I specifically stated that I dissented from the preparedness program."[62] To Kirchwey this was hardly an adequate defense: "To tell the committee privately that you disapprove of preparedness may satisfy your conscience; but a committee like this one exists only to put over its program with the public, and that is what your name and your membership will help accomplish."[63] For Villard, apparently, peace for the United States was the ultimate cause,[64] before which all other principles would bend; for Kirchwey, that cause was the defeat of fascism. In this, Kirchwey was perhaps a more appropriate successor to Villard's grandfather William Garrison, noted nineteenth-century pacifist and abolitionist, who declared, in reference to John Brown's raid on

Harpers Ferry in 1859: "Yet, as a peace man—I am prepared to say: 'Success to every slave insurrection at the South, and in every slave country.' . . . I thank God when men who believe in the right and duty of wielding carnal weapons are so far advanced that they will take those weapons out of the scale of despotism, and throw them into the scale of freedom."[65]

The America First Committee would become the center of isolationist opposition, pursuing similar means of proselytizing its cause as the Committee to Defend America. Both groups circulated petitions and organized rallies, radio broadcasts, letter-writing campaigns, and so on. Both groups enlisted the prestige of prominent Americans to bolster their arguments. Charles Lindbergh became the America First Committee's most prominent spokesman. Together these two groups, working energetically to rally public opinion to their opposing causes, served to highlight every possible advantage and disadvantage of every imaginable policy. Despite what some historians, and indeed the isolationists themselves, have argued, it would be hard to foist a warlike policy on an unwitting American public in a context in which America First was loudly condemning every interventionist measure as an act of war. Anyone politically alive enough to have an opinion about aid to Britain could hardly fail to be aware of both sides of the argument.

One of the proposals that attracted considerable attention from both isolationists and interventionists in the fall of 1940 was former president Herbert Hoover's plan to feed occupied Europe. During the First World War, Hoover, as head of the Food Administration, had organized the distribution of food to the inhabitants of occupied Belgium. He believed that the situation in Nazi-occupied Europe was essentially the same and sought to achieve the same humanitarian end as in the first war. However, the British flatly refused to raise their blockade of the Continent for Hoover's shipments, and the Germans refused to promise not to divert the supplies or to stop plundering the occupied territories themselves, thus exacerbating the shortages.

The issue of the Hoover Plan drove a wedge between the International Section and the U.S. Section of WILPF when it was discussed in October 1940. The debate began with a presentation by Gertrud Baer, who had recently arrived in the United States. She argued that no plan which required the cooperation of the Germans had any guarantee, or even likelihood, of success; that a recent Department of Agriculture publication had confirmed that the only barrier to feeding Europe in the coming winter was German distribution policies, not an absolute shortage of food; and that "the Hoover Plan is contrary to the basic principles of the W.I.L.P.F. . . . [which] has always been against the humanizing of war."[66] The provision of food for Europe, she went on, would only mean more food for the Germans and she suggested that feeding people while they were under the brutal oppression of an occupying army was not compatible with pacifist ideals. Those with religious reasons for wishing to "feed equally friend and foe" should look to other organizations to lobby for such an end—WILPF was "not a humanitarian and not a philanthropic body."[67] For Baer the primary moral imperative was to defeat Nazi oppression—before this all other moral concerns had to give way.

The U.S. National Board was considerably more ambivalent than Baer. Board members expressed a variety of opinions, most notably a concern that some kind of conditions should be attached to the Hoover Plan to allow for greater emigration from the Continent, since it was illogical to embark on a scheme to feed Europe while the governments involved would not allow anyone to leave their countries. Dorothy Detzer moved that the board agree to support the Hoover Plan provided that some such condition was added, but this proposal was rejected in favor of a more general endorsement of any plan to alleviate starvation in Europe. However, a committee was formed to approach Herbert Hoover with the suggested amendment to his proposals. Thus, while the board members recognized the complications and potential dangers of the plan, their desire to prevent possible famine in Europe outweighed their concern about possible aid to the German cause.

At the end of the day, Gertrud Baer made a statement suggestive of some disenchantment with the proceedings. While she made it "clear that it was not her intention to influence the policy of the American Section of WILPF in any way but that she was speaking as a representative of her European co-workers [she also] suggested that unless her position and purpose were completely understood by the Board, she would not like to attend future meetings of the National Board of the U.S. Section."[68]

The Hoover Plan also served to bring the Century Group out of the shadows, as it played a growing role in opposing the scheme and endeavoring to counter the propaganda put out by the America First Committee. With the expansion of its agenda beyond direct pressure on the administration, the Century Group enlisted the aid of Katherine (Kay) Gauss Jackson, daughter of Dean Christian Gauss of Princeton, and Helen Everitt, a writer and magazine executive, to promote the group's goals through women's organizations and women's magazines. To this end, Kay Jackson invited prominent women in the media, religion, and labor to "a series of lunches."

These women were targeted as those who could in turn "reach the greatest number of women—the wide group of 'women in the home.'"[69] Although most of these women were too busy to engage in any regular committee activities, they formed the basis of an informal network of women who worked in cooperation with the Century Group, as a sort of women's auxiliary, to promote U.S. entry into the war. While Kay Jackson enlisted professional women in the cause, Helen Everitt interviewed magazine editors—notably, those of *Ladies' Home Journal, Woman's Home Companion, Redbook, McCall's, Good Housekeeping,* and *Woman's Day*—to discuss ways in which their publications could be used to advance interventionist ideas. Apparently the response was generally favorable. Everitt reported, "Contrary to my personal expectation, there has been only the keenest desire to cooperate from people who felt that they were already doing much."[70] So she contacted both writers and literary agents to encourage the production of useful articles and the adoption of novel approaches to the issue.

However, by February 1941, the results had not proved particularly satisfactory, and Everitt reported that "most editors felt that their women readers needed escape, not realism." Here Everitt faced a traditional stereotype of women as uninterested in questions beyond the home. She proposed that women supporting the Century Group position should write to these editors "assum[ing] a naive line—that there is only one thing that matters now in our lives. You have helped us with our home problems. Why don't you help us with this emergency?"[71] In some ways, this suggested response seems only to bolster traditional stereotypes, playing on images of women as "naive." It also reflected the women's behind-the-scenes approach, attempting covertly to exert pressure on women's magazines to address foreign policy issues: rather than arguing from an authority based on their expertise and knowledge of foreign policy, they preferred to hide behind a veil of naïveté and domesticity.

In early December, the women's auxiliary of the Century Group organized a women's statement opposing the Hoover Plan. The press release that accompanied the publication of the statement declared,

"Twenty-five outstanding American women today united in a declaration asserting that America's own national security would be endangered by any action making easier Hitler's control of the subjugated European countries." The statement criticized the Hoover Plan as an aid to the Nazis, quoting Hoover's own acknowledgment that "it is easier to maintain order, without the use of force, in a population not dying of starvation." Finally, the women allowed that they would support some medical and food aid for occupied Europe, if the British government agreed to it, "but we oppose the application of any pressure whatsoever upon the British people or their government which will jeopardize the outcome of the struggle." The signers included Anna Lord Strauss, president of the New York City LWV; Josephine Schain; Virginia Gildersleeve, dean of Barnard College; Rose Schneiderman; C. Mildred Thompson, dean of Vassar; and Helen Hayes, the actress.[72]

The women's auxiliary to the Century Group cherished its informality but feared being dismissed as an upper-class interest group. Late in December 1940, its members decided to try to expand the range of their petition drives, "to start lining up labor women . . . as we feel strongly that they must be one of our main lines of approach and that we must get away from repetitive lists of elderly and well-heeled ladies."[73] However, sometimes they could not rise above their elitism. On January 9, they heard about the efforts of some New Jersey women to put together a letter to Congress in favor of aid to Britain to be "signed by a great many outstanding New Jersey names" and then published in three New Jersey newspapers as an advertisement. After some consideration, they agreed "to help them release it as a general story if the names *turn out to be good enough.*"[74]

In contrast, the Committee to Defend America, as a grassroots organization with a mass membership, was much less concerned about its class image. Indeed, the organization trumpeted its upper-class members. A press release directed to Maury Paul, society editor of the *New York Journal-American,* in July 1940, proudly declared: "The Social Register has yielded its quota of feminine volunteers in the cause of American defense. . . . Enlistments [in the Committee to Defend America] . . . include the names of debs, post-debs, young-marrieds and dowagers, many of whom are working daily elbow to elbow with their lesser sisters . . . putting their white gloves to the wheel in one way or another."[75] Of course, the women of the Committee to Defend America came from much wider social circles than the Century

Group's women's auxiliary, which had only about fifty-five members,[76] but inevitably, those with the time to become active in the organization were mostly middle- or upper-class, and campaigns such as the Minute Americans were directed at other middle-class women who had the time, and the telephones, to play their part.

While the interventionist organizations rallied their forces, internationalist women's organizations considered their next step. For the NCJW, the year would climax with its triennial convention, a moment when the organization could reconsider its agenda in the light of international developments. The council had strongly emphasized the goal of keeping the United States out of the war in late 1939 and early 1940. It had, however, consistently maintained the principle of aid for the victims of aggression as well. The delegates at the Sixteenth Triennial Convention in New York City in November 1940 reaffirmed those priorities. The council's Committee on International Relations and Peace drafted the resolutions on November 8, just a few days before the convention met, to ensure that they would not already have been made obsolete by the rapidly changing international situation when the delegates considered them. The first of these resolutions, under the heading "War and Peace," affirmed: "We support the declared policy of the President to keep the United States out of war."[77] Next, under the heading "Defense," the council resolved: "We urge as a measure of defense: 1) the strengthening of the policy of aid to nations which are victims of aggression; 2) The imposing of economic restrictions on nations which resort to aggression as a national policy."[78] Together these resolutions suggested continued ambivalence within the organization—an unwillingness to accept the possibility that these goals might turn out to be fundamentally incompatible. But their support for Roosevelt's administration was clear, and that would continue unabated through 1941.

Moreover, Fanny Brin, national chairman of the Committee on International Relations and Peace, may well have had a more realistic attitude. She acknowledged in her report to the convention the vital interest of the United States in the outcome of the war: "Everything depends on who emerges victorious from this conflict. Our existence as a free democratic nation, and the possibility of a democratically organized world, depends upon the victory of the nations that support reason."[79] Even more striking was her comment: "We pray that we may not become involved in the *actual war.*"[80] The phrase "actual war" suggests that Brin drew a distinction between direct military involvement, which might yet be avoided, and moral and economic involvement, which was already a reality.

By the end of 1940, the National LWV had also established its ongoing commitment to aid through its publicity both to members and to the public in general. Moreover, it was engaged in extensive monitoring of the situation in Washington, on the lookout for possible legislative proposals that would require action by the League. League newsletters kept members informed of the developments in Washington and the implications of international events. Florence Kirlin, the League's congressional secretary, commented in the September newsletter: "It seems to be agreed that the Rome-Berlin-Tokyo alliance only makes aid to Great Britain more imperative since the result of the Far Eastern conflict hinges upon the fate of Britain. The most discussed possible next move is the transfer of a portion of the United States Army 'flying fortresses' to Britain."[81] In October, Anna Lord Strauss, president of the New York City League, gave an interview to the *Christian Science Monitor* in which she declared her belief that the United States should "do all in her power to aid Great Britain. That is we should bend our energies to delivering her the supplies she needs."[82] Thus, the League's support of aid to Britain was well publicized in the second half of 1940, even though there were few specific proposals that could be supported.

League leaders in Washington and New York kept a close watch on developments, meeting with State Department officials[83] to find out what kind of aid Britain might need and considering different proposals in detail at National Board meetings.[84] As 1940 drew to an end, there was increasing pressure from some members at the state level for the League to take some action on aid questions. Edna Gellhorn, a National Board member, wrote to Louise Wright in December about Katharine Ludington and Mrs. McCormick: "Both of these women wanted us to assure them that the L.W.V. was going to do something about repeal of the Johnson Act and necessary changes of [the] Neutrality Act to permit money or credit to Great Britain."[85] The LWV's position was well established—it simply awaited a legislative initiative from the administration.

But before Roosevelt could embark on a major new legislative program, he had to secure reelection. So, in the fall of 1940, the nation prepared for a historic election—one that would in some ways be dominated by foreign policy, even though the candidates were largely in agreement in their support for a policy of all-out aid to Britain and the major party platforms on foreign policy were essentially indistinguishable. The Republicans nominated an interventionist—Wendell Willkie—rather than one of the leading isolationist contenders, Arthur Vandenberg or Robert Taft. This decision resulted from effective maneuvering by eastern interventionist Republicans combined with the impact of the fall of France on American public opinion.[86] Willkie's broad agreement with Roosevelt's foreign policy produced a rather paradoxical campaign wherein the challenger avoided specific criticisms of the incumbent's policy, often endorsing the administration's proposals for aid to Britain, but occasionally fired off vague accusations that Roosevelt would get the nation into the war, in some unspecified manner. Freda Kirchwey called these attacks "general and unsubstantiated criticisms of the President's foreign policy."[87] For example, in mid-August Willkie alleged that "there have been occasions when many of us have wondered if he is deliberately inciting us to war."[88]

However, Willkie endorsed the key elements of Roosevelt's foreign and defense policies, even controversial actions like the destroyers-for-bases deal and the introduction of conscription in September 1940. This bill began its life as a private initiative by two congressmen—Democratic senator Edward Burke of Nebraska and Republican representative James Wadsworth of New York—who introduced it in late June 1940. Initially Roosevelt had been reluctant to support the measure publicly. The United States had a long history of hostility to a standing army and a peacetime draft was unprecedented. In private, Roosevelt supported the idea, but he was extremely cautious about making public his views. Only in July, as opinion polls began to show clear majorities in favor of a draft, did Roosevelt start to make positive noises in public. On August 2, he finally made an unambiguous declaration of support, from which he immediately backpedaled when it provoked outrage among the isolationists. Only after Willkie had expressed his support for the draft did Roosevelt really get behind the bill, which he signed into law on September 14.[89]

Freda Kirchwey, who as early as June 1940 had abandoned her traditional left-wing suspicion of the draft, came out strongly in favor of the selective service bill. The crisis facing the United States was, in her view, severe enough to warrant even this level of regimentation and militarization. Indeed, she argued that the United States was really at war.[90] "It is foolish to call the Selective Training and Service Act a measure for 'peace-time conscription.' The United States is not waging military war, but it is only nominally at peace. Openly and officially we have identified ourselves with the nations fighting against Hitler. . . . Mussolini's term 'non-belligerent ally' describes as accurately as any other the actual if unofficial relationship of the United States to Great Britain. . . . [The draft bill] is a war measure, enacted on the assumption that active participation in the struggle cannot ultimately be avoided."[91] Thus, Kirchwey not only endorsed the draft but also explicitly related its passage to the inevitability of direct American military involvement in the war.

Nor was Kirchwey the only prominent woman interventionist to undertake an about-face during the campaign. Even more notoriously, Dorothy Thompson, vigorous conservative, critic of the New Deal, and supporter of the Republican Party, abandoned Willkie in October 1940 and announced her support for a third term for Roosevelt. Her reasons, explored at length in a series of columns throughout October, revolved around the international crisis. Roosevelt, she believed, was better equipped to lead the nation.[92] Moreover, as she pointed out, "The Axis desires the defeat of Roosevelt."[93] A Willkie victory, Thompson argued, would be seen also as an Axis victory: "It makes no difference whether or not there is substantial ground for such an interpretation. . . . the psychological result of the fall of Roosevelt would be Nazi jubilation in Germany and popular depression in Great Britain in a moment when the state of popular morale in both countries is the most important factor in the war."[94] Thompson was roundly criticized for jumping ship, and, indeed, she lost her contract with the Republican *New York Herald Tribune* as a result of her change of heart. However, her column was quickly taken up by the interventionist *New York Post,* and her crusade on behalf of aid to the Allies continued unabated in its columns.

While interventionists rallied to Roosevelt, isolationists campaigned vigorously against a third term. On October 14, Charles Lindbergh indicted America's leaders for their failings and called on Americans to "select leaders who believe sincerely in national defense, but who are whole-heartedly opposed to our involvement in foreign wars." Without mentioning either of the candidates by name, Lindbergh clearly assailed Roosevelt's record: "What we lack today is the type of leadership that made us a great nation; the type that turned adversity and hardship into virility and success."[95]

Until October, however, the Willkie campaign generally focused its attention on domestic issues, especially the failings of the New Deal. Willkie also hammered away at Roosevelt's violation of the two-term tradition, persistently referring to Roosevelt not by name but as the "third-term candidate." As the campaign entered its final month, however, Willkie trailed Roosevelt in the polls and succumbed to pressure from his advisers to exploit the war issue. On October 7, in Newark, he argued that Roosevelt had "pushed America close to the wars in Europe and Asia."[96] In a radio interview the next day, while he expressed his commitment to aiding Britain, which he described as "our first line of defense," he also declared, "I believe we should keep out of war at all hazards," adding, in a jibe at Roosevelt, "We are being edged toward war by an Administration which is alike careless in speech and in action."[97] And as the month went on, his charges became more serious. On October 17, Willkie asked, in a speech in St. Louis, whether Roosevelt had "entered into any secret pact with any foreign powers or is he negotiating any that may obligate this country to enter into war?" He further indicted the New Deal for failing to promote the industrial production essential for American preparedness and charged that Roosevelt would take the nation into the war: "We do not want to send our boys over there again. And we do not intend to send them over there again. And if you elect me President we won't. But by the same token I believe that if you re-elect the third-term candidate they will be sent."[98]

As Willkie climbed in the polls, Roosevelt was moved to respond. On October 23, in Philadelphia, he emphasized the foreign policy laid out in the Democratic Party platform: "I repeat again that I stand on the platform of our party: 'We will not participate in foreign wars and will not send our Army, naval or air forces to fight in foreign lands outside of the Americas except in case of attack.' It is for peace that I have labored; and it is for peace that I shall labor all the days of my life."[99] The very next day, Willkie cited a broken plank of the 1932 Democratic platform and piously hoped that Roosevelt would remember this promise for longer: "If he does not remember it longer, then shortly our boys will be on the transports, sailing for some foreign shore."[100] In response, Roosevelt made his most famous declaration of the campaign: "I have said this before, but I shall say it again, and again, and again. Your boys are not going to be sent into any foreign wars."[101]

Freda Kirchwey was very critical of this approach, arguing that both candidates had compromised their integrity by failing to deal honestly with the foreign policy issues. Addressing the as yet undetermined new president, she said, "I think you should have refused to vie with your opponent in unqualifiedly promising peace. Instead, you should have bravely warned the nation that war may be necessary; that certain possible happenings will be prevented even at the risk of war. You should have told the people plainly that this country is already inextricably engaged in the struggle against Hitlerism and that we shall not draw back from its uttermost consequences."[102] An important opportunity had been missed, she believed, for educating the American people and preparing them for what was to come.

On November 5, Roosevelt won with a greatly reduced margin compared with 1936 (though one that would be the envy of most recent American presidents): 27 million to 22 million, although this gave him a decisive electoral college victory, 449 to 82. Polls suggested that the war issue had, in fact, assisted Roosevelt, with more than 10 percent of his supporters declaring that they had voted for him because of the war; only 2 percent of Willkie voters backed him because of his war policy.[103] In the wake of the election, Americans daily expected the administration to announce new measures for aid to Britain.

While Americans waited, the debate continued, focusing on the nature of the war and America's stake in the conflict. One striking entry into the discussion was a short book by Anne Morrow Lindbergh called *The Wave of the Future.* She gave the book the subtitle: *A Confession of Faith,* but her interventionist sister Constance "wittily corrected [her] by calling it 'A Confession of Doubt.'"[104] In it, Anne Lindbergh attempted to explain why she could not embrace the interventionist view of the war. As she explained to her mother in a letter, "I think the clearest definition of the [book] is that it attempts to give a *moral* argument for isolationism—which I think no one has yet presented. . . . I have wanted to present [this] because I feel that the cause of staying out of this war has been so badly presented, so unjustly criticized and accused, and because I think it is vital to stay out."[105]

Interventionists, in Anne Lindbergh's view, perceived the war in simplistic terms, as a conflict between good and evil. She rejected this, arguing that the world was experiencing a revolution—what she called "the wave of the future." The Axis powers did not represent this future, but they were riding the wave: "The evils we deplore in these systems are not in themselves the future; they are scum on the wave of the future."[106] The Allies, however, represented the forces of reaction—desperately trying to resist the irresistible—"There is no fighting the wave of the future."[107] Lindbergh believed it was fruitless, even destructive, to become involved in the Allies' vain struggle to stop the clock, and that the United States should focus on reforming itself—riding the revolutionary wave to a better future: "It seems to me that our task, instead of crusading against an inevitable 'revolution,' or change, in Europe, is to work toward a peaceful 'revolution' here, or rather, a reformation—to reform at home rather than crusade abroad."[108] Anne admitted both to her mother and to her friend Mina Curtiss that the book was, at heart, a "moral defense of Charles's position."[109]

Predictably, perhaps, the book did not impress interventionists, not least because it was strikingly vague. The central argument of the book was that the "wave of the future" was a positive force. "What was pushing behind Communism? What behind Fascism in Italy? What behind Naziism? Is it nothing but a 'return to barbarism,' to be crushed at all costs by a 'crusade'? Or is some new, and perhaps even ultimately good, conception of humanity trying to come to birth . . . ? . . . Something, one feels, is pushing up through the crust of custom. One does not know what—some new conception of humanity and its place on the earth. I believe that it is, in its essence good; but because we are blind we cannot see it."[110] But Anne Lindbergh had nothing more than her gut feeling to show that it was good. As Clare Boothe Luce, playwright and wife of Henry Luce, a member of the Century Group, commented in a review for *Current History and Forum,* "Anne Lindbergh would have Americans accept or rather appease the terrible *form* of this German born eruption, simply because she believes that the force behind it *must* be good."[111] Moreover, although the book contains many very general condemnations of the horrors taking place in Europe, it is devoid of any specific sense of what the Axis powers were up to—even to the extent of depersonalizing the blitzkrieg. Lindbergh wrote of "the invasion of Holland and Belgium by tanks, machine guns, and bombers,"[112] almost as if no human beings had been behind those weapons.

Indeed, Anne Lindbergh might well have been classified as a "Kneeler" by Alzada Comstock, chairman of the AAUW International Relations Committee. In late 1940, the *AAUW Journal* published an article entitled "The Distant Drum," in which Comstock divided isolationists into four groups: Utopians, Sitters, Kneelers, and Grabbers. The Kneelers, she argued, when faced with the possibility that preserving their way of life might require great sacrifice, wondered whether living under totalitarianism would be so bad. Here she reserved particular blame for women who ignored the special oppression experienced by their sisters under National Socialism. "Women Kneelers, in particular, seem curiously unable to remember that hundreds and thousands of women in conquered territories . . . are put to work in the fields for as long as they last. Women Kneelers, with their one or two children, ignore the totalitarian decrees about women having large families and not being too fussy about paternity."[113] Thus, Comstock appealed to her educated female readership by noting both the exploitation of female labor and also the distortion of the ideals of motherhood and family under Hitler—a double-pronged assault designed to cover all the possible convictions of her readers. Both professional career women and educated housewives and mothers had reason to oppose the Nazis.

It was not, however, that Anne Lindbergh denied these problems but that she believed they were not the heart of the story. To make this point, she drew a parallel with the French Revolution: "No one today defends the atrocities of the French Revolution; but few seriously question the fundamental necessity or 'rightness' of the movement."[114] Critics, of course, completely repudiated this analogy. "The French Revolution," declared Clare Boothe Luce, "born of man's need for Liberté, Egalité, Fraternité, in which great masses of long oppressed men rose to slay and torture their tyrants, has nothing in common with the German Revolution of today in which a few tyrants have, in the name of national oppression, led a bewildered and now infuriated people in a highly organized, cynical, ruthless and greedy crusade to wipe out Liberté, Egalité, Fraternité all over the world."[115]

Interventionists not only rejected Anne Lindbergh's conception of the war but also argued that the United States could not hope to remain aloof from the conflict, as she suggested. Anne O'Hare McCormick, appearing on the radio discussion program *America's Town Meeting of the Air* in November 1940, called upon the rhetoric of Abraham Lincoln to undermine Lindbergh's view. "Whether we like it or not," she declared, "whether we call ourselves isolationists or interventionists, this is our war, in the sense that we are part of the world, and if it is impossible to remain free in a world which is half enslaved, it is equally impossible to live at peace in one hemisphere when the other hemisphere is at war."[116] It was hard to imagine how the United States could conduct a peaceful reformation as Anne Lindbergh suggested, while the rest of the world was consumed by war.

But if interventionists wholeheartedly rejected "the gentle appeasement of Mrs. Lindbergh,"[117] they did not necessarily agree among themselves about the character of the war. At the end of 1939, Dorothy Thompson had offered her readers a vision of the war as a struggle between Christianity—an Anglo-Saxon Christian civilization, in fact—and the forces of barbarism,[118] closely linking Western Christian tradition with the ideals of freedom and democracy that were central to the war.

In contrast, Freda Kirchwey, while acknowledging the power of religion as a motivating force, rejected the assumption that it was necessarily a force for good. "From faith men draw the strength and meaning that carry them through desperate ordeals. But the religious impulse is a fluid which runs as readily into one mold as another. It can be made to fit the uniform of a storm trooper quite as snugly as the habit of a Christian churchgoer."[119] Indeed, Thompson's glorification of Western ideals and her tendency to see the war as a battle between Western, Christian values and German paganism brought her into direct conflict with Kirchwey, who dismissed the Christianizing of the war effort.

In November 1940, Kirchwey explicitly rejected Thompson's religious vision, vigorously asserting the secular character of democracy and thus of the war. "More and more," she complained, "the belief seems to take root that the fight against Hitler is a fight for religion. Oftener and oftener we are invited to go forth to the defense of a 'Christian' civilization. The Christian faith is somehow equated—even identified—with democracy, and the war itself is becoming a holy war: embattled Christianity against the Nazi infidels." She identified Roosevelt as chief culprit: "Last May he proclaimed his belief that the Americas would have to 'become the guardian of Western culture, the protection of Christian civilization.' . . . One can find similar if less powerful expression of it in the writings of Dorothy Thompson and other supporters of the struggle against Hitler." Kirchwey would have none of this. "Democracy has nothing on earth to do with any particular faith," she declared. "Christianity may nourish democracy or dictatorship. . . . The struggle we are engaged upon is not a struggle of Christianity against paganism or of religion against non-religion. It is a secular struggle to establish a society in which men and women shall be free to vote and write and speak as they choose; to follow the dictates of reason rather than of blood; to use methods of discussion and orderly decision rather than violence; to achieve economic security and justice by their common efforts; to follow the faith they prefer or to repudiate religious dogma altogether."[120]

Interventionists were sometimes sharply divided in their perceptions of the war and what was at stake. But they nevertheless united in their conviction that the United States would be vitally affected by the result of the conflict and that American interests demanded that sufficient aid be provided to the victims of aggression to ensure that the Nazis were defeated. As 1940 drew to a close, they waited to see what the third Roosevelt administration would propose to deal with the problem of aiding the Allies.

After postponing Operation Sealion, Hitler turned his eyes eastward and began to plan for the conquest of the Soviet Union. As a result, much of the military activity of the late fall and winter revolved around Mussolini's adventures, or misadventures, in Greece and North Africa. He began by striking from Libya into British-occupied Egypt on September 13. He followed this with a strike against Greece on October 28, motivated by what military historian John Keegan has called "an egocentric wish to emulate Hitler."[121] Although Italian forces greatly outnumbered the Greeks, the campaign was a disaster. The Greeks defended their homeland with a will, throwing back the Italian invaders and counterattacking on November 14. Even reinforcements, rushed in from Italy, could not save the initiative. Mussolini's failure convinced Hitler that a German assault on Greece would be necessary—to prevent the establishment of British air bases within bombing range of vital raw material supplies in the Balkans, notably the oil fields of Ploesti, Romania.

The blitzkrieg had altered American public opinion decisively, creating solid, if not unanimous, support for aid to Britain. Moreover, Roosevelt's reelection reaffirmed the American people's support for his foreign policy while leaving in doubt their stomach for war. By the end of 1940, most women internationalists were committed to aid for Britain and embraced the view that German defeat was vital for the security of the United States. They stood ready to support a major legislative initiative to realize their demands for all-out aid short of war. And this readiness should be understood in the context of their interwar support for discrimination against aggressor nations and their belief that any postwar peace must be based on collective security and international law.

6

The Arsenal of Democracy

The months of late 1940 and early 1941 were comparatively quiet on the military front. The Luftwaffe continued its bombing campaign against the British Isles—many feared in preparation for a spring invasion. But the main ground action occurred in North Africa between British and Italian forces. On December 9, the British in Egypt turned the tables on the Italians, who had invaded in September, counterattacking and taking nearly forty thousand prisoners, and then continuing their advance into Libya. The British captured the port of Tobruk on January 21, adding another twenty-five thousand Italian prisoners of war. They then divided their forces and trapped the remainder of the Italian force in the desert on February 5. The Italian collapse prompted a German rescue mission under General Erwin Rommel, whose forces landed in Tripoli in the early weeks of February. The British enjoyed further successes against the Italians in Ethiopia and Somaliland and inflicted humiliations on the Italian navy by shelling Genoa on February 9 and defeating an Italian fleet in Greek waters on March 28. While these small victories were good for British morale, this theater of the war was clearly peripheral, and the real enemy, the Germans, remained undefeated. In truth, probably the most significant event of the war in these months occurred not on the battlefields of Europe or Asia but in the political arena of a supposedly neutral nation. For it was in these months that the American people and the United States Congress debated and adopted the Lend-Lease Act, a measure that shattered all pretense of American neutrality and established the United States as a nonbelligerent member of an anti-Axis front.

The idea of leasing or lending ships and other war matériel to Britain was first suggested by President Roosevelt in a cabinet meeting on November 8, 1940, three days after his reelection, but the concept was not presented to the American people until mid-December, and the bill was not introduced into Congress until early January 1941. Although isolationists continued to fight against administration policy through the rest of 1941, the lend-lease debate was basically their last significant chance of sustaining American neutrality—once the Lend-Lease Act became law, the United States was publicly committed to the Allied cause. As a result, the whole nation was engaged in the argument that raged in Congress. The hearings were given front-page coverage in most newspapers, and the debate was carried on in opinion pages and letters and on radio discussion programs. Both supporters and opponents of the bill poured out propaganda, and congressmen's offices were flooded with letters from their constituents. A poll conducted at the end of January 1941 showed that 82 percent of Americans were aware of the bill before Congress. Just over two weeks later that figure had risen to 91 percent.[1]

The Roosevelt administration hoped to use the debate over lend-lease to create a meaningful consensus in support of its policy of aid to Britain. However, it hoped to do so by presenting the bill as the best means of avoiding war and playing down the risks inherent in aiding one side over the other in a major international conflict. As the leading historian of the legislation has commented, the administration "was not thoroughly honest and candid in its presentation of the Lend-Lease Bill."[2] It would be a mistake, however, to suppose that that meant the American people did not fully understand the possible consequences of the lend-lease bill. After all, its opponents took every opportunity to point out those consequences, indeed, to present them not just as possibilities but as inevitabilities. Moreover, not all advocates of the bill were as reluctant as administration officials openly to acknowledge the risks involved. In fact, the administration's tactics had little restraining effect on the public debate. Americans were very well aware of the implications of the bill under consideration; and, while support was by no means unanimous, close to a two-thirds majority definitely approved of the government's policy, in full knowledge of what it might mean. The lend-lease debate also produced the most vigorous and public campaigning by American women—on both sides of the issue.

As anticipation grew toward the end of 1940 over what steps the administration would take to aid Britain, National LWV leaders tried to resolve the potential conflict between aid and staying out of war. During December and early January, Marguerite Wells carried on a regular correspondence with members of the National Board, especially Louise Wright, discussing the question of aid. Wells's primary concern was how the League should respond to proposals for aid that seemed likely to result in America's entry into the war, given that the 1940 convention had mandated action specifically as a nonbelligerent. As she explained in a memorandum to Wright in early December, "I cannot seem to satisfy myself to go on with our recommendations to members, leaving them ignorant of implications of which we are aware and which mean going to war."[3] Wells herself seems to have experienced considerable angst over the question of whether war should be risked for the sake of aid, for while she declared that she was "one of those who recognize that there are worse things than fighting," she continued: "I cannot however rid myself of the conviction that our country will be a better country at the end of all this if it is not a country that has suffered war."[4]

Louise Wright replied in mid-December that she did not believe it was possible to anticipate what kinds of aid would lead to war and suggested that "any decision that is made about assistance to any nation can only be . . . based on intelligent opportunism."[5] She confessed that she could "not see any hard and fast distinction between peace and war in these totalitarian days" and argued that if the Axis powers wished to declare war, they could make a casus belli out of any number of issues. Wright did note, however, that if the question of entering the war arose directly, the League had no authority either to support or oppose it and could take no position on the issue.

At a press conference the following day, December 17, Roosevelt gave a clearer indication of the policy he had in mind. Rather than loaning the British money or giving them arms, which would require repeal of the Johnson Act and the Neutrality Act, respectively, Roosevelt proposed "something brand new." The United States would produce weapons and "enter into some kind of arrangement for their use by the British on the ground that it was the best thing for American defense, with the understanding that when the show was over, we would get repaid sometime in kind, thereby leaving out the dollar mark."[6] To illustrate his idea, he created the famous analogy of the man whose neighbor's house is on fire. A sensible man, aware of the danger of the fire spreading, would lend his neighbor a hose to help put out the fire rather than attempting to sell him the hose, expecting only that his neighbor would return it once the fire was out. More details, Roosevelt was reluctant to provide.

The new proposal formed the nucleus of the activities of the women's auxiliary to the Century Group, which organized itself as the Women's Committee for Action in mid-December. This committee operated alongside the Century Group and in close association with it, providing weekly reports of its activities and sharing office space with the men. The Women's Committee for Action conceived of its role explicitly as a counterweight to "the influence of the women lobbyists for peace who are giving Congress very effectively the idea that all women are against war and help to Britain if it involves any danger to ourselves."[7] However, it functioned in a much less public fashion than any of its opponents or the Woman's Division of the Committee to Defend America. There were no big rallies or poster contests; rather, the committee members worked through informal networks of women, to win favorable press coverage for their cause, to spread their message across the country, and to put pressure on Congress and the administration. One of their primary goals in December 1940 was to show support for the president's new aid proposal. To that end, they decided to get up a petition signed by "heads of women's organizations all over the country" supporting "his statement urging that we send war materials to Britain without immediate cash paying, and offering our support for any steps he may take to awake the country to an awareness of [the] national emergency."[8]

The Committee to Defend America also readily embraced Roosevelt's plan, despite its vagueness, announcing, "We are united in our support of the President's proposal to lease war material to Great Britain and have so informed the President."[9] Moreover, in anticipation of one of Roosevelt's famous "fireside chat" radio addresses, scheduled for December 29, in which he was expected to elaborate on the plan, the Woman's Division set up shop on Park Avenue in New York "to aid persons wishing to telegraph President Roosevelt, in advance of his fireside chat tonight, to increase the amount of aid to Great Britain. Telegraph blanks and postcards will be provided those wishing to telegraph and telegraph messengers will be waiting to rush the messages to offices for transmission."[10] Not all Americans were impressed with the committee's stand, however. One critic complained acidly that it should change its name to "the Committee to Keep America Defenseless by Giving Away Everything We Own."[11]

Roosevelt used the December 29 speech to lay the groundwork for the lend-lease plan with the American public. First he declared forthrightly that aid was the best hope for the United States to keep out of the war, although he did allow that there were no guarantees: "I make the direct statement to the American people that there is far less chance of the United States getting into war, if we do all we can now to support the nations defending themselves against attack by the Axis than if we acquiesce in their defeat, submit tamely to an Axis victory, and wait our turn to be the object of attack in another war later on. If we are to be completely honest with ourselves, we must admit that there is risk in any course we may take." Despite this admission, however, his chief object was to emphasize that the goal of American policy was to avoid war. "The people of Europe who are defending themselves do not ask us to do their fighting. They ask us for implements of war . . . which will enable them to fight for their liberty and for our security. . . . Our national policy is not directed toward war. Its sole purpose is to keep war away from our country and our people." Finally, he suggested that the United States could play a vital role through its productive capabilities. "We must be the great arsenal of democracy. For this is an emergency as serious as war itself. We must apply ourselves to our task with the same resolution, the same sense of urgency, the same spirit of patriotism and sacrifice as we would show were we at war."[12]

Senator Burton Wheeler took on the task of responding to Roosevelt's plan on the following day. His speech foreshadowed the primary rhetorical contests of the coming weeks. First, Wheeler set out to define American interests: "Our stakes are our independence, our democracy and our trade and commerce. Every red-blooded American would fight to preserve them." There was, however, conflict over how to defend these interests. Some people believed that this could best be done by aiding Britain, "that England is our first line of defense and that we must go to England's aid every time she declares war." The other group, in contrast, did "not believe that the preservation of the American people or our democracy depends upon any foreign nation." Wheeler argued that the president's plan would lead to war: "If we lend or lease war materials today, we will lend or lease American boys tomorrow." He also suggested that the German threat to the United States was exaggerated: "Our independence can only be lost or compromised if Germany invades the Western Hemisphere north of the equator. . . . Remember, Hitler has already been seven months in vainly trying to cross twenty miles. If Hitler's army can't cross the narrow English Channel in seven months his bombers won't fly across the Rockies to bomb Denver tomorrow." Wheeler also raised the dangers of total war for belligerents on the home front: "War means the end of civil liberties, the end of free speech, free press, free enterprise.

It means dictatorship and slavery, all the things we abhor in nazism, communism and fascism. It means Stalin or Hitler will have achieved their boasts for a totalitarian world without conquering America." Finally, Wheeler criticized interventionists for mudslinging: "We have reached a strange situation in America when those who advocate peace, who do not follow the party line, are branded appeasers or unwitting tools of the dictators."[13] These would be the core arguments that isolationists would present to the American people in the course of the next two and a half months as the nation debated the administration's lend-lease bill.

The day after Roosevelt's speech, Marguerite Wells noted in a memorandum to Louise Wright that the interventionist movement had begun to divide into two camps: "those who balk at war on our part" and those who did not.[14] The question was, In which camp did the League belong? Wells asked the National Board this question early in January 1941, clearly placing it in the context of a war in which the United States was interested both morally and in terms of national interests: "Our people know today something they did not know in the fall of 1939. They know that the war is not between certain nations whose ways we prefer and others whose ways we object to, but that it is a war against democracy. Therefore, that its outcome not only affects us, but affects us vitally. Finally we know that the chances of its being decided to our advantage have decreased. It is because of this growing knowledge that the American people have agreed during the past year to policies entailing more and more sacrifices and greater and greater risks of eventual entanglement in war itself."[15] Thus, Wells posed the question in such a way as to leave the fundamental interventionism of the League undoubted. Against the background of a conflict in which American interests were vitally concerned and the cause of democracy threatened, League support for aid to the Allies was certain. The issue in question was how far the League would be willing to go; were there risks the League was not willing to take?

Since the details of the lend-lease bill were revealed shortly after this memorandum was sent to the board, the board members' responses were mixed in with their views on the new legislative proposals for aid, which served as a test case for board opinion. Many board members shared Wright's view that it was not possible to determine in advance the results of different measures of aid. Thus, the question of whether they should support aid likely to lead to war was moot. As Mrs. Field explained, "I feel that the decision as to whether we go to war officially has passed to the Nazis. The decision consequently as to whether a certain action is more likely to lead us into war than another action is difficult—maybe even meaningless."[16] Field also stated that she believed that, while most League members still hoped the United States could keep out of war, if "the majority of League members were faced with the choice between insufficient aid to Great Britain and belligerency on our part they would choose the official declaration of war."[17] She added, however, that she was from New England—a region where interventionism was strong. Nevertheless, her response suggests that some members of the League, at least, had reached the conclusion by early 1941 that German defeat was a higher priority than American peace.

Harriet Eliel, secretary of the National LWV, took almost as hawkish a position, declaring of lend-lease: "If this is just another roundabout method of not facing an issue with the country or Congress I would vote to oppose it. . . . I am not yet ready to approve the repeal of the 'carry' provision for the only reason that I think it would immediately involve us in a declaration of war and we are not yet ready to take on Japan."[18] Eliel's concern was to *delay* war because of a lack of preparedness. She had already reached the conclusion that war would, perhaps even should, come. Similarly, Jeannette Cheek, chairman of Government and Economic Welfare, supported lend-lease as a delaying tactic: "As far as involvement in the broad sense of the word is concerned, I think we have no choice. We are in it and I'm for the 'defense' bill as the best means in view to protect our interest without *immediate* military action."[19] Thus, as early as January 1941, at least two members of the LWV's National Board had clearly accepted the inevitability of war, even if they had practical reasons for not calling for an immediate declaration of war.

They were not alone in this view. Freda Kirchwey rejected the idea that U.S. policy makers faced a choice between war and peace. Although she advocated an open recognition of the fact that if aid was not enough, Americans would enter the war, she nevertheless attacked the isolationist camp at the start of 1941 for its tactic of equating any support for aid as a covert attempt to secure direct American military intervention in the war. The isolationists, she argued,

> have adopted a trick which is of the utmost value to Hitler. They try to center all discussion on the danger of our going into the war as a belligerent. . . . It may be necessary to send air and naval units

> to England to prevent British defeat. It is more likely that we shall have to convoy supply ships across the Atlantic, running the risk of Nazi attack. . . . But at the moment the odds favor non-belligerent support of Britain, and . . . the more generous and swift the support, the better the chance that it will continue to be nonbelligerent. . . . We cannot afford to let the appeasers and isolationists, or Hitler himself, switch the discussion to the danger of possible American participation in the war. That isn't the point. The point is the defense of freedom.[20]

Kirchwey was, perhaps, well ahead even of the interventionist crowd at this point in the war—she had already accepted the likelihood of direct American involvement, whereas many interventionists still clung to the hope that it could be avoided, if only enough material aid could be given.

On January 6, 1941, the president addressed Congress in the traditional State of the Union Message. "I find it unhappily necessary to report that the future and the safety of our country and of our democracy are overwhelmingly involved in events far beyond our borders," he announced. "The need of the moment is that our actions and our policy should be devoted primarily—almost exclusively—to meeting this foreign peril. . . . [W]e are committed to full support of all those resolute people everywhere who are resisting aggression and are thereby keeping war away from our hemisphere. . . . [W]e are committed to the proposition that principles of morality and considerations for our own security will never permit us to acquiesce in a peace dictated by aggressors and sponsored by appeasers. We know that enduring peace cannot be bought at the cost of other people's freedom." Having established the nation's needs and goals, he explained how they might be achieved. First, a great effort to increase arms production was necessary, accompanied by increased appropriations from Congress. Roosevelt also asked Congress "for authority and for funds sufficient to manufacture additional munitions and war supplies of many kinds, to be turned over to those nations which are now in actual war with aggressor nations. Our most useful and immediate role is to act as an arsenal for them as well as for ourselves." Roosevelt also attempted to counter isolationist concerns that lend-lease might provoke the Germans to declare war on the United States: "Such aid is not an act of war, even if a dictator should unilaterally proclaim it so to be. And when the dictators—if the dictators—are ready to make war upon us, they will not wait for an act of war on our part. They did not wait for Norway or Belgium or the Netherlands to commit an act of war." The great concern for American production and aid to Britain now was speed: "The happiness of future generations of Americans may well depend on how effective and how immediate we can make our aid felt."[21]

Having made his case for the forthcoming lend-lease bill, Roosevelt ended his speech with a compelling statement of American war aims: "In the future days which we seek to make secure, we look forward to a world founded upon four essential freedoms: . . . freedom of speech and expression, . . . freedom of every person to worship God in his own way, . . . freedom from want, . . . [and] freedom from fear."[22] Simply by establishing American goals in the war, Roosevelt implied a greater American involvement. Genuinely neutral nations cannot, by definition, have war aims.

The speech was extremely well received by many interventionists. The Executive Committee of the National Committee on the Cause and Cure of War, meeting the day after the speech, agreed to send the president a congratulatory message, signing as individuals (rather than as representatives of their respective organizations), emphasizing in particular their support of the goal of aid to Britain and the ideals expressed in the four freedoms.[23]

The WTUL also took up the issue in the wake of Roosevelt's speech. Margaret Stone wrote to the members of the Executive Board on January 9, asking them for authority to act in support of whatever legislation might be introduced. She prefaced this request by describing the seriousness of the international situation: "Observers everywhere are convinced that Hitler is planning a knockout blow against Britain in the near future, and that is why the next ninety days are so important. Whatever action the United States decides on should be taken quickly, so that no precious time will be lost in the moment of acute crisis. It might very well mean the difference between victory and defeat for Great Britain; and for the United States, the difference between the possibility of living peaceably in the world and . . . the necessity for arming to the teeth with accompanying regimentation and heavy taxation prolonged indefinitely."[24] In such a context, the need for action to increase aid to Britain was extremely urgent. Moreover, as Stone pointed out, the League's general position had already been established: "The Executive Board of the WTUL has gone on record twice in favor of discriminatory treatment for victims of aggression. *It is a question now of how far our National League is willing to go in this direction, and how grave we think this crisis is.*"[25]

The board voted toward the end of January to support the Lend-Lease Act with a time limit amendment. In an explanatory letter to League secretaries and international relations chairmen, Margaret Stone, national chairman of the International Relations Committee, noted that the board's decision "follows logically on its previous stand" of supporting aid to victims of aggression.[26] Thus, the National Board consciously saw the wartime policy of interventionism as a logical extension of its interwar peace policy of collective security.

Similarly, the National Committee of the NCJW readily endorsed the Lend-Lease Act.[27] In an explanatory letter to local peace chairmen, Brin noted: "The Act gives unprecedented power to the executive and in a great measure sets aside legislation which limits this country's action in case of war."[28] In other words, it largely dismantled the neutrality legislation of the 1930s, including the "cash" half of cash-and-carry, which the NCJW had specifically advocated as a measure that would lessen the danger of the United States being drawn into the war. Brin acknowledged the danger: "We believe that though this bill involves risks, it may help the victims of aggression and check further conquest. If so, it would turn the tide that threatens to destroy the civilization of the remaining free nations of the world."[29] Thus, Brin argued that the risk of war was worth taking to promote an Allied victory; the balance in the NCJW had shifted, and German defeat had become the priority.

Freda Kirchwey took a similar view, arguing strongly in support of the lend-lease bill but recognizing that even that level of aid might not be enough. As a result, she interpreted the president's speech in the most interventionist terms possible, calling for a frank understanding of the growing likelihood of direct military intervention. "The fact remains that . . . the British and their allies may face defeat. If the President's words mean anything, we would fight to prevent that defeat—and the fascist peace that would follow. I stress this possible alternative because I believe it must be accepted as real and then used, not as an argument for inaction, but rather as a spur to a more intense effort to pour weapons into Britain's arsenals."[30] Kirchwey was not yet calling for war, but she was demanding a clear understanding that there would be no limits put on American aid to Britain.

The LWV National Board conducted a mail poll of its members on the issue of lend-lease, resulting in a vote of 10 to 2 in favor of supporting the bill, and the League embarked on a vigorous campaign to promote its passage. However, the bill was supported as a measure that would *help to keep the United States out of war,* not, as some board members saw it, as a way to buy time. Louise Wright clearly saw the bill as an embodiment of the discriminatory principle, which the League had pursued for years in connection with the Neutrality Acts. She regretted that the bill's authorization of aid to any country whose defense was deemed vital to the security of the United States was theoretically more limited than the League's prescription of "victims of aggression," but she recognized also that under the circumstances there was little practical difference and that the defense argument would carry more weight with the American public.[31] However, despite the long-standing principles dictating League support for lend-lease, when Marguerite Wells wrote to the state presidents to inform them of the board's decision, her rationale was quite different: "The Act to Promote the Defense of the United States is of such far-reaching implications that it cannot be operated without sacrifice, public and private, present and future, comparable to the sacrifices demanded by war itself. Yet it is not an act providing for war. On the contrary it is a *substitute for war.*"[32]

Wells's decision to present the League's position in this way was a reflection of her own convictions, her own hesitance to accept what some other board members had—that direct U.S. involvement in the war was necessary if Germany was to be defeated and their hopes for a peaceful postwar world protected by a world organization based on collective security and international law were to be fulfilled. As she explained to Louise Wright, "I myself have come to a position of support of the Act . . . based on the fact that it seems to me the bill is a sincere and bold attempt to do what everybody wants to do without going to war about it and that that is of the very essence of our long continued program to find a substitute for war. . . . I should be dismayed if I thought my bold assertion that the League sought to avoid war was not justified. It is to me of the very essence of the present attempts, nor can I justify the present act in any other way."[33] This last comment is particularly significant, since it shows that Wells had not yet come to the conclusion that aid was worth any risk. Indeed, her correspondence throughout the period of war before American entry displayed an anguished uncertainty as her conviction that the Axis must be defeated battled with her horror of war and her hope that the United States could refrain from full-scale military involvement.

On January 10, the lend-lease bill was introduced in Congress, with the rather coy title "A Bill to Further Promote the Defense of the United States and for Other Purposes" and the suspiciously fortuitous number H.R. 1776. The act defined the key term, *defense article,* as broadly as possible and then provided the following grant of power to the president: "Notwithstanding the provisions of any other law, the President may, from time to time, when he deems it in the interest of national defense, authorize the Secretary of War, the Secretary of the Navy, or the head of any other department or agency of the government: 1. To manufacture in arsenals, factories and shipyards under their jurisdiction, or otherwise procure, any defense article for the government of any country whose defense the President deems vital to the defense of the United States. 2. To sell, transfer, exchange, lease, lend, or otherwise dispose of, to any such government, any defense article."[34] In a final, broad grant of power, the bill declared, "The President may, from time to time, promulgate such rules and regulations as may be necessary and proper to carry out any of the proposals of this act; and he may exercise any power or authority conferred on him by this act through such department, agency or officer as he shall direct."[35]

The reaction of isolationists was predictably ferocious. Clearly, if the bill became law, all pretense of American neutrality would be destroyed, but this was not the isolationists' only concern. In particular, they condemned the tremendous power that the bill vested in the executive. Senator Hiram Johnson of California led the charge, declaring, "I regard the bill as presented today as monstrous. I decline to change the whole form of my government on the specious plea of assisting one belligerent. The bill presents squarely to Congress whether it shall create a dictatorship. . . . It is up to Congress now to determine whether our government shall be as ordained or become a member of the totalitarian states."[36] He was joined by Senator Taft of Ohio, who complained that "the proposed bill combines all the faults of the worst New Deal legislation, including unlimited delegation of authority and blank-check appropriations. In addition it authorizes the President to make war on any nation in the world."[37]

Isolationists outside Congress also attacked the bill for the powers it delegated to the president. An editorial in the *Chicago Sunday Tribune* on January 12, 1941, carried the headline "A Bill to Destroy the Republic." In it, the editors of the *Tribune* denounced the lend-lease bill, declaring: "This is a bill for the destruction of the American republic. It is a bill for an unlimited dictatorship with power over the possessions and lives of the American people, with power to make war and alliances for war. With this power, Mr. Roosevelt could do almost anything, notwithstanding, as is provided, 'the provisions of any other law.' Mr. Roosevelt's power to do anything he pleased with the person and property of an American citizen to aid any governments he pleased to aid in any conflict which he chose to make his own would be unlimited."[38] If this seems a little paranoid from the perspective of the twenty-first century, it should be understood in the context of the extraordinary expansion of federal and executive power involved in the New Deal; and of Roosevelt's attempt to expand the Supreme Court in 1937, packing it with justices who would not oppose his policies.

The standard pro-bill response was to deny that the bill involved any extraordinary powers, but Dorothy Thompson took an entirely different tack, pointing out that the will of the American people, so far as it could be determined, was essentially contradictory: "It is to achieve an objective while limiting the means of achieving it. 'Do not let Britain be defeated and do not go to war.' It is like saying 'see that we have our cake and eat it, too.' Yet, it is *possible* of accomplishment. . . . But it demands completely unified command."[39] The powers given to the president in the lend-lease bill, she suggested, made this goal attainable. Moreover, she argued: "Time and again democratic republics have saved themselves by freely and voluntarily suspending the routines of peaceful and prosperous times and resorting to what amounts to a limited dictatorship. . . . Indeed we misuse the word 'dictatorship,' confusing it with despotism and tyranny, which are quite different things."[40]

Anne O'Hare McCormick also seems to have been unconcerned by the dangers of dictatorship; rather, she presented Roosevelt's request for complete control over lend-lease allocations as a sign of how confident and well-informed he was: "Just the development of the brand-new policy of buying exemption from actual fighting, of winning a victory without the use of man power—and this is the President's aim and hope—requires an almost superhuman skill and sagacity."[41]

These and many other arguments were rehearsed in great detail in the congressional hearings on the bill, which began before the House Committee on Foreign Affairs on January 15. On January 24, Charles Lindbergh appeared before the committee. Lindbergh's formal statement, however, made no specific reference to the bill but rather focused on his area of expertise—aviation. The development of aviation had, he argued, greatly increased the defensive position of the United States, "first, because it is impossible for an enemy to invade this continent by means of aircraft alone; second, because transoceanic bombing is indecisive; third, because our own air force makes it more difficult than ever before for an enemy to approach our shores."[42] In this way, Lindbergh contributed significantly to a key isolationist contention—that the United States was not dependent on the survival of Great Britain for its national security. The threat of German invasion was negligible, they believed.

Lindbergh's views naturally attracted a great deal of comment in the newspapers, not least from Dorothy Thompson, who was unrelenting in her criticism of his position. In a column responding to his testimony, she argued that "Col. Lindbergh's reasoning is as fallacious in the things he does not take account of as in the things he counts. There is nothing in any of his speeches to indicate that he is conscious of the power and pull of economic factors. . . . Col. Lindbergh's viewpoint shows a complete lack of knowledge of history and of naval, economic and cultural factors."[43] He might be an expert on aviation, in other words, but he knew precious little about anything else, according to Thompson. But she was kinder to him than to Philip La Follette, of the progressive Wisconsin political family. Her column on his contribution was entitled "Are We Dumb?"[44]

The American people were also sharply divided over the question of the danger of invasion. As one woman, who described herself as "a sane and devoted mother," commented to the editor of the *Chicago Tribune*: "They try to tell us we will be attacked, but you know and I know that is just a crazy fancy."[45] But not all the *Tribune*'s correspondents were so sanguine. One woman proclaimed, "I don't see how any one can be so blind as not to see that if England falls, and we have to fight alone against the whole of Europe, then we would have these bombs falling in our own backyards. What good would our dollars do us then? I am a mother of three sons and I'd rather give everything I have than see this country torn like Europe and my children living in holes in the ground."[46] While the majority of women explicitly claiming maternal authority for their views were isolationist, correspondents such as these suggested that the relationship between motherhood and isolationism was not a straightforward one. In fact, there were mothers on both sides of the debate, who all believed that their actions were calculated best to protect their children.

On January 28, the House committee heard its only two women

witnesses, Dorothy Thompson and Florence Harriman, the United States minister to Norway. Thompson attracted some fierce questioning from the bill's opponents on the committee, but she remained unshaken. Thompson's case for supporting the lend-lease bill revolved around one central idea—that the defeat of Britain would be disastrous for the United States, possibly militarily, certainly economically. As she asserted, "When the charge is made that Britain wants to get us into the war, it is well to remember that there is one simple act of Britain that will almost certainly get this country into war, or into a catastrophic defeat without war, and that is to surrender to Germany, thus bringing about the establishment of a pro-Nazi government in England. . . . If Great Britain falls, we will be encircled in two oceans. . . . And Great Britain subjected would not be out of the war but would be the base from which the Germans seek the domination of the Atlantic Ocean."[47] More than any military threat, however, Thompson spelled out the economic implications of a Nazi-dominated Europe, warning that "German-dominated Eurasia will offer to buy our cotton, wheat, oil, and so forth, provided—provided we have a President in the White House who suits them."[48] In particular, Thompson predicted that the Nazis would target South America, which was economically dependent on European export markets: "There will be no frontal attack on the United States, and no attempt at invasion at this time. There will be, and immediately, a tremendous penetration of South America and of this country. . . . Every single wholesale commercial penetration of the Nazis has ended in the long run by their controlling the countries politically as well."[49]

When she was done with her prepared statement, Thompson then faced tough questions from some of the committee's leading opponents of the bill. Hamilton Fish, of New York, asked her directly if she wished to see the United States enter the war. Thompson responded, "Mr. Fish, I am in favor of preserving the freedom and independence of the United States of America, without war if possible, with war if necessary. . . . I think we still have a chance of winning this war without fighting with actual belligerence in Europe, and I am counting on that chance, but not 100 percent."[50]

Edith Rogers of Massachusetts then attempted to undermine Thompson by recalling her 1931 dismissal of Hitler after she met him, but Thompson was willing candidly to admit her error: "Mrs. Rogers is casting doubts upon my reliability as a witness. . . . I only wish to say that I was very wrong in this article in 1931."[51] However, it was

Representative Karl Mundt of South Dakota who really got to the heart of the issue, by way of questions about the British fleet. He asked, "If England should lose, do you think the fleet might go to the totalitarian powers?" Thompson responded in the affirmative, commenting, "If we let Britain down and aren't in the war, why should she send us her fleet?" Mundt then made his real point: "It would not be good policy for us to extend part of our fleet unless we gave England assurance that we were going to stick with her to the end; is that not correct?" Thompson agreed. Mundt continued: "If that brings war, we would have to enter the war?" Thompson had to answer "yes."[52]

Thompson was followed by Florence Harriman, recently returned from Norway. She declared, "My recent experience in Europe has left me with the profound conviction that merely a desire for peace will not keep a nation out of war." Harriman emphasized the dangers posed by the "fifth column," asking, "Is anyone credulous enough to believe that these subversive forces are not now active in our own country? Having seen this tragedy take place in one country because of its confidence that it would not be attacked, when I find here among those who oppose this bill the same arguments being used, I fear for the ultimate safety of this Nation, notwithstanding the geographical dis-similarity between the United States and Norway, for modern invention is eliminating space, and an ocean is no longer a barrier, especially an ocean if controlled by a hostile power."[53] Harriman emphasized the view of the bill as the best hope to avoid more direct involvement in the war. She quoted Roosevelt's fireside chat of December 29 to the effect that Europeans needed arms, not men, and continued, "The President emphasized that we must get these weapons to them in sufficient volume and quickly enough so that we and our children will be saved the agony and suffering of war which others have had to endure."[54] Her experience in Norway had had a significant impact on Harriman, challenging her to rethink her past pacifism. Asked if she would still declare herself a pacifist, she stated, "No; I could not say today that I was. I think with a Hitler loose in the world, that we have to change our tactics."[55]

Outside the hearing room, the battle also continued in public. The main thrust of the Women's Committee for Action's work for lend-lease was a letter campaign. The committee's lobbyist in Washington, D.C., reported: "We are getting groups of people organized all over the country, each of whom will get five people in their state and one outside their state to get five more, etc., trying to start some sort of chain, to send more letters into Washington than were ever seen there before. And quicker."[56] This approach was indicative of the informal nature of the committee's activities. Where the Woman's Division of the Committee to Defend America relied on women in local chapters, the Women's Committee for Action depended on networks of friends and associates to reach out to women across the United States.

The letters that went out asking for support for lend-lease described the Women's Committee for Action as "a most informal non-partisan one, [which] came together simply because a group of us felt very strongly that we, as individuals, had to do everything in our power to get aid to Britain and to arouse this country to a sense of its own danger."[57] Members of the committee believed that it was extremely important to maintain a nonpartisan stance and to do everything possible to win the support of Republican women (and men) for intervention.

Mrs. Hendrik Van Loon Jr. acted as the Women's Committee for Action Washington lobbyist in January 1941, and she received considerable help and cooperation from the White House, through Eleanor Roosevelt.[58] Her reports on the progress of the bill and the success of militant antiwar women in packing congressional galleries during the debates led the committee to attempt to organize a pro-bill group "to have at least ten good clappers there each time."[59] This sort of informal organizing was typical of the Women's Committee for Action, which depended on social contacts and networks to promote its agenda.

In addition to these activities, the debate was conducted in the pages of national newspapers and journals. On January 25, 1941, Freda Kirchwey considered the motives of the opponents of aid to Britain in a column entitled "Loyal Opposition." Many of these opponents expressed conservative fears about the future of England—that it might involve some kind of socialism. Kirchwey believed that if they "would rather risk fascism than the chance of social change, their preference is shared by very few people."[60] In this she was joined by that archconservative and anti–New Dealer Dorothy Thompson, who frequently promised that a new, more democratic England would emerge from the war.

A poll taken on January 23, 1941, showed that 68 percent of Americans favored aid to Britain even at the risk of war,[61] and in a radio broadcast during the debate Dorothy Thompson analyzed these poll results for her listeners: "In January 1941 two thirds of us have realized that we cannot have our cake and eat it, that we cannot help England without running the risk of war, and that we would rather run the risk of war than fail to help bring about a defeat of the Axis dictators."[62]

On January 27, the Senate hearings opened, and isolationists rallied to provide as much compelling anti-lend-lease testimony as they could muster. The women who testified before the House committee were interventionists. Before the Senate came a series of isolationist women. Nor were they simply isolationist. With one exception, they represented the mother's movement, a movement of the extreme right wing of American politics, incorporating a range of views that included virulent anti-Semitism, tremendous Anglophobia, and traditional conservative ideas about the sanctity of the family and motherhood. These women played a significant role in creating the impression that American women were predominantly opposed to the bill.

However, the first woman to appear was Fay Bennett, the secretary of the Youth Committee Against War, an organization, she explained, that represented "American young people who are firmly dedicated to the ideals of democracy and who are vigorously opposed to every form of dictatorship, whether Hitler's, Mussolini's, or Stalin's. We want to keep this country out of war because we believe that such a policy alone can promote the defense of the United States and make possible a genuine contribution to the welfare of the rest of the world."[63] Bennett raised the twin specters of war and dictatorship, expressing her concern about "the powers which [the lend-lease bill] gives the President, both in matters of foreign policy—which we believe to be war powers—and in matters of domestic policies, which we believe to be virtual dictator powers."[64] Moreover, unlike many opponents of the bill, Bennett questioned whether Britain was truly a worthy recipient of American aid: "Is there anyone here who will argue that complete democracy pervades every part of . . . the British Empire?"[65] Many isolationists argued that no war to protect Britain could be a war for democracy given the British imperial record. Bennett also argued that American safety was not dependent on events in Europe—a standard isolationist belief. As she explained, her committee's opposition to the Lend-Lease Act was "based on our denial of the assumption upon which the bill is based, namely, that the defense and security of the United States rests with what happens to countries several thousand miles away."[66]

Working from this assumption, many isolationists went on the offensive against the interventionist position, claiming that if the war was really America's war, then it was cowardly and dishonest to pay others to fight it. Catherine Curtis, chairman of the National Women's Committee to Keep the United States Out of War, testified that supporters of the bill "maintain that speedy adoption of this measure is necessary in order that we may buy time to adequately arm and protect ourselves. . . . If their position is correct, then they are in effect saying that this is our war, but we will not fight it. Rather in shameful cowardice, they suggest we buy our protection with the blood of thousands of sons of another nation."[67] However, not all her listeners drew the same lesson that she did from this observation. One man commented angrily to the *New York Times:* "One cannot help wondering if courage and bravery are going old-fashioned. As I see it, the British, Greeks, Finns and Germans are the only fighting men left. The French cave in, the Italians run away and we Americans have to promise faithfully that our boys shall never follow in their fathers' footsteps. In fact, I wonder the mothers don't insist on Beautyrest mattresses for the draftees."[68] This man's reference to "the mothers" is an indication of how much attention the right-wing isolationist mothers' movement had garnered for its anti–lend-lease protests.

Curtis was at the center of this campaign, organizing small groups of women to talk individually with senators, as well as testifying before the Foreign Relations Committee. Her views combined a paradoxical maternalist feminism with anti-Semitism and an analysis of the war that focused on economic issues.[69] As she told the Senate committee, the war was "just another of Europe's recurring trade wars, through which Britain is endeavoring to enthrone her trade control everywhere."[70] Passage of the lend-lease bill would lead to American entry into the war, she believed: "Send the materials of war into the war zones in our ships, convoy them with our naval vessels, and a ship flying our flag will be sunk. Then we are in this war, and under a military dictatorship."[71]

Despite their strong antiwar stance, few in the mother's movement were pacifist. Rosa M. Farber, acting national chairman of the Mothers of the United States of America, explained to the Senate committee: "So that we will not be misunderstood, may I state here that we are not pacifists. We are ready and willing to fight and have our sons fight to defend our country—but we repudiate the contention that only on foreign continents can we defend the United States of America. We are in favor of national defense, and, in addition, we demand that our defense be strengthened by keeping arms, munitions, and airplanes here and not lend, lease, or give away any of our defense equipment."[72] Farber also feared that the bill would create a dictatorship, a danger she perceived as dating from the earliest days of the New Deal, whose measures constituted the start of "a premeditated drive toward ultimate dictatorship."[73] The bill, embodying as it did, in her view, both war and dictatorship, threatened fundamental American values. It was, she declared, "part and parcel of an alien program to destroy the security of our homes, the respect for our women, and nullify the God-given right of parenthood over children."[74]

A similar brand of rhetoric was deployed by Mrs. Cecil Norton Broy, president of Americans United, another group in the mothers' movement.[75] Broy declared that she spoke not just for herself, but "for the women of our organization, and for the millions of American women who believe as we do, but cannot leave their homes or other duties to be here today." Her agenda was simple. "We insist upon three things: (1) Defense for our country, (2) revitalization for our American people, (3) peace."[76] Broy explained that her organization favored a strong national defense policy but believed that there should be a negotiated peace in Europe. "American mothers, wives, and sweethearts are calling to you in tears today with heavy hearts to do your duty well, and to let your conscience only be your guide in the consideration of this dangerous bill. Now, on the other hand, if our country is ever attacked, we, the mothers, the wives, and the sweethearts of the American men, will take our places in the fight even as the brave women of the other countries have done and are doing. But we are convinced that this is not our war."[77] However, Broy may have undermined her credibility with many members of the committee by quoting from a speech made by Hitler to the Reichstag just a few days earlier in support of her belief that the Germans had no interest in attacking the United States.[78]

As the Senate Foreign Relations Committee considered these arguments, the House Foreign Affairs Committee reported out the bill, with eight dissenters who issued their minority report on January 31. Their case was simple. Although they declared themselves fully in support of the administration's desire to aid England, they argued that the lend-lease bill was not the best way to achieve this and involved two significant dangers. The first was war: "If we assume the direction of the war, we underwrite the success of the war. The ultimate result must be the American people will pay the full cost of the war, and that means we will be obligated to put our material resources and our men into the struggle." The second was dictatorship: "This bill gives the President unlimited, unprecedented and unpredictable powers, literally to seize anything in this country and to give it to any other country without limit in law." The minority report also presented an alternative proposal, centered on a $2 billion credit to be given to Britain, with certain limitations, including bans on repairing belligerent ships, using American ships to deliver goods to belligerents, and using the American navy to convoy ships across the Atlantic.[79]

Once the bill had been reported out of committee, the debate shifted to the floor of the House of Representatives, with occasional comment from the gallery. On February 5, a woman named Margaret Russell, a member of the mothers' movement, interrupted Representative Stephen Young of Ohio as he denied that the bill created a dictatorship, rising from her seat in the gallery, wearing a black robe and a skull mask, and shouting "My Novena! My Novena!" This, she later told police, meant "Victory is mine—death."[80] Indeed, as the month of February wore on and a decision on the bill approached, the extent of the public debate widened as both sides increased the urgency of their pitch to American public opinion.

On February 6, the Committee to Defend America organized a mass meeting on Long Island in support of the bill. One of the speakers was Ellin Berlin, wife of the famous songsmith Irving Berlin. She declared, "There is only one way to stop a conqueror. To defeat him. The only way to stop Hitler is to defeat him and if we don't help Great Britain to defeat him over there we shall some day have to surrender to him or defeat him over here."[81] Berlin's speech addressed a number of significant issues in the debate. A central concern was time—interventionists increasingly worried about the delay in enacting the lend-lease bill. "Our immediate objective in our battle against Nazism is the passage of the Stop-Hitler Bill—the 1776 Bill—and we want to pass this bill without amendments that would destroy its effectiveness and we want to pass it quickly!"[82] Berlin also considered the nature of the war, rejecting isolationist assertions that it was a traditional European conflict over territory and trade: "The war . . . is a war between free men and an empire of slaves. Actually it is a war between good and evil. That is an old-fashioned thing to say, but this is an old-fashioned war. In spite of his mechanized army and his fifth column and his skillful propagandists Hitler is as old as Xerxes and the courage of the free people of Great Britain is as old-fashioned as the courage of the Greeks at Thermopolae."[83]

In addition, Berlin took some potshots at the isolationist opposition, highlighting the strange bedfellows on the other side of the debate: the Communist newspaper the *Daily Worker* echoed the arguments of leading American industrialists such as General Wood of Sears Roebuck, Henry Ford, and Kathryn Lewis, daughter of prominent unionist John L. Lewis. Moreover, Berlin dismissed concerns about the increasingly ugly tenor of the debate. "It isn't fair, we are told, to call a man a pro-Nazi. Why not? They may call us pro-British. We don't mind. We are. . . . It is equally fair to ask the man who opposes aid to Great Britain if he is pro-Nazi. What helps Great Britain hurts Hitler. What hurts Great Britain helps Hitler, so those who oppose aid to Great Britain at this moment by opposing the 1776 Bill are knowingly, or unknowingly, serving the cause of Hitler. We are told that we must not criticize a man if he is sincere. I think that is nonsense. Hitler is probably the most sincere man alive."[84]

A few days later, the Committee to Defend America organized a bevy of prominent speakers across the nation for a half-hour broadcast advocating aid to Britain. The host was the movie star Douglas Fairbanks Jr., and the speakers included Alice Hixon, chairman of the Women's Division of the Layman's Association of the Episcopal Diocese of Chicago, who was invited to speak for the women of the Midwest. Her comments are instructive because they demonstrate clearly the tremendous flexibility inherent in contemporary assumptions about women: "The great majority of women with whom I have talked are 100% for aid to England. Possibly women, with their love of home and security, feel the necessity of giving all possible help more closely than many others, but regardless of our sex, such aid is a personal matter for all of us."[85] Rather than assuming that women's domestic nature would lead them to oppose aid, Hixon assumed just the opposite—because she believed that Germany posed a serious threat to the United States. "We must put this world fire out. We can help do it now with only materials, but if we fail in our duty by playing the game as Hitler wants, we may literally lose our home. Unless we do that, we are not doing our part as a citizen to keep war away from our home and country."[86]

One of the other speakers was Mary McLeod Bethune, director of the Division of Negro Affairs in the National Youth Administration and a leading figure in the National Council of Negro Women. She spoke for African-Americans, rather than women, and her support for aid reflected the hopes of African-Americans in seeing the ideals of democracy realized in the crucible of war. "The present European crisis must be regarded as the clash of two ideals—democracy versus dictatorship. The American Negro sees in the ideal democracy, his chance for equality of opportunity, the protection of his civil rights, his inclusion in all the individual and group benefits that flow from national progress." She ended with a clear call for action: "Let us speed the passage of the Lend-Lease Bill. Let us push with all possible speed the effective aid so necessary to England's success and America's protection—and God grant that our efforts be not too late."[87]

The program featured speakers from seven cities across the country, ending up in Hollywood, where actress Constance Bennett had the last word. Hitler, she declared, was a "mad director," one who had "had too many box office smashes." She called on listeners to support the lend-lease bill: "In the Congress today is a Bill known as 1776. That startling combination of numbers might have been thought up by someone in the movies—it has that kind of dramatic and historical significance. . . . We Americans can't live in Hitler's world. No freedom-loving person can. We want Hitler and everything he stands for wiped off the face of the earth. We are all united in our desires to write one well-known movie term on Hitler's career. And that term is—Fade Out."[88]

On the same day, Winston Churchill gave a broadcast speech over the BBC. It was in large part an appeal to the United States, albeit a cautious one. He had to be careful not to give ammunition to the isolationist side. The speech was calculated, rather, to reassure Americans that with sufficient aid—in other words, with lend-lease—the British could prevail in Europe without more direct American intervention. Churchill declared, "It seems now to be certain that the Government and people of the United States intend to supply us with all that is necessary for victory. In the last war the United States sent 2,000,000 men across the Atlantic. But this is not a war of vast armies, firing immense masses of shells at one another. We do not need the gallant armies which are forming throughout the American Union. We do not need them this year, nor next year; nor any year that I can foresee. But we do need most urgently an immense and continuous supply of war materials and technical apparatus of all kinds. We need them here and we need to bring them here."[89] Thus, he emphasized, Britain needed American materials and supplies, not men. Churchill finished his speech with an eloquent, and famous, appeal to Roosevelt and the American people: "Put your confidence in us. Give us your faith and your blessing, and, under Providence, all will be well. We shall not fail or falter; we shall not weaken or tire. Neither the sudden shock of battle, nor the long-drawn trials of vigilance and exertion will wear us down. Give us the tools and we will finish the job."[90]

In her column the following day, Anne O'Hare McCormick considered the likely impact of Churchill's words on the American public. As she well understood, most Americans still clung to the idea that military involvement could be avoided and that the lend-lease bill could help to keep the United States out of the war. "To most people 'war' still means sending armies to fight, and the only real conflict in the American mind at this stage of our participation in the struggle against Hitler is neither on the matter of all-out aid to the British nor even on the amount of power to be given to the President. As the debate proceeds, it centers less and less on this point and . . . more and more on the question whether our now open commitment to British victory means armed intervention if other means fail."[91] McCormick believed that Churchill's speech had been tremendously successful because, she argued, it had "restored to the aid-to-Britain policy the phrase 'short-of-war' as war is understood by the general public."[92] In other words, Churchill had specifically challenged the isolationist contention that the bill would make American military involvement in the war inevitable.

As the Senate debate began on February 13, the domestic conflict entered its last desperate stages. On February 18, Catherine Curtis sent out an emergency mailing addressed "To All Citizens of the United States," calling on them to write to their senators, contribute money to her committee, and "devote your every moment to protesting H.R. 1776." The lend-lease bill, she declared, was "an Abdication Bill—an abdication of your Congress." If the bill became law, she argued, "you will not only live under a Dictatorship—under a regimented economy—but you may also find your liberties—your properties—and even your CITIZENSHIP placed at the disposal of a foreign power and you will be without any method or means to object!"[93]

In mid-February, *Life* magazine published an editorial by its owner, Henry Luce, with the title "The American Century," complicating the debate over the meaning of the war by dividing interventionists between right and left. Into the cauldron of debate over lend-lease, Luce poured a vision of a Pax Americana, a world that *might* emerge from the current war, dominated by American ideals and values. "The American Century" was a mid-twentieth-century manifestation of the American tradition of manifest destiny—perfectly constituted to appeal to Dorothy Thompson, who saw the war as a battle between the forces of Christian, democratic, Anglo-Saxon civilization and the forces of barbarism. Upon reading Luce's vision in February 1941, Thompson raved: "It was more than an editorial; it was an essay, and I have an idea that it is more than either—that it is an American document."[94] Luce had described Thompson's vision more eloquently than even she could, and she quoted him at length in her column. Luce's version of American internationalism was, Thompson maintained, the destiny of the United States. "Internationalism means taking up the full responsibility that destiny has placed in our hands as a nation of 130,000,000 people occupying the greatest land space between the Atlantic and Pacific Oceans. It means taking upon ourselves the complete responsibility of leadership which is ours for the taking." The war was creating an amazing opportunity to reshape the world in the image of the United States. "We are having a revolution—a world revolution—which is turning and changing political structures, economic structures and social relationships from Scotland to Peiping. The question, however, is whose revolution? . . . To Americanize enough of the world so that we shall have a climate and environment favorable to our growth is indeed a call to destiny."[95] By destroying the old world order, the war would allow the United States to take its place at the forefront of nations and spread the blessings of democracy and capitalism throughout the world.

Freda Kirchwey, in contrast, was not the least bit carried away by Luce's grandiose vision. Rather, she recoiled from it and contemptuously dismissed Thompson's eloquent praise as "language that might have come straight out of a spring seed catalog."[96] Warning darkly of the dangers of this "new brand of imperialism," she characterized the "American Century" as "nothing more than Kipling in modern dress."[97]

In particular, she denounced the notion of a world dominated by an English-speaking Union—an idea proposed on several occasions by Thompson. Indeed, the week before Luce's article was published, Thompson had advocated "a voluntary federation of the English-speaking world . . . [through which] the Anglo-Saxon world, which has carried the banner of liberty and freedom on every hemisphere for centuries, would be able to raise it again, in a better way than it has ever been raised before, and set the example to all nations."[98] Thus, John Winthrop's idea of a Puritan "city on a hill" might be reincarnated in an Anglo-Saxon, democratic union.

Kirchwey uncompromisingly condemned this idea as "smug, self-righteous, superior, and fatuously lacking in a decent regard for the susceptibilities of the rest of mankind."[99] Luce and Thompson were the Cecil Rhodes of the mid–twentieth century, propagating a "new myth of superiority." Kirchwey rejected any notion of the domination of the postwar world by such a federation: "The fact is," she proclaimed, "no democratic basis for national dominance can be found in any formula, no matter how you slice it. . . . You don't nourish an honest internationalism with nonsense about 'destiny' and 'Anglo-Saxon traditions' and an 'American century.'"[100] Kirchwey did of course support international cooperation and organization, but she clearly envisaged an egalitarian system in which no single nation would dominate. Luce's vision exposed a significant fault line within the interventionist movement. If the isolationist industrialists were peculiar allies of the Communist Party, as Ellin Berlin had suggested, Thompson and Kirchwey were hardly less surprising comrades-in-arms on the interventionist side.

Meanwhile, the mothers continued to inundate their congressmen with anti-lend-lease mail, and many of them marched on Washington and made the rounds of senators and representatives, seeking to secure their votes. On February 23, members of the Mothers Crusade to Kill Bill 1776 attempted to hang an effigy of Dorothy Thompson on the gates of the White House, although the police stepped in and confiscated it before they succeeded. The women continued to demonstrate, however, parading before the White House waving American flags and banners, one of which read, "Kill Bill 1776, Not Our Boys."[101] Thompson remained unrepentant, however.

A few days later, Elizabeth Dilling, leader of the Mothers Crusade, and a group of some thirty women demonstrated outside the office of leading interventionist Senator Carter Glass of Virginia. Glass was furious, and, although the police broke up the crowd and arrested Dilling, he remained unsatisfied, calling upon the FBI to investigate the group's finances. The women had, he complained, created "a noisy disorder of which any self-respecting fish-wife would be ashamed," adding "that it would be pertinent to inquire whether they are mothers. For the sake of the race, I devoutly hope not."[102] Glass did not have the last word, however. The following day, during a recess in her trial for disorderly conduct, Dilling denounced Glass: "You will be known to millions as a traitor to the republic, another Benedict Arnold, an overaged destroyer of American youth."[103] She was, nevertheless, fined twenty-five dollars for her conduct.[104]

Nor did interventionists concede that the mothers movement represented American women. In an article for the *Hyde Park Herald,* the Hyde Park LWV responded directly to the "mothers'" claims: "'The mothers of the country' are by no means united behind that much publicized group in Washington." In support of this, it cited the comments of some of its leading members. Mrs. John Barden advocated the passage of the lend-lease bill because it would reduce the danger to her son: "As a mother of a son of military age, I believe our risk will be less if we do not let England go down." Barden shared the hope that lend-lease would keep the United States out of the war. Another Hyde Park mother emphasized the unhappy consequences of a German victory: "Unless Hitler is stopped, I feel that the future will be bleak and hopeless for my son and the other young men and women of our times."[105]

Hattie Caraway, Democratic senator from Arkansas, also challenged the mothers' claims, using maternalist rhetoric to promote aid rather than oppose it. She argued, in a speech over the radio at the end of February: "I am the only woman member of the United States Senate. Because of that fact, I have received a great many communications against the bill that would not otherwise have come to me. They urge that because of my sex I should, in support of their views, vote against this proposed legislation." But Caraway was not swayed by such attitudes:

> I have two sons already in the military service. . . . I do not want war. I do not know of any Senator favoring this bill who is for war. Many of them have sons as have I. These sons are either already in the military service or will be called sooner or later. . . . [F]or my part I state to the mothers and fathers of America, and I repeat to the young men of my country, that it is my firm belief that the pending measure, if enacted into law, will do much to keep the war from our shores. As a representative of a sovereign state, as an American mother, as one who has been a constant advocate of peace, as one who believes that humanity is at stake and that some measure must be taken to safeguard it, I will cast my vote for the Lend-Lease Bill.[106]

Caraway thus countered the claim implicit in much of the rhetoric of the mothers' movement that the supporters of lend-lease had no personal stake in peace; argued that aid offered the best hope of maintaining peace; and finally suggested other sources of obligation, as well as motherhood, from which to derive an opinion about foreign policy.

She also expressed the belief that the United States had a very real stake in the struggle—a view that was fundamental to the interventionist position: "If Hitler wins, we will face not only a hostile Germany but a hostile world. There can be no doubt but that Hitler desires to impose his system upon the whole world, including the United States. He has said so." Finally, while criticizing isolationists for their predictions of war, and pointing out that similar arguments had been made about the repeal of the arms embargo in October 1939, Caraway was cautious about making any guarantees, saying only that "in this fight, I do not believe England needs or wants our men to go overseas. She does want materials and munitions of war in order to carry on her fight. . . . I believe that the enactment of this bill into law will *do much* to prevent our being drawn into the conflict."[107]

Meanwhile, the Women's Committee for Action launched a petition drive among the mothers and wives of servicemen to counter "a campaign of fear and misrepresentation, claiming that these women were not behind the defense program and a program of aggressive aid to the democracies, and that a vigorous foreign policy was urged only by those with no personal stake in the situation today."[108] The petition was sent out to women with a request that they secure twenty-five signatures and pass along five copies to other women to do the same. In case they were not acquainted with twenty-five "defense wives and mothers," they were referred to the local draft board, recruiting office, American Legion, and Veterans of Foreign Wars. The petitions were to be sent to senators, with copies to the Women's Committee for Action, which would compile a full copy to be forwarded to the president. The petition declared: "We are not timid, confused or irresolute. We are glad, with our sons, husbands and fiancees, that they are privileged to meet the greatest challenge that has ever been presented to our country, and our democracy. . . . As Americans with the greatest stake in this emergency, we stand with President Roosevelt, . . . and the great majority of Americans who want to stop Fascism now, here, and forever."[109] The wording of the petition not only attempted to reclaim women for the interventionist cause but also implicitly attacked opponents of that cause for their timidity and lack of resolution.

In addition to its efforts to challenge the isolationist claim to represent women, the Women's Committee for Action played a central role in organizing college students into the Student Defenders of Democracy early in 1941—to challenge another isolationist contention that only those too old to fight favored an interventionist policy. Dorothy Overlock, a recent graduate of the University of Chicago, served as head of the group, which got together over the Christmas vacation to prepare a statement for release to the press. This statement declared: "We, as individual American students, pledge ourselves to the defense of progressive American democracy with a full sense of the sacrifices that pledge may entail."[110] It was signed initially by eighteen students, nine women and nine men, mostly from colleges in the Northeast, and then sent out to other student leaders for their support.[111] At the same time, the committee was organizing a "youth petition to be signed by young men and women of combatant age, to counteract the propaganda that suggests that all interventionists are old fogies."[112] The petition was drafted in February and suggested that, contrary to isolationist charges, older people might have an interest in appeasement, in delaying war for a few years, but that the young would have to live out their lives in a Nazi-dominated world and were ready to take risks and make sacrifices to avoid that. By February 20, some 330 signatures had been gathered.[113] Both the "youth petition" and the creation of the Student Defenders of Democracy reflect the Women's Action Committee's determination to prevent the isolationist movement from claiming a monopoly of support from the young.

As the bill neared a vote, interventionist women attempted to prevent a congressional filibuster from delaying its passage. On March 5, a group of these women sent a telegram to Henry Wallace, the vice president, and party leaders, urging "that there be no further delay in passing the Lend-Lease Bill. We regard the right of intelligent debate as inseparable from the practise of American democracy, but resort to prolonged and repetitious argument serves no useful purpose, and thwarts the manifest will of the majority. Facing as we do one of the great crises in our history, we sincerely hope there will be no filibuster—declared or undeclared—on the Bill or on proposed amendments." Thirty leading American women signed the telegram, including Dorothy Thompson, Elizabeth Christman, Carrie Chapman Catt, and Ellin Berlin.[114]

The following day, as the Senate discussed various possible amendments to the bill, Senator Hattie Caraway made a rare speech on the floor, again deploying maternal rhetoric in the interventionist cause: "I want to speak for the mothers who are not afraid. I have two sons in the Army and I believe they will be much safer if we do not amend this bill. I'm standing for the bill as it is."[115] One thing the mothers' movement had clearly done was to encourage interventionist women to appeal more explicitly to their own sex and to do so with maternalist language.

As the debate continued, the tenor of the discussion continued to deteriorate, and accusations of warmongering and pro-Nazi sympathies became increasingly common. Senator Wheeler alleged in the Senate debate that the Committee to Defend America was financed by and represented the interests of international bankers—playing on American sensitivity to the idea of financial motives for war, dating from the Great War. Ernest Gibson, national chairman of the Committee to Defend America, in issuing his denial, turned the accusation around and questioned the funding of leading isolationist organizations: "I want to answer once and for all the charge made by Senator Wheeler in the Senate that the Committee to Defend America by Aiding the Allies is made up of or in any way a tool of international bankers. Such a charge is absolutely unfounded. It is very likely that if he will investigate the groups that are supporting him—namely, the America First, and No Foreign War and other kindred groups—he will find a strange conglomeration of business appeasers, bundists, Communists, fascists and, of course, some sincere but misguided Americans." Gibson pointed out that his organization had given to a New York newspaper a list of all donors of sums greater than $100, giving permission for that list to be published when the newspaper obtained similar lists from America First and the No Foreign War Committee. That it had not yet appeared in the newspaper was evidence not of the Committee to Defend America's reluctance but of the reluctance of these isolationist groups to acknowledge the sources of their funding.[116] Naturally, America First had its own version of events. It declared its willingness to release a list of contributors but explained that "because of the bitterness which has been created, we have felt it only fair to consult our contributors before making their names public. We have not heard from all of them. When we do the list will be made public."[117]

As a vote in the Senate approached, the mothers' movement launched a "last-ditch" effort to defeat the bill, involving demonstrations both in the Senate and outside the White House. Elsie Canefa was removed from the Senate gallery after displaying a banner declaring "H.R. 1776 Means War—Vote No," and some fifty women paraded up and down Pennsylvania Avenue in front of the White House, claiming "that they represented 'thousands of other women in churches, trade unions and community peace committees' who protested passage of H.R. 1776 and charged that 'already the policy of the administration has brought America into the orbit of war.'"[118]

The isolationists were not alone, however. Advocates of the bill also made a final drive for passage. On March 8, Elizabeth Morrow once more took to America's airwaves, calling for enactment of lend-lease "without weakening amendments or strangling clauses." The United States should provide all possible aid, she declared, "to give Britain, who is fighting for our democratic faith, the assurance of victory. To give the United States the assurance of security. To fulfil a moral obligation assumed by our country. The American people have declared in favor of aid to England. I have spoken of honor—are we to go back on our promise? I believe the bill should pass by a majority large enough to show the President the great popular support which exists here for the policy of aid to Britain." She also rejected isolationist accusations that the measure would lead to war: "I cannot see that to do stingily, badly and late what we have already promised to do will make us more vulnerable than to give aid generously, efficiently and promptly."[119]

On March 8, the Senate voted decisively for the lend-lease bill, without significant amendment, 60 to 31. Three days later, on March 11, the House finally passed the Lend-Lease Act by an overwhelming majority of 317 to 71. Roosevelt signed the bill at 3:50 P.M. and five minutes later authorized the first transfer of materials to the British and the Greeks. He also announced that he would present to Congress a request for a $7 billion appropriation to fund lend-lease.[120]

The following day, Winston Churchill spoke about passage of lend-lease: "The most powerful democracy has, in effect, declared in solemn Statute that they will devote their overwhelming industrial and financial strength to ensuring the defeat of Nazism in order that nations, great and small, may live in security, tolerance and freedom. By so doing, the Government and people of the United States have in fact written a new Magna Charta, which not only has regard to the rights and laws upon which a healthy and advancing civilization can alone be erected, but also proclaims by precept and example the duty of free men and free nations, wherever they may be, to share the responsibility and burden of enforcing them."[121]

The Lend-Lease Act marked a vital shift in the debate over American foreign policy. Embodying, as Churchill suggested, an unequivocal statement of support for the British, an unmistakable marriage of

American interests and the British cause in the war, it ushered in a year in which American public opinion gradually came to terms with the inevitability of American military involvement in the war. Having decided to support the British war effort to the fullest potential of American industry, the American people were confronted with the fact that should this prove inadequate, military intervention would be necessary.

Once the act had been passed by Congress, there was little left for interventionists to advocate other than war. The only possible exception to this was the use of American ships to convoy aid, but many Americans, interventionist and isolationist alike, agreed that convoying would lead to incidents in the Atlantic, which would amount to war and would almost inevitably lead to an official acknowledgment of war, if not by the United States then by Germany. With passage of the Lend-Lease Act, the interventionist movement split. Some felt that the measure should be given a fair chance at success and focused on boosting American production to the levels required to provide meaningful support to the British; others went further and advocated the use of convoys to ensure the delivery of aid, thus risking war but not demanding it; the most determined interventionists went furthest of all and called for an immediate declaration of war against Germany.

On March 17, the Committee to Defend America issued a new statement of policy. It called for "the full mobilization of American economic life for greater production. . . . Immediate and adequate appropriations under the Lend-Lease Act. Use by the American government of whatever means are necessary to insure prompt delivery of war materials to the Allies, including . . . convoy of ships with American naval vessels if need be. Our slogan will be 'Deliver the goods to Britain now.'"[122] This was not, however, an ambitious enough agenda to satisfy the more hawkish attitudes of some interventionists, notably the Century Club, which organized the Fight for Freedom Committee in the first months of 1941. Some members of the group hoped, during the winter, that one of the grassroots interventionist organizations would adopt a position of unqualified support for direct intervention in the war, but they were disappointed.[123] So, in March 1941, the Fight for Freedom Committee was organized, with Bishop Henry Hobson as chairman and Senator Carter Glass of Virginia as honorary chairman. Hobson introduced the Fight for Freedom Committee in a national radio broadcast on April 19, 1941, declaring that the United States was "in the immoral and craven position of asking others to make the supreme sacrifice for this victory which we recognize as essential to us. Once the United States accepts the fact that we are at war we shall at last find a peace within ourselves which can never come as long as we seek safety at the cost of others' sacrifices."[124]

When the Women's Committee for Action discussed the Fight for Freedom early in April, there seem to have been some initial doubts about the strategy of forming a new grassroots organization. Mrs. Goddard Leach suggested that a letter planned by Grenville Clark, a member of the Century Group, might be a better tactic to achieve the current goal—convoys—but the committee eventually decided to endorse the new organization.[125] The reluctance of some members of the committee to give unqualified support to the Fight for Freedom was in keeping with the committee's perception of itself as a rapid-response group, which complemented grassroots organization rather than being an alternative to it. In February 1941, in a letter soliciting help in recruiting the Willkie Clubs, Kay Jackson expressed this idea explicitly: "You may wonder how we fit in with the William Allen White Committee. We work with them all the time but we have found that as a very small and loosely organized group, we are able to work more directly with problems as they come up without having to go through cumbersome committee machinery. We have found that an interchange of ideas between two such groups, one an idea group, the other an organizational group, can be very effective."[126] Thus, the Women's Committee for Action valued its informality and small size as an advantage in responding quickly to specific developments; and when it endorsed the Fight for Freedom, the statement issued reflected the particular policy question that the committee thought was most important at that moment—convoying. The undated release in the Fight for Freedom files declared: "Believing that only by prompt and decisive action on the part of the United States can the Nazi forces be defeated and our own future assured, the Women's Committee for Action heartily endorses the aims of the Fight for Freedom Committee in all that they are advocating and especially in their stand that we now use our navy and our air force to safeguard the transportation of vital supplies across the ocean, and in their statement that 'We must throw our full weight now into the fight for freedom, knowing that if this means war, it also means the surest and swiftest road to peace.'"[127]

The Women's Committee for Action seems to have been absorbed into the Fight for Freedom. A handwritten note across the bottom of this press release noted that the names should be added to the Fight for Freedom, and, indeed, a membership list dated April 28, 1941, shows five of the thirteen signers as members; three others became members of the national committee of the Women's Division when it was formed in November 1941.[128] Moreover, in April 1941, the records of the Women's Action Committee cease—suggesting that its members were incorporated into the new organization.

The creation of the Fight for Freedom Committee seemed in some ways to confirm the isolationist critique of the Lend-Lease Act as a back door to war, despite the basic contention of the administration and many of the bill's advocates that it was actually the best and/or only hope of keeping the United States out of the war. But more fundamentally, the debate over the bill had addressed the central question of whether the United States really had any national interest at stake that was significant enough to warrant the risk of war. In this way, the debate over lend-lease uncovered and examined in great depth and detail the basic assumptions underlying American foreign policy and showed that a majority of the American people genuinely supported the policy of aid to Britain. Support for the Lend-Lease Act ran consistently at about 54 to 58 percent, during the debate, with a further 8 to 15 percent expressing a "qualified opinion," which probably indicated the wish to see some amendment or other added before the bill was passed.[129] More than just supporting the policy of aid, Americans did so even in the knowledge that the policy might lead to war and conscious of the fact that the commitment embodied in the bill meant that the United States would go to war if aid proved insufficient to the task of defeating Hitler. Polls showed that throughout the lend-lease debate some 60 percent of Americans believed it was more important to help England even at the risk of war than it was to keep out of the war.[130] As the *New York Times* commented two days before the bill became law, "The historic fact established by this debate is nothing less than the end of American isolation."[131]

Although the isolationists were not yet ready to give up, opinion polls during 1941 reflected steady support for the policy embodied in the Lend-Lease Act, in full knowledge of the possible consequences. In late March 1941, the number believing that aid to Britain should be supplied even at the risk of war had risen to 71 percent from 55 percent in early December 1940, and that figure remained steady at about two-thirds throughout the rest of 1941.

However, while many Americans were prepared to risk war rather than see Britain defeated, considerably fewer supported an immediate declaration of war. Polls showed consistently between 14 and 24 percent of Americans in favor of such a declaration, leaving some 40 to 50 percent willing to risk war but not yet quite ready to go to war. Two polls conducted on May 20, 1941, by the same organization—the American Institute of Public Opinion—asking if people would favor going to war if Roosevelt said that Britain would be defeated soon otherwise, showed 49% and 54% in favor and 43% and 40% opposed.[132] These figures suggest that the majority of those willing to risk war were also prepared to go to war, if they really believed that it was necessary to save Britain, but that another group also existed—those who were willing to risk war but could not quite bring themselves to support a declaration, whatever the circumstances might be.

Women interventionists spread out along this spectrum of opinion in 1941. The LWV, in the absence of any authorization from its biennial convention to make policy on the question of war or peace, avoided even the controversy of publicly supporting convoying and focused on making good the promises of lend-lease, through its "Battle of Production" campaign to mobilize Americans behind defense production. Some members of the League were not satisfied with this level of activism, however, regarding it as inadequate, and joined the Fight for Freedom Committee. These included, most notably, the president of the New York City LWV, Anna Lord Strauss,[133] who had also been a part of the Women's Committee for Action. Similarly, many women members of the Committee to Defend America by Aiding the Allies also moved on to the Fight for Freedom Committee.

The Lend-Lease Act marked the final turn in the road for interventionists. Right through its passage, interventionists could argue sincerely that they favored aid to Britain as a means to keep the United States out of the war. By the end of March 1941, however, many interventionists were convinced that American participation in the war was necessary; and few could doubt that further measures to aid Britain, most notably convoying, would lead, at the very least, to an undeclared war. While this proved a sticking point for some, a significant number of Americans were ready for immediate war, and a majority supported the fullest aid to Britain, whatever the consequences.

7

The Battle of Production

On April 6, German forces embarked on the conquest of the Balkans, attacking Yugoslavia and Greece as a prelude to the coming Russian campaign. The Yugoslav army was overwhelmed in a matter of days, while the Croat and Slovene minorities exploited the crisis to claim independence, preferring a subordinate relationship with Nazi Germany to incorporation in Yugoslavia. Serb leaders signed an armistice with Germany on April 17. Greek forces, supported by three British divisions, put up rather more of a fight, but a strategy that relied on the Yugoslavs to protect a vulnerable flank proved disastrous, and defeat followed rapidly before the end of April.

The situation in the Atlantic was scarcely more promising. After the fall of France in June 1940, the Germans were able to use French ports as bases for U-boat operations in the Atlantic. They employed what was called the "wolf-pack" tactic for dealing with convoys. A single submarine might easily miss its opportunity to attack a convoy, but a group of submarines spread out in a line, and attacking on the surface where their speed was greater than that of most merchant ships, could inflict tremendous damage. In the early months of 1941, the British began to lose shipping at a rate far greater than their capacity to replace it, raising serious doubts about their ability to keep open the Atlantic supply line. Inevitably, this led to calls for the U.S. Navy to begin convoy duty in the Atlantic.

Stimson and Knox, the secretaries of war and navy, advocated convoying as early as January 1941; Admiral Harold Stark, chief of naval operations, agreed. But Roosevelt feared that convoys would lead to American casualties at sea and thus to war, and that the American public was not yet ready to make that commitment. There had been some pressure for the addition of an amendment to the Lend-Lease Act prohibiting the use of American ships for convoying, and Roosevelt hesitated to undertake such a controversial measure.

In contrast, interventionists outside the administration were less deterred by the possible consequences. However, with the passage of the Lend-Lease Act, the interventionist movement began to split—between those who favored full American participation in the war and those who could not quite bring themselves to that point. In some ways, convoying served as a sort of no-man's-land between these two positions, simply because, although almost everyone assumed that convoys would lead inevitably to war, it continued to leave the decision in someone else's hands.

At the vanguard of the interventionist movement was the Fight for Freedom Committee, which called for immediate American entry into the war. Although the Committee to Defend America endorsed convoying in the wake of the passage of the Lend-Lease Act,[1] it never advocated a declaration of war. As the Fight for Freedom Committee was forming in April 1941, proclaiming dramatically, "We are for *war*,"[2] the Woman's Division of the Committee to Defend America was organizing a song contest. It is perhaps not surprising, therefore, that many women members of the Committee to Defend America signed up with the Fight for Freedom. Among them were Mary Ellen Chase, professor of English at Smith College; Dean Virginia Gildersleeve; actress Helen Hayes; Freda Kirchwey; Judge Dorothy Kenyon; Elizabeth Morrow; Rose Schneiderman; and Ellin Berlin.[3]

Closer to the Fight for Freedom Committee than the Committee to Defend America was the AAUW, coming from behind the pack in May 1941 when it held its biennial convention. In 1939, at the start of the war, the Board of Directors of the AAUW had decided that, in the absence of an opportunity to consult the members of the association, it would not be appropriate to make any public pronouncement in support of the revision of the Neutrality Act. The board had maintained that silence on foreign policy questions for over a year and a half because it believed that the war so changed the situation of the United States that no decisions made by the convention *before* the war could accurately reflect the views of members *during* the war. Only in 1941, when the organization again met in convention, could the views of members be ascertained.

The foreign policy resolution offered to the AAUW convention in May 1941 read, "recognition of a common cause with all nations resisting totalitarian aggression and the furnishing of whatever economic and moral aid we can give to make this resistance effective." The delegates, however, led the way. The very first contribution to the discussion was an amendment, offering a substitute item. It read: "We recognize a common cause with all nations resisting totalitarian aggressions, and since we are already committed in the Lend-Lease bill to a policy of all-out aid to Britain, we endorse whatever measure in the judgment of our Government will make this aid effective—even to active intervention."[4] To produce a more concise resolution, the delegates rejected this amendment as offered but kept its fundamental meaning by deleting the words "moral and economic" that had qualified "aid" in the original resolution. The item adopted thus read: "recognition of a common cause with all nations resisting totalitarian aggression and the furnishing of whatever aid we can give to make this resistance effective."[5] In this context, it was very clear that the convention intended this resolution to cover military intervention in the war.

This was the most radical position on aid adopted by any women's organization before the United States entered the war. Significantly, there were no speeches that took issue with the desire to provide whatever aid the Allies needed. The only delegate to express any reservations about the resolution did so on the basis that the branches had not authorized delegates to vote on the possibility of military aid, since that question had not been on the program. She did, however, comment that "personally I would vote for active intervention. I have come to the conclusion that we have to."[6]

In support of the resolution, delegates emphasized the oppression that women experienced under National Socialism. Mrs. R. C. Dexter, from Boston, pointed out to the convention: "A year ago women were holding meetings like this in various democratic countries in Europe that they cannot hold now. They tried to limit their aid to the people who were fighting to economic and moral aid. . . . They helped them as they could but they tried to keep out of war. They have been picked off one by one. . . . [W]e've got to have the courage to make up our minds, and as a mother, as a citizen, as a person who has given years of her life for the work of peace, I beg you all to face the facts that we are in a critical time and that the sands are running out. (Applause)"[7] This delegate used the example of women in other nations whose desire for peace had, in her view, betrayed them, and she claimed an authority derived from her maternal role and her past commitment to peace to urge intervention in the war. For her, and for the majority of women at the convention who voted for the resolution advocating "whatever aid we can give," the cause of defeating National Socialism, a political philosophy that exploited and oppressed women, took priority over every other consideration. Having spent the first part of the war in comparative silence on the issue of aid and intervention, the AAUW leaped to the forefront of women's organizations campaigning for greater American involvement, as the first, indeed the only one, to vote in full convention for military aid if necessary.

The WTUL's National Board could not go that far, but it did favor convoys, even in the knowledge that this might well lead to war. As Margaret Stone argued, "Since the Board supported the Lend-Lease Bill, it would seem logical for it to support legislation designed to make sure that the aid extended to Britain actually arrives. This is no time for half-way measures."[8] Seven of the nine National Board members voted to support convoys, one was opposed, and one did not vote due to illness. The one opposing vote was cast by Agnes Nestor, long a halfhearted advocate of aid, because of her determination that the United States should not enter the war. While Nestor declared herself in favor of "all aid to Britain short of war," she rejected convoys because she believed that they would lead the country into war, and she regretted the apparent abandonment of the qualification "short of war" by the administration.[9]

In contrast, another board member, Pauline Newman, supported convoys even while explicitly acknowledging the likelihood that they would result in war: "It seems to me that there are few other possibilities which will do the job as effectively as convoying our aid. We may as well fight now as later."[10] Thus, some WTUL board members had, by May 1941, reached the conclusion that the defeat of the Axis was more important than keeping out of the war, and that aid should be provided to Britain whatever the risks. The attitude of members at the local level is less clear—a letter to local leagues in June asking for action on this question apparently elicited only one response.[11] However, the National Board did inform the president of its resolution in favor of convoys, and the commitment of the League's leaders to the cause of defeating Germany was clear—even U.S. entry into the war was a risk worth taking.

In this view they were joined by some members of the U.S. Section of WILPF. That organization had been experiencing a fairly precipitous drop in membership since the start of the war, reflecting the unhappiness of some members with the pro-neutrality policy pursued by the National Board. In the year 1940–41, the Santa Barbara branch lost 70 of its 125 members; the Carroll County branch, in Maryland, lost nearly 100 out of 371; the St. Paul branch, in Minnesota, lost 104 out of 324; and in New York, Brooklyn lost 188 out of 334, and Manhattan's membership roll dropped from 426 to 160. Some branches did report increases, but they were small by comparison, and the net figure was a loss of over 1,000 members out of a national figure of about 14,000.[12]

Moreover, Mildred Olmsted, the national organization's secretary, reported that some WILPF branches and members were engaged in fund-raising activities for much more financially secure organizations, "such as the American Friends Service Committee—not to mention such unneutral activities as Bundles for Britain."[13] Clearly, not all WILPF members who disagreed with the policy of the National Board went so far as to quit the organization. Supporting Bundles for Britain, a humanitarian aid campaign, was a minor transgression from national policy, however, compared with that of the Chicago branch members, who added the following appendix to the annual meeting minutes of 1941: "Believing that a Nazi victory would imperil peace and freedom for the whole world and plunge it still further into darkness and slavery, [we] wish to clarify our attitude toward the National W.I.L. . . . since we believe in aid to Britain."[14]

While they apparently did not resign from the organization, they could scarcely have formulated a more complete repudiation of the policy of the National Board. Nor were these Chicago members alone. In November 1941, the Executive Committee considered the case of the Princeton branch, which had "announced their members oppose our point of view, and wish either to resign, or to go on as a W.I.L. branch but rejecting our policies."[15] Representatives from Princeton appeared before the Executive Committee and reported that their membership had been cut in half "because the majority of the members cannot follow the national program in *keeping America out of the war.*"[16] Of the thirty-five remaining members, only three supported the national policy. The Princeton members had rejected not only the "pro-neutrality pattern" but also one of the original common goals—to keep America out of war. Faced with National Socialism, they opted for freedom over peace.

In contrast, the LWV never moved much closer to war in terms of policy than supporting lend-lease aid. In May 1941, the General Council debated the question of convoys but rejected the idea of undertaking any kind of action in support of their use. Rather, the council adopted a formula that abdicated responsibility for ensuring the delivery of lend-lease supplies: "We recognize that there *is* a problem of transportation, but . . . our position is that it is the job of the Administration and that we hope the Administration will find a way to see that the goods reach their destination."[17] Instead the League decided to focus on the question of producing enough goods for lend-lease to be effective.

Wells believed that the key role for the United States in the war lay in the arena of production. It was her hope that American industrial power would supply Allied armies with everything they needed to secure victory, thus making U.S. military involvement unnecessary. Her focus on production began to emerge as early as December 1940 and found its full expression in mid-1941 with the LWV's "Battle of Production" campaign. Wells argued that production was the real issue in a memorandum to Wright in December 1940: "The essential next step in 'aid to Britain' is to speed production."[18] With the passage of the Lend-Lease Act in March 1941, this became especially true. Having made the choice to back the British war effort with the full force of the American economy, a good deal now rested on what that economy could produce.

The Battle of Production campaign was developed at the start of May 1941 during the National Board meetings before and after the League met in General Council. On May 5, the National Board voted to "initiate an immediate campaign to increase public support for American Foreign Policy as adopted in the Lease-Lend and national defense measures."[19] On May 10, the board developed a series of ideas for the campaign, which would emphasize that every citizen had a part to play, without attempting to tell people specifically what they should be doing. On May 13, Marguerite Wells wrote to state league presidents, announcing the campaign and noting the absence of any concerted effort to build public support for defense production: "No citizens' organization has undertaken to rally support of the country's program for preparedness and aid to nations now the victims of aggression, a program which may well be called the Battle of Production."[20]

States were left in charge of their own campaigns, but the National Board kept a steady supply of publicity ideas flowing to the states. The Leagues produced buttons and banners bearing the slogan "Win the Battle of Production!"; members gave speeches and worked with newspapers to provide news coverage of their efforts and favorable editorials; the national League published a pamphlet entitled "The Battle of Production: It Can Be Won"[21] and a flyer that declared: "More planes, more tanks, more guns, more goods—faster; more getting-together, more sacrifices, more taxes, more work—now. Do everything to help, say nothing to hinder the Battle of Production."[22] There were even special "movie screen flashes" created for the week of July 4, which connected the present struggle to produce with the Revolutionary past: "The Spirit of '76 lives on, the spirit that gave us liberty can produce the goods to keep us free. Let's go America! Win the Battle of Production."[23] The League was extremely successful in creating a rash of publicity for the Battle of Production. On June 26, Virginia Mannon, the League's publicity secretary reported to Marguerite Wells that the campaign had produced 16 editorials, 11 front-page stories, and 29 features and had been mentioned in 278 other articles.[24]

The rhetoric of the campaign was clear in its intent. League spokeswomen steadfastly refused to make any connection between the Battle of Production and any policy issue as yet undecided by Congress, in other words, things such as convoying and direct military intervention. Rather, the battle was intended to make effective a policy already endorsed by the nation in the form of the Lend-Lease Act. When asked whether the League supported U.S. entry into the war in a radio interview conducted early in June, Marguerite Wells explained: "Our campaign has nothing to do with going into the war or staying out of the war. The campaign is based on our country's plan for defense by all-out production, for use at home and aid abroad."[25] Thus, the League attempted to sidestep further debates over policy by focusing on the issue of pursuing the current policy to its fullest extent. Indeed, those who were concerned with promoting other interventionist steps were criticized for failing to recognize the importance of production and distracting vital attention from the problem. In a radio speech on July 15, Louise Wright noted: "While production lags people argue about whether the United States should go into or stay out of the war but too few talk about the one area of agreement which has been determined by the entire nation, that of being the economic ally of those nations who are fighting Hitler."[26] This was probably a reference to the recently formed Fight for Freedom Committee, which was calling for an immediate declaration of war by the United States, a step that League leaders had decided they could not endorse, even had they been united in support of the idea.

The Woman's Division of the Committee to Defend America, however, was more in sympathy with the LWV's position, pursuing its own "speed production" campaign in the spring of 1941. The centerpiece of this campaign was the winning poster from the previous year's competition.[27] Local chapters were asked to approach outdoor advertising companies, which controlled billboard space, and ask for free space to display the winning poster. The Outdoor Advertising Association of America had endorsed the idea and written to its members indicating its approval, but since the companies were independent, they had to be approached on the local level. Grace Manners, secretary of the National Woman's Division, wrote to local chapter chairmen on March 13, announcing that the San Francisco chapter had already procured 264 billboard spaces and that more had been promised in four states in the east, as a source of inspiration for their efforts.[28] In this way, the Woman's Division plastered the committee's message on billboards across the country.

The Woman's Division also sponsored a song contest, launched in April 1941, that targeted radio audiences and hoped to "produce a great rallying song to sweep the country."[29] Major national music groups, such as the National Federation of Music Clubs, the National Association for American Composers and Conductors, the American Society of Composers, and the Song Writers' Protective Association, cooperated with the national Woman's Division to promote the contest. Some 1,675 entries were submitted, and the winning song, "Me and My Uncle Sam," was broadcast on NBC on July 8, 1941. As a "great rallying song" it left something to be desired, however, and it has faded into deserved obscurity, doubtless because of the lyrics:

> For we never start a fight in this great country
> but when freedom is in danger we prepare
> And with justice from above
> All this whole world does need is love.[30]

Meanwhile, the attempts of the LWV to steer the debate away from the issue of entry into the war and toward production were made more difficult by the conviction of some Americans that the kind of commitment and sacrifice required from the people to achieve the desired production levels would be forthcoming only in wartime. In other words, it was suggested that the people would make the necessary sacrifices only if the very existence of their nation was threatened by war.[31] They could not be persuaded to do so by rhetoric or pop songs. Marguerite Wells acknowledged that a national unity and commitment unprecedented except in time of war was necessary, but she consistently argued that such a spirit could be roused without direct U.S. involvement in the war. A League press release announcing the Battle of Production declared: "This plan can succeed only if the people recognize the emergency, and work and sacrifice with the unity of purpose hitherto characteristic of war. The LWV has faith in the American people and in their capacity to carry out the plan they have adopted [Lend-Lease]. . . . We reject the slander that only through war can a people achieve a spirit of national unity."[32] In this way, the Battle of Production allowed the League to focus the energies of its members in the cause of an interventionist policy, while avoiding taking any further steps toward direct military involvement.

Despite the League's reluctance to venture further in the debates over entry into the war, the tone and rhetoric of the speeches promoting the Battle of Production left no doubt as to the vital interest of the United States in the war. Indeed, most of the speeches simply assumed an American part in the war, even if that part was defined economically rather than militarily: "Against the forces that have become a mortal danger to our way of life, a great struggle is being fought. The battle that uses guns and tanks and bombs and airplanes is being fought by Britain in the Atlantic, in the Near East, and in Africa; by China in the Far East. There is another battle that is equally crucial in this struggle. That is America's battle—the battle of production."[33]

This speech clearly equated Britain's and China's military battles with the United States' economic battle as two halves of the war effort. The rhetoric of the Battle of Production de-emphasized the idea of aid, which had some semblance of detachment from the war, and firmly located American production within the context of a war being fought by all the democracies, including the United States, albeit in different ways. Louise Wright declared in a Battle of Production campaign speech: "The people of this country may not know all there is to know about foreign policy but they know what they want. After long and thorough discussion we selected our role in the world war. By the vote of a substantial majority of Congress we voluntarily chose as our part in the war against aggression the providing of material with which modern wars are fought."[34] The United States might not be engaged on a military level, but it *was* involved in the war, and it had a vital part to play. Thus, while the Battle of Production campaign was in some ways an alternative to taking further steps toward active involvement in the war during the spring and summer of 1941, the shift in the way American women (and men) were thinking about the war was apparent in the rhetoric of the campaign.

The League's approach reflected an undeniable reality—as much as people might believe in a cause, few will actively embrace war. While American public opinion clearly supported lend-lease, and polls showed that a majority backed aid to Britain even at the risk of war, there was also very clearly a huge majority that opposed immediate entry into the conflict. Americans would cling desperately to the semblance of peace right up to the attack on Pearl Harbor. And isolationists exploited that attitude by pointing endlessly to the majority against direct intervention and interpreting that as evidence that a similar majority would oppose measures that they believed would lead to war. For example, Anne Lindbergh interpreted the occupation of Iceland in early July 1941 as a denial of democracy. "This is a move *into* war," she believed. But "the President does what he wants, regardless. There could not be a more compelling majority to stay out of this war. All the polls show an overwhelming mass of the people want to stay out. . . . The interventionists pooh-pooh any talk of a referendum. They deceive the people and draw them along closer and closer into the war, *against their will.*"[35] But Anne Lindbergh misread the polls. Although about 80 percent of respondents consistently declared themselves opposed to entering the war in the course of 1941, some 60 to 65 percent consistently said they favored aid to England *even at the risk of war.*[36] It is not hard to understand why people might hesitate to take the final plunge into war before they absolutely had to; but it was nevertheless a tremendous distortion to see those people as advocates of the isolationist position. Roosevelt far more accurately represented American public opinion than either of the Lindberghs or America First ever did.

To counter this isolationist tactic, interventionists attempted to argue that the obsession with direct American involvement in the war was misplaced. As Freda Kirchwey put it, "Today we must insist that war is not the primary issue; the defeat of Hitler is the issue. If we can encompass his defeat without fighting, we shall be fortunate. . . . But whether we should fight or not is now a question of strategy."[37] The policy decision aligning the United States with Britain had already been made. All that remained was to determine how best to go about winning the war. "The pressing issue of convoys and naval patrols must be rescued from the isolationists, who will, if they are allowed, reduce it to a choice between committing acts of war or avoiding them."[38] That was no longer the point. The United States was already in the war. The question was how to fight it. But Kirchwey was not advocating an expeditionary force. "Our job," she explained, "is to combine today with Great Britain . . . to defeat Hitler by all the forces at our joint disposal. If this means sending an army to England or Africa we must do it. Certainly it does not mean that now. We have no army ready to send, and if we had, the sending of it would interfere with tasks that need doing immediately and at top speed."[39] At this point in the war, Kirchwey believed, the United States was not yet prepared to make a significant military contribution, and an attempt to do so would divert resources from Britain, where they were urgently needed.

Although, after the passage of the Lend-Lease Act, isolationists were fighting a losing battle, they did not give up. In May, in anticipation of Mother's Day, the Women's Division of the America First Committee issued a publicity flyer, calling on mothers to take action: "*This* Mother's Day, May 11, Make it a *real* Mother's Day—Do something for your son—our sons—Mothers! Send this S.O.S. [Save Our Sons] to President Roosevelt. Demand! . . . No Convoys. No War. Save Our Sons."[40] This sort of emotional appeal owed a lot to the example of the mothers' movement, but it touched a powerful chord—so powerful, in fact, that the Committee to Defend America's Woman's Division had to respond in kind. On May 6, Florence Harriman called on "all mothers of conscripted men to visit their sons at training camps on Mother's Day." Her appeal read as follows: "We mothers have long been the recipients of favors on Mother's Day. In this time of crisis it is fitting that all mothers now rally to prove to their sons that we are proud of the manner in which they are accepting their responsibilities. . . . I am certain, too, that the mothers will be thrilled to see how camp life is benefiting the men of the country. Speaking as a great-grandmother, I am proud to make this appeal to all mothers. Let us show our sons that we are behind them."[41] If maternalism was a powerful rhetorical device, it could be employed effectively by both sides.

In the spring of 1941, as interventionists campaigned for convoys, Charles Lindbergh embarked on a speaking tour representing the America First Committee. One of his primary contentions was that the United States was not prepared to conduct a successful war: "Not only is the performance of some of our vital types of service aircraft inadequate, but our total air force in the United States today, both Army and Navy, both modern and obsolescent types, is not more than

Germany can produce in a few weeks." He condemned the thoughtlessness of Americans who would take the nation into a war it was not ready for, comparing the nation's likely fate with that of Britain and France: "In England, in France and now in my own country, I have listened to politicians and idealists calling upon the people for war without hardly a thought of how that war is to be fought or won. I have seen France fall; I see England falling, and now I see America being led into the same morass. I knew, in 1939, that England and France were not prepared to wage war successfully and I know that America is not prepared today to wage a successful war in Europe."[42] In such a context, Lindbergh believed, American involvement in the war would be a disaster. "I have never wanted Germany to win this war," he declared, "but I know that England is not in a position to win it, even with our help. That is why I have constantly advocated a negotiated peace."[43]

Interventionists were quick to challenge Lindbergh. Freda Kirchwey devoted a full editorial to him on May 10. "If Charles A. Lindbergh is right and Hitler is indeed invincible, if the powers resisting Nazi aggression even backed by the full industrial and fighting strength of the United States are doomed to defeat, then the American future may as well be written off. For Lindbergh's happy faith that a victorious Germany will prove no threat to the United States is too silly to consider as an alternative." Moreover, Kirchwey argued, "Lindbergh tacitly recognizes the absurdity of his own hope of peace by insisting that the United States must build up an impregnable defense."[44] Indeed, isolationists were fighting a rearguard action at this point. Public support for lend-lease had been strong, and they had effectively lost the battle over whether or not the war affected American interests.

By the spring of 1941, as a result, isolationists fell back heavily on the long-standing fear that war would mean the end of democracy in the United States. As Lindbergh put it, "I now oppose our entry into the war because I do not believe that our system of government in America . . . or our way of life can survive our participation."[45] Lindbergh further alleged, in a speech in Minnesota, that the democratic process had been undermined the previous November because both candidates had falsely promised to keep the nation out of war. The reality was that voters had had no real choice: "Many a sincere Democrat and Republican voted with full confidence that his man if elected would keep our country out of war. But it now seems doubtful that we even had two political parties last November, at least as far as the

Presidential candidates were concerned. The people of this nation were not given the chance to vote on the greatest issue of our generation, the issue of foreign war. And yet now we are told that we must go to Europe to fight for the very principles of democracy that were denied to us in our own country last November."[46] He also suggested that the government would soon act to stifle his dissenting voice, noting that he already faced a smear campaign designed to paint him as a Nazi sympathizer. "And," he declared portentously, "I do not know how much longer free speech will be allowed in this country."[47] Reading these speeches, it is hard to suppress the feeling that Charles Lindbergh actually hoped that the government might attempt to silence him—that at least would have given the movement new ammunition and credibility.

As the month of May came to an end, Americans prepared for a radio broadcast by the president—the first since his fireside chat of December 29. Interventionists hoped that it would signal brave new measures to increase aid to Britain. The president had signed an executive agreement with the Danish government-in-exile in early April, allowing the United States to take over the defense of Greenland, thus extending the reach of the U.S. Navy farther into the Atlantic. But he had held back from authorizing American ships to engage German vessels threatening Atlantic supply lines. The day before the speech, the Committee to Defend America released to the press an open letter to Roosevelt from Florence Harriman, now also a vice chairman of the committee, and Lewis Douglas, president of the Mutual Life Insurance Company and chairman of the Committee to Defend America's National Policy Board. The letter, which was also signed by some two thousand other prominent Americans, declared:

> We await your address on May 27 in the belief that you will tell what we must do to insure the security of the United States by hastening the defeat of the aggressors. . . . We have prayed that we might be spared from involvement in the war, but we cannot close our eyes to the wholesale murder of liberty. Most of all we cannot ignore the threats to our own security uttered and progressively enforced by those tyrants who are dedicated to the proposition that democracy must die. . . . The challenge is inescapable. We cannot meet it with mere words nor with mere dollars. We know that strong action, even armed action, entailing greater sacrifices will be required of us.[48]

This was as close to a call for war as the Committee to Defend America ever came. In the context of May 1941, and given its vagueness, it seems more like a call for vigorous action on the Atlantic than for full-scale military intervention in the conflict.

If the interventionists were hopeful, isolationists were fearful. In the afternoon of May 27, a group of congressional isolationists, led by Senator Burton Wheeler, appealed to the president to be cautious, commenting that "we have tested out sentiment in our districts and throughout the country . . . and we find that over 80 per cent of the people are opposed to any course which will take this nation into the European war." Moreover, they pointed out that the Constitution reserved to Congress the power to declare war and argued that "by every sound principle of government the same requirements must extend to acts which mean war, such as convoys and direct naval action."[49]

As it turned out, neither side would be completely happy with the speech, although the isolationists clearly had more to worry about. In what the Administration insisted on describing as a "fireside chat," despite the fact that it was eighty-four degrees in Washington when he began to speak, Roosevelt declared unequivocally that the Nazis were bent on "world domination." The United States could not hope to remain outside the fray. "Nobody can foretell tonight just when the acts of the dictators will ripen into attack on this hemisphere and us. But we know enough by now to realize that it would be suicide to wait until they are in our front yard." In declaring a state of unlimited national emergency and calling on the American people for unity and, in particular, their participation in measures for civilian defense and the expansion of industrial production, Roosevelt emphasized the importance of maintaining the freedom of the seas. But he stopped short of announcing explicitly that the United States would begin to convoy goods to Great Britain. Instead, he said simply that "all additional measures necessary to deliver the goods will be taken."[50] Indeed, the speech did not identify any specific actions that the administration planned to take to meet the national emergency thus declared. At a press conference the following day, moreover, Roosevelt confirmed that he had no plans to ask for the repeal of the Neutrality Act, and when reporters asked if his determination to ensure that lend-lease supplies reached Britain meant the introduction of convoys, he denied this, "explaining that escorting was outmoded."[51]

Any hope that interventionists might have had that Roosevelt intended serious action on the Atlantic was further undermined by the administration's indifferent response to the sinking of the *Robin Moor* in early June. The *Robin Moor,* an American freighter, was attacked and sunk by a German submarine in the South Atlantic, outside the official war zone. As such the incident seemed to offer the perfect grounds for expanding U.S. naval operations. The Fight for Freedom Committee certainly thought so, declaring: "The cold-blooded ruthless sinking of the Robin Moor demonstrates to us once again the futility of appeasement. There was no contraband on the ship. This sinking shows how futile our Neutrality Act is because now the Nazis have themselves gone into neutral waters to harass American shipping."[52] The committee called for a shoot-on-sight policy in response, as well as the repeal of the Neutrality Act. Roosevelt, however, was not ready to act. At this point, American vessels were engaged in extensive patrols of the western Atlantic, extending from the United States to Greenland, but the president had specifically prohibited them from engaging the Germans.

Interventionists continued to press the issue nevertheless and express their confidence that the United States would not allow Germany to control the seas. As Dorothy Thompson put it in mid-June, "The moment the oceans of the world become involved in war, that moment the United States, the greatest oceanic power in the world becomes involved. . . . Here we are today having to decide whether to let ourselves be pushed right off the seas and back to our shores with the Atlantic turned into a moat, or whether we shall go out to clear up the Atlantic, driving submarines out of its waters and bombers of ships out of the skies. And, of course, we shall decide to do the latter. There is not the slightest question that we shall decide to do the latter. There never has been any question—not from the beginning."[53] The question was, *When* would the United States do it?

While Americans pondered that question, Hitler prepared to launch Operation Barbarossa—the conquest of the Soviet Union. On June 22, 1941, three German armies invaded the Soviet Union, descending on Leningrad, Moscow, and Kiev. The German attack on the Soviet Union presented a serious threat for interventionists—that Americans' anticommunism would undermine their commitment to Hitler's defeat. As Kirchwey noted, "A genuine danger exists that Hitler will be able to accomplish his immediate aims in America. . . . Communism is an unpopular nostrum in this country. . . . And the conversion of the Communist Party, now that Russia is fighting, is likely to create more contempt than sympathy. . . . To concentrate on the mental contortions of the comrades is to follow a course laid out for us by Hitler. We who know he must be defeated, whether Russia is his enemy or his ally, cannot afford to fall in with his plans."[54]

More significant even than American anticommunism, however, was the American perception that Soviet involvement made it far less likely that the United States would have to intervene directly in the war. Isolationists had long argued, with considerable merit, that even if the British could avoid defeat and occupation, they could not hope to liberate the Continent without American troops. Now, though, perhaps the additional manpower necessary to defeat the Germans could come from the Soviet Union. And, in fact, many isolationists greeted the news of the attack on Russia with relief. As Herbert Hoover said, "Now it is not necessary for us to enter the war."[55]

Others, however, rejected any idea of supporting Communist Russia. As Charles Lindbergh declared in a speech at an America First rally in San Francisco on July 1, "I would a thousand times rather see my country ally herself with England or even with Germany, with all of her faults, than with Soviet Russia." Anne Lindbergh commented in her diary that she had wished Charles to leave out this statement, knowing how it would be received.[56] And she was right to be concerned. In an extremely bitter attack, Secretary of the Interior Harold Ickes denounced Lindbergh as a "Nazi scuttlefish." "Lindbergh now denounces communism because it defends itself against the aggression of Hitler, but I have never heard this Knight of the German Eagle denounce Hitler or nazism or Mussolini or fascism." In a final snide aside, Ickes referred to Lindbergh's work with a French doctor to develop an artificial heart, commenting, 'I could tell ex-Colonel Lindbergh where he could readily locate an artificial heart with the aid of an X-ray machine."[57]

Most interventionists welcomed the addition of the Soviets to the ranks of anti-Nazi fighters. Dorothy Thompson was even ready to endorse the extension of lend-lease aid to the Soviet Union after the Nazis turned east in June 1941. Early in the war, she had argued that Nazism and communism were twin evils: "No possibility of human renewal, no reconstruction or renaissance can come from these two movements. All their still unburied corpses can do is to breed disease and corruption."[58] However, the invasion of the Soviet Union provided, Thompson believed, an unprecedented opportunity for the West to influence the future direction of the Russians: "The fate of Russia now lies in the hands of the democracies—not the fate of the democracies in the hands of Russia. . . . Why in the world, under those circumstances, should we fear Russia? For the first time there is a chance of an evolution in Russia toward a socialist democracy."[59]

Less surprising was Kirchwey's endorsement of lend-lease for the Soviets: "Hitler must be defeated and destroyed, not because yesterday he was in league with Stalin or because he is fighting Stalin today, but because he represents the one overwhelming menace to the Western democracies and to freedom throughout the world. This most Americans realize." Kirchwey called for all possible action to exploit the opportunity created by Hitler's move—first for an extension of lend-lease aid to the Soviet Union, but also for increased aid to Britain and the repeal of the "obsolete Neutrality Law" to speed delivery of such aid. "Russia's war is democracy's opportunity, perhaps its last one for a long time to come."[60] In the end, the American people would support the decision to extend lend-lease aid to the Soviet Union, despite their hostility to communism, because it seemed to increase the chances that they would be spared military involvement themselves.[61]

Some of the more hawkish members of the administration, like Knox and Stimson, hoped to exploit the distraction of the Russo-German war to make some progress in the Battle of the Atlantic. But Roosevelt remained cautious, always looking over his shoulder at the isolationists in Congress. The decision to send American troops to Iceland at the start of July might have heralded a new policy of convoying ships of any nationality between the United States and Iceland, but Roosevelt lost his nerve and rescinded his original order to this effect.[62]

As the Germans locked horns with the Russians in the east, the Japanese considered their position. During the early months of 1941, the United States had gradually expanded the list of items subject to export ban under the terms of the National Defense Act of July 1940, and by the spring, Japan was starting to feel the effects. American-Japanese negotiations, aimed at resolving the differences between the two nations in the first half of 1941, collapsed partly due to diplomatic blunders, but it is not clear that negotiators could ever have bridged the gulf between the American ideal of open-door trade in Asia and Japanese ambitions for an Asian economic bloc. The German assault on Russia left the Japanese with two options. They could join the German campaign against the Soviet Union, thus dealing permanently with their northern neighbor. Or they could move south—into Indochina, Malaya, and the East Indies, which offered supplies of raw materials sufficient to make good the deficits created by U.S. sanctions. Given the increasing shortages that their war machine faced, the Japanese decided to pursue the southern strategy early in July, and their troops moved into southern Indochina on July 24.

The American government responded by freezing all Japanese assets in the United States on July 25, effectively preventing any further exports to Japan. Of particular importance from the Japanese perspective, this meant that they could no longer obtain vital supplies of oil from the United States. With only about a year's supply of oil on hand, this confirmed their decision to attack the East Indies in pursuit of alternative sources. Although the United States continued to seek some kind of modus vivendi with the Japanese in late 1941, the two sides were too far apart, and Japanese plans for war with America proceeded all the while.

Meanwhile, in August, after the sort of initial dramatic success that people had come to associate with the blitzkrieg, the German advance into Russia had begun to slow down. The problem with the success of Soviet resistance was that it had the wrong effect on American public opinion. As Freda Kirchwey commented, "The greater the resistance of Russia, the more complacent becomes the attitude of the United States."[63] And this was a serious problem, in Kirchwey's view. By this point in the war, the United States was pursuing a vigorous policy of interventionism much along the lines she had advocated. The only fly in the ointment was the continued isolationist rhetoric of individuals such as Lindbergh and the fact that the American public had not yet fully accepted the reality that U.S. military intervention in the war would be necessary before the day was won. What was necessary to deal with the lag in public opinion was honest and effective leadership from Roosevelt. Kirchwey had already criticized him in 1940 for fudging the issue during the election campaign. In August 1941, she resumed the attack:

> It is possible that nothing short of a declaration of war will awaken the country to an understanding that we are in any case involved in war and, as surely as Britain, face victory or defeat. If this is so, then a campaign should be undertaken to bring the truth home to the people. But before such a course is determined upon, the other policy should be fully exploited. The President . . . should tell the people what the situation of Britain demands of this country. And he should act upon that demand. If it means a

> system of full convoy instead of a patrol, he should order convoys. If it means shooting, he should order the navy to shoot. . . . But the President will have to buttress his acts with the sort of courageous honesty that has made Churchill's leadership a work of genius. Under such leadership this country could be quickly brought to realize what we face and what we must do.[64]

And Kirchwey was not the only interventionist to criticize Roosevelt for failing to lead the nation where they wanted to go.

In June 1941, Anne O'Hare McCormick defined the problem in the following way: "From Washington the picture of America is the picture of a growing minority of urgent interventionists, a dwindling minority of non-interventionists, and in between a slow-moving majority resigned to the inevitability of war."[65] The administration's reluctance to precipitate U.S. entry into the war, she argued, was due to the fact that the people were "merely resigned." Kirchwey believed that it was the duty of the administration to explain the likelihood of war to the public, and that such a frank explanation would be sufficient to win the support of the majority of Americans. In late July 1941, Kirchwey asked her readers, "Shall We Declare War?" Her answer was no. "To ask for such a declaration today would precipitate a battle in Congress and the country that might stall rather than accelerate the program of defense and help for Britain. The war between the isolationist and interventionist forces would distract the public mind from the greater war in which, without any declaration, we are inextricably engaged." However, Kirchwey believed that there was a serious danger in the administration's failure to address the American people's reluctance to take that final step into war. "It means that too little may be done at any one time. . . . A declaration of war is not what this country needs. It needs instead a course of action broadly conceived, honestly explained to the people, and courageously carried out by men and women who know what the fight against fascism means and what it demands of American democracy."[66]

Thompson shared Kirchwey's concern. In September 1941, in a column calling for a recognition of the fact that the British could not win the war alone, she noted that "the people have been kidded along, until we have reached a political situation where every one fears to take real leadership. Apparently the President does not believe that the people are capable of enduring the full truth. . . . The public is treated like a patient who must be spared shock."[67]

The Atlantic Charter helped to move the United States a little closer to where Kirchwey and Thompson wanted it to be. This document was the product of a secret meeting between Winston Churchill and President Roosevelt between August 9 and 12. The charter was designed to describe the kind of postwar world that would result from the defeat of the Axis. Roosevelt hoped that the statement of principle would reassure Americans that association with the Soviet Union in the war against Germany would not compromise American ideals.[68] Its eight points included self-determination, freedom of the seas, a rejection of any territorial ambitions in the war, a commitment to a liberal trade policy, and the creation of "a wider and permanent system of general security."[69] Although the charter involved some compromises for the British, especially over trade, Churchill accepted them because he understood the symbolic value of a joint declaration of war aims—the very act bound the United States more fully than ever to the British cause. As Kirchwey pointed out, "We are now associated with the coming peace in a sense that commits us to winning the war. . . . I cannot see how the promise of the eight points can be translated into reality unless the country is prepared for measures that do bring us 'closer to war.'"[70]

The Atlantic Charter was a bold act for Roosevelt. Nations not at war do not generally have war aims, and so the charter was a tacit acknowledgment of the reality of American involvement. Predictably, isolationists were upset, but the principles were very popular with the American public, so the issue could not be used against the president to much effect. The Atlantic Conference also involved military discussions, and Roosevelt, once again, approached the brink of ordering the U.S. Navy to undertake convoy duty; but, once again, he drew back, fearful of public reaction.

However, in early September, an incident in the North Atlantic gave Roosevelt the excuse he felt he needed to justify convoying to the American people. On September 4, a German submarine fired upon the U.S. destroyer *Greer* as it made its way to Iceland. The *Greer* deployed depth charges in return, but neither side found its target. The truth of the matter was that the *Greer* had been pursuing the submarine for several hours, working with a British patrol plane, also armed with depth charges, and that the Germans had fired on the *Greer* in self-defense. Nor was it even clear that the German commander had known that his surface pursuer was an American ship.[71]

A week later, however, Roosevelt described the attack on the *Greer* as "piracy legally and morally." Moreover, he placed the incident in the context of others, including the *Robin Moor*, arguing, "The important truth is that these acts of international lawlessness are a manifestation of a design that has been made clear to the American people for a long time. It is the Nazi design to abolish freedom of the seas and to acquire absolute control and domination of these seas for themselves. . . . This attack on the Greer was no localized military operation in the North Atlantic. This was one determined step toward creating a permanent world system based on force, on terror and on murder." Thus, Roosevelt outlined the situation for Americans, leading them toward the conclusion that some action was essential to preserve American rights at sea. "We have sought no shooting war with Hitler. We do not seek it now. But neither do we want peace so much that we are willing to pay for it by permitting him to attack our naval and merchant ships while they are on legitimate business. . . . These Nazi submarines and raiders are the rattlesnakes of the Atlantic." Having laid the groundwork of American innocence in this way, Roosevelt then announced his new policy—what was called the "shoot-on-sight" policy. "In the waters which we deem necessary for our defense American naval vessels and American planes will no longer wait until Axis submarines lurking under the water, or Axis raiders on the surface of the sea, strike their deadly blow—first. . . . [O]ur patrolling vessels and planes will protect all merchant ships—not only American ships but ships of any flag—engaged in commerce in our defensive waters. They will protect them from submarines; they will protect them from surface raiders." Finally, Roosevelt argued that the decision was a defensive one, thereby attempting to reassure Americans that it ought not to be taken as a provocation by the Germans: "It is no act of war on our part when we decide to protect the seas that are vital to American defense. The aggression is not ours. Ours is solely defense."[72] And, despite isolationist complaints, the American public accepted Roosevelt's argument, supporting the policy by the same 60 to 65 percent majorities that had backed all the major interventionist acts by the administration.[73]

On the same night that Roosevelt announced the new shoot-on-sight policy, Charles Lindbergh made his most infamous speech at an America First rally in Des Moines, Iowa. In it, he finally identified the forces that he believed were behind a conspiracy to get the United States into the war, forces that he had referred to before but refused to name: "The three most important groups which have been pressing this country toward war are the British, the Jewish and the Roosevelt

Administration."[74] Anne had tried to warn him of the likely reaction to this statement. "When I say that it will be taken as Jew-baiting, he says that of course he does not mean to do that."[75] And, of course, she was right. Charles had tried to place his allegation in a relatively sympathetic context, explaining, "It is not difficult to understand why Jewish people desire the overthrow of Nazi Germany. The persecution they suffered in Germany would be sufficient to make bitter enemies of any race. No person with a sense of the dignity of mankind can condone the persecution of the Jewish race in Germany." Unfortunately he went on: "But no person of honesty and vision can look on their pro-war policy here today without seeing the dangers involved in such a policy both for us and for them." And as if that was not bad enough, he also made what could easily be read as a veiled threat: "Instead of agitating for war, the Jewish groups in this country should be opposing it in every possible way, for they will be among the first to feel its consequences."[76] Lindbergh was not really pro-Nazi; he was certainly not disloyal, as many suggested, but he had what is perhaps a common failing of celebrities—an exaggerated sense of his own importance, of his own abilities. He imagined that he understood the situation in Europe much better than he really did—and perhaps even more damaging to his public image at this point and since, he seems to have lacked the sort of gut-level outrage and horror at National Socialism that informed the views of so many interventionists; that Anne herself felt and that caused her such anguish.

Interventionist reaction to the Des Moines speech was predictable. As Anne commented, "He is attacked on all sides—Administration, pressure groups, and Jews, as now openly a Nazi, following Nazi doctrine."[77] The family, however, was more sensitive. Anne noted in her diary for September 17: "Mother calls me up but we do not talk about the speech. She would not, of course. She would understand."[78]

The America First Committee stood behind Lindbergh, charging that it was the interventionists who had "inject[ed] the race issue into the discussion of war or peace." On September 24, the committee issued a statement in defense of Lindbergh. It declared, "Ever since the nation-wide effort to keep America out of war began the interventionists have sought to hide the real issue by flinging false charges at the America First Committee and at every leader who has spoken out against our entry into the European conflict. The present attack on Colonel Lindbergh is merely another case in point. . . . Behind a smoke screen of groundless charges this nation is being led to war in violation of the Constitution of the United States. There is but one real issue—the issue of war. From this issue we will not be diverted. We will carry on the fight until it is won."[79] America First's indignation rang rather hollow, however. Interventionists were by no means alone in their mudslinging. For every accusation of Nazi sympathizing made by interventionists, an isolationist somewhere was condemning them for warmongering.

Although the *Greer* incident and the shoot-on-sight policy heralded an undeclared naval war in the Atlantic, Freda Kirchwey remained discontented with Roosevelt's failure to lead public opinion. On September 20, she complained, "What one can wish, with passionate regret, is that the President had prepared the American people for the war that will sooner or later emerge from the policy to which the country is now committed."[80] The danger of the president's policy in the Atlantic was not, in her view, that it might lead to war. Kirchwey had long been reconciled to that. Rather, she feared that it would lead the United States into war for the wrong reasons. "But war against Hitler must be waged as a war for freedom and our democratic institutions—not for shipping."[81]

Dorothy Thompson agreed. Before she went on vacation in October 1941, her final column called on the American people to answer some vital questions: "The basic question is not whether the Nazis sink our ships carrying our goods in waters we have declared to be essential to American defense. . . . if we go to war, . . . we should go to war, not only in defense of the United States, but in defense of humanity, for the noblest of causes and the loftiest of aims. . . . if we fight, let us fight for fundamental things; let us fight for the basic issue of freedom and equality, as between persons and nations. Let us not fight over 'incidents.'"[82] Her primary concern was that the United States should enter the war not because of some naval incident in the Atlantic but because it was in American interests and in support of American ideals.

By this point, as Americans daily awaited news from the Atlantic that would take them into war, there remained, however, a Neutrality Act, unrepealed through all the dramatic interventionist moves of 1941. Admittedly, the passage of the Lend-Lease Act had gutted the law of any real meaning, but it was still on the books, now prohibiting only the arming of American merchant ships, the movement of those ships through combat zones, and travel by American citizens on belligerent ships. In the context of the war in the Atlantic, however, even those restrictions seemed limiting. So in the fall of 1941, interventionists began to pressure Congress and the president finally to repeal the Neutrality Act altogether.

In September 1941, a group of interventionist women planned a trip to Washington to lobby Congress to repeal what was left of the Neutrality Act—the last vestige of American neutrality. Rose Chayes, of the New York chapter of the Fight for Freedom Committee to Defend America, organized the trip, writing to a number of women in late September for advice on an appropriate statement of aims and on how to arrange activities. Initially, the idea was to lobby Congress as an independent group of women: "We prefer to seem a spontaneous crusade by women not given to large scale demonstrations. We are not taking a name. We are not associated with this committee [Fight for Freedom] or any other."[83]

This was probably a response to the sense, which the isolationist community had successfully created, that ordinary American women were opposed to U.S. involvement in the war. However, within ten days the agenda had changed, apparently for publicity reasons, and Chayes was writing again to women: "The 'nameless' group of women which contemplated an assault on Washington has turned into a full-fledged Women's Committee of FIGHT FOR FREEDOM, INC. This change was the result of advice that we were a better story that way—and that we would not then need the lengthy description which would discourage using our story."[84] The statement that was issued to accompany the visit to Washington, nevertheless, made explicit the women's intent to provide striking evidence of women's support for the interventionist position:

> We are a group of women who have enlisted in the FIGHT FOR FREEDOM. We want it known that the hysterical women who have been demonstrating in Washington do not speak for us. We feel deeply and acutely the threat which the Axis presents to our families, our homes and the fundamental principles of civilized society. We have taught our children that decency should guide their conduct. . . . We are convinced that the Nazi machine must be outlawed by the civilized world, and that we and our families will not be enabled to return to constructive efforts and justified hopes for peace until the Nazi machine is completely annihilated. We are determined to do our share to safeguard our future.[85]

This statement was followed by a call for the revision of the Neutrality Act. These women explicitly claimed the authority of the defenders and nurturers of family and decency to promote an interventionist agenda. They rejected the isolationist claim to represent American women and staked out new ground for themselves as women who put the cause of freedom before the cause of peace.

This sort of maternal rhetoric had become more common among interventionist women in 1941, no doubt in response to the very vocal efforts of the mothers' movement and other isolationists to claim women as their constituency. For example, a Fight for Freedom member, Mrs. Philip Morgan of Worcester, Massachusetts, declared in September 1941: "I am a housewife. My husband served eighteen months in France during the war as an enlisted man. We have two sons, seventeen and sixteen years of age."[86] In this way, she established her authority to speak about the war, as one who had sons who would likely be drafted; her potential loss gave her words added force. She went on to attack the isolationists, particularly for the argument that the United States would be better off building up its own defenses and then, if Hitler did decide to attack, Americans could defend themselves rather than fighting in another foreign war. "Why, in Heaven's name do they want him to get over here? . . . Don't the isolationists know what war is, that they so bravely talk of fighting it here? . . . Do the isolationists want to see war come out of the sky on homes, women and children? They say 'We don't want to send our brave boys to fight on foreign land.' I believe that our soldiers would rather fight all over the world than have their families go through a Blitzkrieg."[87] This statement worked on several levels: the prospect of war in the United States was raised, with its concomitant threat to civilians, especially women and children, appealing to the instinct both for self-preservation and for the protection of the innocent and helpless. Morgan finished off by characterizing the war as "a war of dictators vs. democracy; tyranny vs. freedom. I believe in our American way of life. . . . I believe in fighting to preserve it for our children and our children's children."[88] Thus, she appealed to women's nurturing instincts for the defense of freedom, in the name of the younger generation.

The debate over repeal of the Neutrality Act drew the LWV back into legislative activity in the fall of 1941. The League embraced the cause of repeal enthusiastically, arguing, "The basic principle of the Neutrality Act—equal treatment of all belligerents—has been repudiated by the American people. It is time that the Act itself be wiped off the statute books. It confuses public thinking, inhibits the Congress in acting on questions of foreign policy, gives aid and comfort to aggressor nations."[89] Early in October, the National Board voted almost unanimously in favor of repeal, with several of the members basing their votes on the argument that it was necessary to make the policy of aid to the victims of aggression effective.[90] Thus, League policy had developed logically from prewar advocacy of collective security and measures to penalize aggressor nations through increasing stages of aid to the Allies, although it did not quite reach the logical next step of calling for direct military involvement, before the question was settled for it by the Japanese attack on Pearl Harbor.

The NCJW also called for repeal in October 1941. "The United States is no longer neutral," it declared. "With each Axis victory, the American people have realized more clearly the threat to their own security and freedom."[91] As the October issue of the *International Relations Digest* explained, the NCJW believed "that a freedom-loving nation should not be neutral, but should distinguish between right and wrong; punish an aggressor and aid his victim." Finally, the *Digest* noted, "In a poll taken of the National Committee on International Relations and Peace with members throughout the country, the overwhelming majority favored outright repeal."[92] Both American national interests and the demands of morality, in the council's view, required this stand. From a position of emphasizing the need to keep out of the war in late 1939, the NCJW had shifted to the point of supporting all-out aid whatever the risk of war.

Freda Kirchwey, of course, had long advocated the repeal of the Neutrality Act. In October 1941, she likened it to another great legislative fiasco of the interwar period: "The Neutrality Act has been not unlike the Prohibition Act in effect on our national life. Both were designed to keep us out of trouble. But like most regulations, public or private, which conflict with genuine desires and interests, it was in each case the law itself that got us into trouble."[93]

Roosevelt, however, remained anxious about the strength of congressional isolationists and, instead of asking for repeal of the Neutrality Act on October 9, limited his request to repeal of the prohibition against arming American merchant ships. Although the Senate expanded Roosevelt's proposed revision to allow U.S. ships to enter combat zones, the debate was conducted in the context of the first American casualties in the undeclared naval war—11 dead on the *Kearny*, attacked on October 16; 115 lost in the sinking of the *Reuben*

James on October 31. These deaths provided sobering evidence of the costs of the administration's policy. Nevertheless, the revisions made it through Congress, albeit with rather narrow margins. The closeness of the votes reinforced Roosevelt's concerns about the fragility of public support for a more aggressive approach to the war.

Despite this, Freda Kirchwey welcomed the revisions as a declaration of hostilities: "Last Friday the House of Representatives adopted a declaration of naval war against the Axis powers. . . . [A]t last the United States has wiped out the pretense that it is a neutral in this war. That pretense has been an empty one ever since the Lend-Lease Act was passed, but it served as a cloak for appeasement-mongers and as a wet blanket on the enthusiasm of the interventionist majority."[94] The reality, however, was that no declaration of war had been made. Moreover, any attempt by Roosevelt to secure such a declaration could well have met with defeat—the American people and their government had traveled a great distance toward war, but they could not quite bring themselves to take that last fatal step. Instead, the United States was pursuing, in both European and Pacific theaters, a policy so provocative, so little different from actual war, that it was merely a matter of time before either the Japanese or the Germans decided to formalize the situation. As historian Robert Divine put it, "It was now only a question of who would strike first."[95]

8

"Brave Women and Fair Men"

With the nation seemingly on the brink of war in November 1941, the Fight for Freedom Committee decided to organize a Women's Division. It seems to have been a product both of a desire to exploit the resources of women—their greater leisure time (an indication of the overwhelmingly middle-class membership of these organizations) and the extensive networks created by women's groups across the nation—and of a belief that women needed to prepare, and be prepared, for the task of maintaining unity and morale on the home front when the United States entered the war. This latter concern reflected the shift in public opinion that occurred over the summer of 1941, as most Americans gradually accepted the inevitability of direct U.S. involvement in the war. The promoters of the new division believed that "women have a combination of leisure and zeal which should be utilized in the fight for freedom."[1] Moreover, an internal Fight for Freedom memorandum pointed out that women were "already so highly organized in groups (13,000,000 women in clubs in the U.S.A.)" that they could "be used to get a larger audience for FFF, more members, and for money-raising." It also argued that women would play a central role in the war, "maintaining unity and democracy at home if we are to have a real democratic victory."[2] This constituted a clearer, more explicit rationale for a woman's division than the Committee to Defend America had developed, but since the division was disbanded a few weeks after the attack on Pearl Harbor, on December 29, it is impossible to determine whether it would have attempted to address women more specifically and directly than its predecessor in the Committee to Defend America.

The Women's Division of the Fight for Freedom attempted to put together a national committee that would be representative of American women and would give the organization prestige and influence. The provisional list included "a doctor, lawyer, merchant, and 6 chiefs of women's organizations, and about 18 women's organizations well represented in all. There are three prominent Catholics, three Jewish women, 2 YWCA and two prominent Protestant Churchwomen."[3] Those who agreed to join included Margaret Forsyth, international relations secretary of the YWCA; Kathryn Starbuck, professor of law at Skidmore and chair of legislative recommendations for the National Federation of Business and Professional Women; Carrie Chapman Catt, suffragist and leader in the interwar peace movement; Ada Comstock, president of Radcliffe College; Deans C. Mildred Thompson and Virginia Gildersleeve; prominent Catholics, Margaret C. Banning and Mrs. Carlton J. H. Hayes; and Rose Schneiderman, president of the WTUL. The national committee had no policy-making function, however; rather, the idea was that members would provide occasional advice, particularly on the mood of the public in their locality, and adorn the committee's letterhead.

The new Women's Division was introduced to the world on November 21, 1941, in a speech by its new honorary chairman, Elizabeth Morrow. There was some discussion regarding the best timing for this speech, which was broadcast nationally by NBC. Early options were November 19 or 20, the Thursday and Friday of the Thanksgiving holiday. A Women's Division memorandum suggested that the latter was preferable, since the speech should be billed "as a big message to American Women. Women with a large family party the next day will not invite other people in to listen to a broadcast or pay much attention to it themselves at 6:30 when they are either eating dinner or cooking it."[4] In the end, the day after Thanksgiving was settled on, and the speech was broadcast at 5:45 P.M. on Friday evening.

Morrow began her address by referring to her speech of June 1940 and commenting on the way in which the changing world situation had shaped her views and brought her finally to the conclusion that war was necessary: "I consider the consequences of a German victory so disastrous for us that I think this country should, if necessary, enter an all-out war to prevent that victory."[5] Morrow, and indeed other members of the Fight for Freedom Committee, faced a difficult rhetorical problem. As advocates of all-out aid to Britain, they had been able to argue that their policy was best designed to keep the United States out of war and American boys out of battle. Now, however, they supported war. Morrow acknowledged the problem candidly: "As I address you in the name of the Fight for Freedom this evening, I feel myself to be a *sheep* in wolf's clothing." Women faced an unenviable choice, she believed: war or oppression—neither was anything a mother could want for her children—and she chose war. Women, Morrow argued, needed to be brave enough to face the facts. The essence of the Fight for Freedom's platform was "that we frankly meet the risk of war and our foreign policy is not founded upon fear, subterfuge or deception." Here she seemed to be challenging the isolationist accusation that interventionists sought to dupe the American people, leading them into a war that they did not want.

But Morrow had a strong incentive not to engage in the mudslinging that had become typical of the debate between interventionists and isolationists—the harmony of her own family. As a result, she made a striking appeal not to the opposition but to her allies. "Let me believe," she asked, "that this Committee is made up of *brave women and fair men.* I misquote with malice. I hope desperately that we can all be not only good fighters but *fair* fighters. There are honest, conscientious and honorable citizens who hold that involvement in the European war will not help our national defense and will not preserve the American way of life so precious to us all. We must respect the sincerity of their opinions while differing with them. . . . 'War Monger' is an unpleasant name, but 'Unpatriotic' and 'UnAmerican' are equally disagreeable adjectives. When it comes to motives, let us leave the role of omniscience to God." The previous months could not have been easy for Elizabeth Morrow. Few hearing her words could fail to have been aware of the personal meaning behind them. What they may not have understood so clearly was how her family's divisions mirrored those of the nation as a whole.

Morrow then switched gears and appealed to women's own interests: "I would remind you that my sex has always fought for freedom." She enumerated the gains of the women's movement in economic and political freedom and access to higher education and pointed out the vulnerability of those gains if the Nazis won the war: "The Nazi ideology does not allow women to use their mental or spiritual powers much less expand them. We have an immense stake in the combat." Thus, women were encouraged to join the Fight for Freedom to protect and defend their own rights.

Morrow could no longer easily appeal to women as mothers hoping to keep their children safe from war, so instead she spoke to them about their own interests and appealed to all Americans on a moral level. She emphasized the threat to democracy and appealed to Americans' honor: "Let us as—Brave Women and *Fair* Men—face the worst fear. Let us imagine a victory of Nazism and realize *beforehand* the remorse we will suffer, feeling that we might have turned the tide of battle in favor of democracy. Let us face a miraculous hope—let us imagine a victory for the British, bought for us by their sweat and blood and tears alone and realize *beforehand* the shame we will feel at accepting their sacrifice. The reproach of Henry IV to his General Crillon will be ours forever—'Go hang yourself brave Crillon, we have won a great victory and *you were not there.*'"

But, of course, Americans were there. Within three weeks of Morrow's broadcast, the United States was at war with all three Axis powers. On the morning of December 7, 1941, Japanese forces launched a full-scale attack on the American Pacific Fleet stationed at Pearl Harbor. The attack was the first step in a larger offensive in Asia—a calculated gamble on the part of the Japanese government, designed to secure access to vital raw materials from the Dutch and British East Indies, which were no longer available from the United States. Although many interventionist women daily expected the outbreak of war, few were not shocked when it finally happened—not least because so many of them had their eyes firmly focused on the undeclared naval war in the Atlantic.

Dorothy Thompson commented that a friend had supposed that she was not surprised; "but I was. . . . Over and over again the same pattern and always the same surprise. . . . And I felt it too. 'Not to us. They can't do that to us.' Even when I'd known all the time that they could, and they would."[6] Anne O'Hare McCormick also noted the shock with which Americans greeted the news of the attack on Pearl Harbor, reflecting on the irony of the situation: "In days to come, when we recall the circumstances in which war came to America, the utter astonishment caused by the first shot may strike us as the strangest aspect of the event; for our incredulity is only the last echo of the surprise of all peoples to whom the same thing has happened."[7] There was some good to come of it, however, in McCormick's view. The thing that was so shocking to Americans—the very directness of the attack—irrevocably ended any possibility of debate or accusations that the administration had conjured up an excuse for war, or so McCormick thought, and united the American people in support of the war.[8]

Freda Kirchwey also recognized the new unity of the American people. "The horror has made America one," she commented. "We are one—all of us. Senator Wheeler and Cordell Hull and you and I and our sons."[9] Nevertheless, Kirchwey worried that Americans would not learn the proper lessons from the experience—that they would see the war with Japan as separate from the struggle against fascism. "Our long appeasement of Japan brought on this war," she argued, "but so did our sell-out of Spain, our futile bargaining with Franco and Pétain. Each is part of a whole—and the whole is the betrayal of the anti-fascist front against aggression and terrorism and tyranny. And the final cost of that betrayal is yet to be met. The war with Japan is only the beginning. Whether we realize it fully or not, we are now in the World War—not in an isolationist Pacific war."[10] What she feared was that Americans might turn away from the conflict in Europe and focus on the war in the Pacific, which had now become *their* war. Even in the face of Japan's assault on the Pacific Fleet, the war, for Kirchwey, was an antifascist war—one whose center of gravity unquestionably lay in Europe.

As it turned out, even before her concern was expressed in print, Germany and Italy had declared war on the United States, making her point more convincingly than she ever could have done. Anne O'Hare McCormick interpreted the German declaration as an inevitable conclusion. The United States, the world's greatest democracy, by definition had also to be National Socialism's greatest enemy. Their clash could not have been avoided. "Those who understand this struggle have seen from the beginning that American participation was inevitable. They knew that while this country stands, Hitler's revolution cannot win. We represent the true antithesis to his system, the eternal obstacle to his aims. . . . By delivering the first open blow, by 'beating' us to a declaration of war, Hitler . . . has proved to the last doubter that our participation was inevitable."[11]

American entry into the war allowed women's organizations, and indeed all internationalists who had advocated a greater role for the United States, to focus on the next step, to look both at winning the war *and* winning the peace. Louise Wright wrote to Marguerite Wells on December 9 about an appropriate stand for the LWV to take: "It seems to me that the League must orient itself to the war. We must plan our activities so that we make a contribution to the war and also make our members feel that they are each being helpful."[12] At the next biennial convention, in Chicago in April 1942, Louise Baldwin, first vice president in charge of legislation, reported: "The first drive of the League was toward preventing war in the world. When war began to seem inevitable, the drive was toward attempting to stop it before it spread to the United States. Now, the original goal of the

League must not be lost sight of. When this war is won, the problems that lead to war will remain and new attacks on them will have to be made. The League experience of the past twenty-two years, its watchfulness and work during this war, can be counted upon to lead it to effective action in the post-war period."[13]

The WTUL also committed itself to the war effort. At a meeting held just after the Pearl Harbor attack, the Executive Board voted to send a letter of support to the president, stating, "As representatives of organized working women we can assure you of our willingness to accept the responsibilities and burdens necessary for the achievement of the high purpose of the struggle in which our Nation is engaged."[14] They also urged the president to apply the principles of the four freedoms to domestic production by appointing representatives of labor to wartime production agencies and by prohibiting racial discrimination. They concluded, "We are aware that in the essential production program that must now be so greatly accelerated, labor will have a responsibility equal to that of the armed forces. We are ready to assume this responsibility and the sacrifice that it will involve, with the assurance that victory will mean for us, as it will mean for the rest of the world, a future in which the human spirit may be free."[15] Similarly, the AAUW greeted the war with a collection of reflections in the *AAUW Journal,* in January 1942, entitled "Nothing to Fear—Much to Do," in which national and local leaders urged the membership to play an active role in war work, especially by putting their educations and skills to good use.[16]

The impact of Pearl Harbor on WILPF was devastating, as the organization seemed for many to lose its relevance. By 1944 the membership had dropped from a prewar figure of 14,000 to 4,708.[17] WILPF's deep-rooted commitment to democratic processes meant that it had little choice but to accept U.S. entry into the war. On December 10, 1941, the National Board issued the following statement: "Since it is the basic policy of the Women's International League not to obstruct the carrying out of the will of the majority, we shall try to serve our country by cooperating with the British section of the Women's International League in directing our joint energies toward the problems of the postwar world."[18] In some ways, though, the final involvement of the United States in the war was a blessing in disguise for the U.S. Section of WILPF. Although membership dropped, the rump organization was able to survive now that the critically divisive question of peace versus freedom had been answered.

For interventionists, especially those in the Fight for Freedom, the final outbreak of war in many ways came as a relief. In fact, Anne Lindbergh complained to her diary that "Fight for Freedom has come out with a gloating exultant full-page ad, starting with a huge headline: 'It's America First now'! This makes me sick."[19] If interventionists rejoiced, they did so only because at last the United States had to face the facts—facts that they had long accepted—that the nation could not escape the war, and that Americans would have to fight for what they believed in.

Fight for Freedom disbanded at the outbreak of war but not before contemplating a continued existence as a committee to maintain morale and fight for a just peace. On January 16, Bishop Hobson contemplated circulating a four-point agenda of war aims: "To fight for the maintenance of the free way of life in our own country; To win an all-out victory against the Axis powers; To insist upon the making of a righteous peace; To insure American participation in world affairs after the war."[20] In particular, the last two of these aims highlight the fundamental goals and assumptions of American internationalists, shared not only by the interventionist organizations but also by the women's organizations considered here.

These organizations had spent the interwar years pushing for American participation in an international system of collective security. When the Second World War began, that dream lived on, but before it could be realized the Axis powers had to be defeated. Women's organizations that had spent the 1930s calling for discriminatory action against aggressor nations accepted the logic of aid to the Allies and, as the Allies' predicament increased, were ready to support increasingly interventionist aid policies. Many of the women in these organizations continued to hope that direct military intervention by the United States would not be necessary, but this hope gradually took second place to their commitment to the cause of defeating Germany. The shift in their thinking that took place during the first months of the war was clear in the way they debated the issues. In late 1939, revision of the Neutrality Act was advocated largely on the basis that it would help keep the country out of the war; in late 1941, repeal was advocated on the basis that the act was contrary to the declared policy of the nation and a hindrance to the provision of full aid to the Allies. The hope of the first months of the war was gone, leaving a firm commitment to the Allies' cause, which, they believed, was also America's. Although some of these women debated the issues within a gendered framework—emphasizing at different times women's maternal instincts and the fate of women under National Socialism—their advocacy of interventionism was based on their commitment to internationalism and collective security, a commitment that was shared by many American men. Although they functioned in a social and political context that assumed women's commitment to peace above all else, and this was indeed their long-term goal, they were not bound by the expectations of this ideal of womanhood. Rather, their position was paradoxical, and they knew it. In the end, they believed that the only way to establish a meaningful and lasting postwar peace might well be through war.

Unlike their male counterparts, however, female internationalists rarely had easy access to the corridors of power. As a result, they fought for their ideals in public marketplace of ideas and, in the best traditions of participatory democracy, lobbied Congress and the executive through petitions, letters, and visits. Some of them, notably Dorothy Thompson, Freda Kirchwey, and Anne O'Hare McCormick, were lucky enough to have established access to the media when the war began, facilitating the expression of their views. Their outspokenness did not go unremarked, however. It was no coincidence that the mothers' movement chose to hang an effigy of Thompson on the gates of the White House, rather than any male interventionist leader. Thompson offended not simply by her views but also because she was a woman, stepping beyond the acceptable bounds of woman's sphere, in the very conservative view of the mothers. Less prominent women were obliged to work on the grassroots level, either through the preexisting institutional framework of women's organizations or, if those groups did not pursue a sufficiently interventionist line, through the women's divisions of the Committee to Defend America and the Fight for Freedom Committee. This grassroots activism, whether getting up petitions, writing congressmen, telephoning neighbors, promoting the "Battle of Production," securing billboard space for interventionist posters, or simply raising the money to finance these and many similar operations, played a significant role in publicizing their message.

Sometimes these women claimed authority to speak, indeed, demanded to be heard, by virtue of their status as mothers. To a considerable extent, this tactic was a response to the isolationist claim to speak for American women that relied heavily on the rhetoric of motherhood. Isolationists suggested that women's maternal nature and nurturing role meant that they were opposed to war—except perhaps a war in defense of the United States. Interventionists responded by arguing that aid to the Allies represented the best means of avoiding direct U.S. involvement in the war and thus of saving American lives. As the war progressed, however, and increasing numbers of interventionists became convinced that aid alone was no longer enough, they recast their use of maternal rhetoric to support a call for war. Women must be brave, they said, and accept their suffering and sacrifice, so that their children and grandchildren could live free from the Nazi menace. This required a reevaluation of moral priorities. Rather than accept, as many isolationists and pacifists did, that women were innately designed to value life above all other things, women interventionists reordered their assumed moral priorities and argued that some things were worse than war—and Nazi domination was one of those things.

It is natural to wonder whether the activities of women in the interventionist committees and women's organizations had any impact on the formulation of American foreign policy in this period. The relationship between public opinion and foreign policy can be very difficult to determine, and one thing is clear: in the context of the Second World War, events abroad were the primary engine driving American foreign policy. As Freda Kirchwey commented in June 1940, "The rush of Hitler's legions to the Channel; the threatened invasion of England; the imminent drive toward Paris—these are making American policy."[21] Beyond this, with so many factors involved, attributing relative significance is fraught with problems. What we can say is that President Roosevelt was aware both of the assumption that women would oppose warlike measures and of the activities of interventionist women. As the Lend-Lease Act neared passage in early March 1941, for example, Roosevelt wrote to Marguerite Wells of the LWV, thanking her for a letter expressing the League's support for the legislation: "I want you to know how deeply I appreciate your clear statement of the position of the League of Women Voters on foreign policy. It is indeed encouraging to know that you and your organization are supporting the lease-lend bill."[22] If interventionist women, and indeed interventionists in general, did not create American foreign policy in the crisis of the Second World War, their voices were nevertheless heard.

The activities of interventionist women were more significant perhaps for a slightly different question about the relationship between U.S. foreign policy and public opinion in this era. Historians have long debated the extent to which American public opinion was isolationist in the years 1939–41. Some have argued that Roosevelt deceived a reluctant American public, manipulating the nation into a war that it strongly wished to avoid. Others have praised his insight, regretting only that he was constrained by isolationist opinion, which prevented him from doing more, earlier, to assist the Allied cause. Still others have criticized his failure to take a stronger stand, suggesting that more decisive leadership from Roosevelt would have allowed him to act more effectively. Clearly, Roosevelt was not always as candid as he might have been either about the dangers created by the war and about the risks of the policies he advocated. But it is one thing to say that Roosevelt was reluctant to lay out the truth before the American people and another to assume that as a result they were unaware. Such an assumption does little credit to Americans of the late 1930s and early 1940s.

The story of American women interventionists, moreover, shows how inaccurate such an assumption is. The women studied here were far too well-informed about the international situation to require the administration to educate them about it, or explain the risks of supporting the Allies; nor were they likely to be deceived by whatever rhetorical spin the administration wanted to put on measures such as lend-lease. The administration might emphasize that the intent of the Lend-Lease Act was to keep the United States out of the war, but interventionists understood that with that hope came a significant risk. And if they had not understood, there were plenty of isolationists around pointing it out to them. All this is to say that the ideas and activities of women interventionists, in the interventionist committees, in women's organizations, and in the press, demonstrate that one significant segment of the American public, at least, clearly understood all the possible repercussions of the aid policies that Roosevelt advocated, and indeed, many of them demanded a more aggressive approach than the president himself was willing to take. They were neither led nor manipulated into the war. Rather, they understood and accepted the necessity of war—both for immediate American interests and security and for their hope of a peaceful future.

Appendix: Women's Organizations and Officers

American Association of University Women (AAUW)
- Esther Caukin Brunauer: Associate for International Education
- Alzada Comstock: Chairman of the International Relations Committee

League of Women Voters (LWV)
- Marguerite Wells: President
- Louise Wright: Chairman of Department of Foreign Policy
- Anne Hartwell Johnstone: Secretary of Department of Foreign Policy
- Jeannette Cheek: National Board member

National Council of Jewish Women (NCJW)
- Fanny Brin: National Chairman of the Committee on International Relations and Peace

National Women's Trade Union League (WTUL)
- Rose Schneiderman: President
- Elisabeth Christman: Secretary-Treasurer
- Margaret Stone: National Chairman of the International Relations Committee

Notes

Chapter 1. "Does America Deserve a Miracle?"

1. Elizabeth Morrow, "Does America Deserve a Miracle?" pamphlet with transcript of radio address, June 4, 1940, Box 57, Elizabeth Cutter Morrow Papers, Sophia Smith Collection, Smith College, Northampton, Mass. (hereafter cited as Morrow Papers).

2. Ibid.

3. Ibid.

4. Ibid.

5. Cited in Rhodri Jeffreys-Jones, *Changing Differences: Women and the Shaping of American Foreign Policy, 1917–1994* (New Brunswick, N.J.: Rutgers University Press, 1995) 97–98.

6. Morrow, "Does America Deserve a Miracle?"

7. "Florence Munson to Elizabeth Morrow," June 5, 1940, Box 57, Morrow Papers.

8. "Katherine Searles Pilliod to Elizabeth Morrow," June 13, 1940, Box 57, Morrow Papers.

9. "The Committee for Sound Americanism to Elizabeth Morrow," June 5, 1940, Box 57, Morrow Papers.

10. "Anonymous letter from Hackensack, N.J.," June 5, 1940, Box 57, Morrow Papers.

11. Morrow, "Does America Deserve a Miracle?"

Chapter 2. Imagining Neutrality

1. Harriet Hyman Alonso, *Peace As a Women's Issue: A History of the U.S. Movement for World Peace and Women's Rights* (Syracuse, N.Y.: Syracuse University Press, 1993), 90.

2. Louise M. Young, *In the Public Interest: The League of Women Voters, 1920–1970* (New York: Greenwood Press, 1989), 2.

3. Faith Rogow, *Gone to Another Meeting: The National Council on Jewish Women, 1893–1993* (Tuscaloosa: University of Alabama Press, 1993), 178.

4. Young, *In the Public Interest,* 119, 125.

5. "1936–1938 Program," Box 1882, "International Relations: Basic Documents, 1930–56," Series IV, Papers of the National League of Women Voters, Library of Congress (hereafter cited as LWV Papers).

6. "Report of the President to the National Convention," May 1936, Box 7, Headquarters Records, Folder 2, May–September, 1936, *Papers of the National*

Women's Trade Union League, microfilm of Library of Congress collection, Reel 7 (hereafter cited as NWTUL Papers).

7. Nancy Schrom Dye, "Rose Schneiderman," in *Notable American Women: The Modern Period* (Cambridge, Mass.: Belknap Press of Harvard University Press, 1980), 631–33.

8. "AAUW 1939 Convention Proceedings: Thursday Afternoon Session, June 22, 1939," Series II, Reel 8, *American Association of University Women Archives, 1881–1976* (Sanford, N.C.: Microfilm Corporation of America, 1980) (hereafter cited as AAUW Archives).

9. Publicity for Esther Caukin Brunauer, Folder: Esther Caukin Brunauer, Series I, Reel 1, AAUW Archives.

10. "A Peace Platform," Box 94, Group I, International Relations and Peace, 1938–43, no. 5, Records of the National Council of Jewish Women, Library of Congress (hereafter cited as NCJW Records).

11. These organizations were the National Board of the Young Women's Christian Association; the General Federation of Women's Clubs; the American Association of University Women; the National Federation of Business and Professional Women's Clubs; the National Home Demonstration Council; the NCJW; the National Committee of Church Women; the National LWV; the WTUL; the National Woman's Christian Temperance Union; and the Women's Conference of the American Ethical Union.

12. See Carrie Foster, *The Women and the Warriors: The U.S. Section of the Women's International League for Peace and Freedom, 1915–1946* (Syracuse, N.Y.: Syracuse University Press, 1995), 209–17, for a discussion of Detzer's role in the creation of the Senate committee.

13. Robert Divine, *The Reluctant Belligerent: American Entry into World War II,* 2d ed. (New York: Knopf, 1979), 23–24.

14. The "peace groups" cited were the National Council for the Prevention of War and the Women's International League for Peace and Freedom on the mandatory side and the League of Nations Association on the discretionary side. "Reference Memorandum on Neutrality," March 20, 1936, Box 1710, Folder 5, Series IV, LWV Papers.

15. Ibid.

16. Ibid.

17. Frank A. Warren III, *Liberals and Communism: The "Red Decade" Revisited* (Bloomington: Indiana University Press, 1966), 69.

18. Sara Alpern, *Freda Kirchwey: A Woman of "The Nation"* (Cambridge, Mass.: Harvard University Press, 1987), 118.

19. Warren, *Liberals and Communism,* 189.

20. Alpern suggests that while Kirchwey denounced the pact, she was nevertheless convinced that it could not last and "never considered it as reprehensible as others did." *Freda Kirchwey,* 126. In contrast, Warren argues that *The Nation* adopted "a sharply critical position. Russia, the editors believed, had timed the pact to give Hitler 'the greatest possible benefit.'" *Liberals and Communism,* 201.

21. Alpern, *Freda Kirchwey,* 116.

22. "Civil War and Intervention," *The Nation,* August 29, 1936, 229. At this point, *The Nation* was not publishing signed editorials by Kirchwey. I have worked on the assumption that she had significant input into the main editorial line taken by the journal at this time, not least because it is consistent with the positions taken by her in later, signed, editorials.

23. Robert Dallek, *Franklin D. Roosevelt and American Foreign Policy, 1932–1945* (New York: Oxford University Press, 1979), 127.

24. "Pro-Fascist Neutrality," *The Nation,* January 9, 1937, 33–34.

25. Ibid., 34.

26. Quoted by Peter Kurth, *American Cassandra: The Life of Dorothy Thompson* (Boston: Little, Brown, 1990), 218. The quotation is from Margaret Case Harriman, "The 'It' Girl," *New Yorker,* April 20 and 27, 1940.

27. Kurth, *American Cassandra,* 232.

28. Ibid., 331.

29. Dorothy Thompson, "Chance vs. Certainty," *New York Herald Tribune,* March 23, 1937, 23.

30. Dorothy Thompson, "Peace! It's Wonderful!" *New York Herald Tribune,* May 3, 1937, 15.

31. Ibid.

32. Ibid.

33. Oswald Garrison Villard, "Another Word on Neutrality," *The Nation,* May 1, 1937, 508.

34. *The Nation,* May 1, 1937, 495.

35. "The President's Speech," *New York Times,* October 6, 1937, 1, 16.

36. Quoted by Pois, "The Politics and Process of Organizing for Peace," 427.

37. Letter from Frederick Libby addressed "Dear Friend," August 21, 1937, Headquarters Records, May–August 1937, Reel 7, NWTUL Papers.

38. Margaret Stone to Frederick Libby, August 27, 1937, Headquarters Records, May–August 1937, Reel 7, NWTUL Papers.

39. "Carrie Chapman Catt to Frederick Libby," December 15, 1937, Box 5, Correspondence, Schain Papers, Sophia Smith Collection, Smith College, Northampton, Massachusetts (hereafter cited as Schain Papers).

40. "Report of the Committee on International Relations to the Board of Directors," November 8, 1938, Series V: Reports of the Chairman to the Board of Directors, Reel 104, AAUW Archives.

41. Ibid.

42. "Elizabeth Christman to Frederick Libby," June 30, 1938, Box 7, Headquarters Records, May–August 1938, Reel 7, NWTUL Papers.

43. "Jeannette Cheek to Marguerite Wells," August 19, 1937, Box 368, Series II, LWV Papers.

44. Ibid.

45. Louise Leonard Wright, *American Neutrality* (Washington, D.C., 1936).

46. "Minutes of Pre-Convention Meeting," April 22, 1938, *Papers of the League of Women Voters, 1918–1974,* Part I, Meetings of the Board of Directors and the Executive Committee (Frederick, Md.: University Publications of America, 1985), Reel 6 (hereafter cited as LWV microfilm).

47. "National Program, 1938–1940," Box 1882, Folder "International Relations: Basic Documents, 1930–56," Series IV, LWV Papers. During the debate in convention, Louise Wright, chairman of the Department of Government and Foreign Policy, noted that the National Board's decisions about neutrality legislation over the past few years had already established a precedent for this item. Part II, Series A, National Conventions and General Councils, Reel 18, LWV microfilm.

48. "Report of the Committee on International Relations to the Board of Directors," November 8, 1938, Series V: Reports of the Chairman to the Board of Directors, Reel 104, AAUW Archives.

49. "Stone/Christman to Mme. Malaterre-Sellier," May 12, 1938, Box 7, Headquarters Records, May–August 1938, Reel 7, NWTUL Papers.

50. "Anne Hartwell Johnstone to Cordell Hull," June 27, 1938, Box 7, Headquarters Records, May–August 1938, Reel 7, NWTUL Papers.

51. Alonso, *Peace as a Women's Issue,* 139.

52. "America's Role in the War Crisis," *The Nation,* September 17, 1938, 256.

53. Ibid., 257.

54. "A Challenge to America," *The Nation,* September 24, 1938, 285.

55. "America Supports Japanese Aggression." Box 94, Group I, International Relations and Peace, 1938–43, no. 4, NCJW Records.

56. "Recommendation adopted by the National Committee on the Cause and Cure of War," October 19, 1938, Box 94, Group I, International Relations and Peace, 1938–43, no. 4, NCJW Records.

57. "A.A.U.W. News and Notes: Japanese Embargo," *AAUW Journal,* 32, no. 3 (1939): 177. Series III, E. Publications, 1900–1976, AAUW Journal, vols. 29–38, Reel 25, AAUW Archives.

58. "Fanny Brin/Mollie Weintraub to Peace Chairmen," January 3, 1939, Box 94, Group I, International Relations and Peace, 1938–43, no. 5, NCJW Records.

59. *New York Times,* January 5, 1939, 12.

60. Ibid.

61. "The President's Message," *The Nation,* January 14, 1939, 52.

62. "Isolation Is Not Enough," *The Nation,* March 18, 1939, 308.

63. Minutes of the National Board Meeting, January 19, 1939, Box 9, Folder 1, Reel 10, *Records of the Women's International League for Peace and Freedom United States Section, 1919–1959* (Wilmington, Del.: Scholarly Resources, 1988) (hereafter cited as WILPF Papers).

64. "The Pro-Neutrality Pattern," Branch Letter, Frame 308, Reel 94, WILPF Papers.

65. "Poll of W.I.L. Opinion," Branch Letter, Frame 320, Reel 94, WILPF Papers.

66. Ibid., Frame 321, WILPF Papers.

67. "The Pro-Neutrality Pattern," Branch Letter, Frame 308, Reel 94, WILPF Papers.

68. Ibid., Frame 309, WILPF Papers.

69. "Poll of W.I.L. Opinion," Branch Letter, Frame 322, Reel 94, WILPF Papers.

70. Branch Letter No. 74, May 25, 1939, Frame 342, Reel 94, WILPF Papers.

71. "National Committee on the Cause and Cure of War: Program for 1939," January 21, 1939, Box 10, Peace Organizations, Schain Papers; Box 440, Cause and Cure of War, Series II, LWV Papers.

72. Quoted by Freda Kirchwey, "Loving Hitler Less," *The Nation,* March 25, 1939, 337.

73. Freda Kirchwey, "Let's Mind Our Own Business," *The Nation,* April 15, 1939, 421–22.

74. Dorothy Thompson, "Freedom of Action," *New York Herald Tribune,* April 7, 1939, 19.

75. Dorothy Thompson, "Secretary Hull Cuts the Gordian Knot," *Washington Post,* June 2, 1939, 11.

76. "National Security Week flier," Box 94, Group I, International Relations and Peace, 1938–43, no. 5, NCJW Records.

77. "The American People Want Peace, Justice, National Security flier," Box 1893, International Relations, Neutrality 1937–42, Series IV, LWV Papers.

78. "Florence Kirlin to Louise Wright, memo," April 7, 1939, Carton 1, Folder 26, Louise Wright Papers, Schlesinger Library, Radcliffe Institute for Advanced Study, Cambridge, Massachusetts (hereafter cited as Wright Papers).

79. "Neutrality Statement Before Senate Foreign Relations Committee," April 13, 1939, Box 1712, Folder 1, Series IV, LWV Papers.

80. Interestingly, once the war had begun in Europe, concern for the effect

of cash-and-carry on the Far Eastern situation took second place to concern for Allied access to the supplies they needed, and these organizations all supported the institution of cash-and-carry trade.

81. "Neutrality Statement Before Senate Foreign Relations Committee," April 13, 1939, Box 1712, Folder 1, Series IV, LWV Papers.

82. "Showdown on Neutrality," *The Nation,* May 13, 1939, 548.

83. Freda Kirchwey, "Short of War," *The Nation,* April 29, 1939, 484.

84. "Edith Abbott to *The New York Times,*" May 1, 1939, Carton 1, Folder 26, Wright Papers.

85. "Anne Talbot Donaldson to Edith Abbott," May 8, 1939, Box 1, Folder 2, Louise Wright Papers, 83-M110, Schlesinger Library, Radcliffe Institute for Advanced Study, Cambridge, Massachusetts (hereafter cited as Wright Papers, 83-M110).

86. "Report of the Committee on International Relations to the Board of Directors," September 15, 1938 to May 31, 1939, Series V: Reports of the Chairman to the Board of Directors, Reel 104, AAUW Archives. There were 845 branches of the AAUW in May 1939, so slightly more than 25 percent were active in support of the association's foreign policy. "Biennial Report of the General Director at the 11th National Convention," May 1939, Series II, Reel 8, AAUW Archives.

87. "Minutes of the Board of Directors meeting," November 14, 1938, Part I. Meetings of the Board of Directors and the Executive Committees: Minutes and Related Documents, 1918–1974, Reel 6, LWV microfilm.

88. "Marguerite Wells to State League Presidents," March 13, 1939, Carton 1, Folder 31, Wright Papers.

89. "Minutes of pre-Council meeting of the Board of Directors," April 23, 1939, Part I. Meetings of the Board of Directors and the Executive Committees: Minutes and Related Documents, 1918–1974, Reel 6, LWV microfilm.

90. "Minutes of post–Council meeting of the Board of Directors," April 27, 1939, Part I. Meetings of the Board of Directors and the Executive Committees: Minutes and Related Documents, 1918–1974, Reel 7, LWV microfilm.

91. "Memorandum to State Presidents," June 2, 1939, Box 1893, "International Relations: Neutrality, 1937–1942," Series IV, LWV Papers.

92. "Statement on Neutrality," June 29, 1939, Box 94, Group I, International Relations and Peace, 1938–43, no. 5, NCJW Records.

93. Freda Kirchwey, "Two Foreign Policies," *The Nation,* July 29, 1939, 116.

94. "Press release," July 11, 1939, Carton 1, Folder 31, Wright Papers.

95. Louise Wright to Marguerite Wells, Oct. 30, 1937, Government and Foreign Policy, Wright, Mrs. Quincy, Box 370, Series II, LWV Papers.

96. "Red Star and Swastika," *The Nation,* August 26, 1939, 211–12.

97. Anne O'Hare McCormick, *New York Times,* September 25, 1939.

98. Quoted by Marion Turner Sheean, ed., *The World at Home: Selected Writings of Anne O'Hare McCormick* (New York: Knopf, 1956), x.

99. Nan Robertson, *The Girls in the Balcony: Women, Men, and* The New York Times (New York: Random House, 1992), 21.

100. James Reston, "Introduction" to Sheean, *The World at Home,* vi.

Chapter 3. Rethinking Neutrality

1. Anne O'Hare McCormick, "Gambler's Throw Threatens the Crash of a Continent," *New York Times,* September 2, 1939, 16.

2. Freda Kirchwey, "Europe's Last Stand," *The Nation,* September 2, 1939, 232.

3. Russell D. Buhite and David W. Levy, eds., *FDR's Fireside Chats* (Norman: University of Oklahoma Press, 1992), 149–51.
4. Press Release, September 8, 1939, Folder 2, Box 1712, Series IV, LWV Papers.
5. Statement of Policy, September 19, 1939, Folder: International Relations and Peace, Box 94, NCJW Records.
6. *New York Times,* September 15, 1939, 1.
7. Ibid., 12.
8. Ibid.
9. Dorothy Thompson, "On the Record: Neutrality Today," *Washington Post,* September 18, 1939, 7.
10. Ibid.
11. *New York Times,* September 16, 1939, 9.
12. Anne O'Hare McCormick, "Second Turn of the War, Like the First, Called in Moscow," *New York Times,* September 16, 1939, 16.
13. Freda Kirchwey, "1939 Is Not 1914," *The Nation,* September 16, 1939, 284.
14. Dorothy Thompson, "On the Record: Neutrality Today," *Washington Post,* September 18, 1939, 7.
15. *New York Times,* September 16, 1939, 9.
16. Dorothy Thompson, "On the Record: Col. Lindbergh and Propaganda," *Washington Post,* September 20, 1939, 11.
17. Statement of Policy, September 19, 1939, Folder: International Relations and Peace, 1938–43, no. 5, Box 94, NCJW Records.
18. Press Release, September 19, 1939, Folder 31, Carton 1, Wright Papers.
19. Marguerite Wells to National Board Members, September 14, 1939, Folder: Board Referenda, 1940–41, Box 440, Series II, LWV Papers.
20. Ibid.
21. Jeannette Cheek to Marguerite Wells, September 18, 1939, Folder 2, Carton 1, Wright Papers.
22. Ibid.
23. Marguerite Wells to state presidents, September 19, 1939, Folder: Neutrality Act—Request for Action, 1939, Box 424, Series II, LWV Papers.
24. The General Council meeting in April 1939, while amending the League's program in less specific terms, had apparently expressed a consensus in favor of repealing the embargo provisions of the Neutrality Act, without any insistence on substituting cash-and-carry. Press release, April 26, 1939, Part II, Series A: National Conventions and General Councils, Reel 18, LWV microfilm.
25. "A Plea for Calm," September 27, 1939, Folder 2, Box 1712, Series IV, LWV Papers.
26. *New York Times,* September 22, 1939, 1.
27. Press release, September 19, 1939, Folder 31, Carton 1, Wright Papers.
28. Freda Kirchwey, "What Americans Want," *The Nation,* September 23, 1939, 307.
29. Ibid., 308.
30. Dorothy Thompson, "A Call to Reason," *Washington Post,* September 27, 1939, 11.
31. Ibid.
32. Freda Kirchwey, "War in Washington," *The Nation,* September 30, 1939, 336–37.
33. Dorothy Thompson, "For Freedom of Action," *Washington Post,* October 2, 1939, 11.
34. *New York Times,* October 3, 1939, 14.

35. Ibid.

36. Kirchwey, "War in Washington," 336–37.

37. Dorothy Thompson, "The Shape of Things to Come," *Washington Post,* October 4, 1939, 11.

38. Dorothy Thompson, "What Is Neutrality?" *Washington Post,* October 4, 1939, 15.

39. Martha Gellhorn to Marguerite Wells, September 27, 1939, Folder 4, Carton 1, Wright Papers, 83-M110.

40. Ibid.

41. Margaret Stone to NWTUL members, October 26, 1939, Folder: Headquarters Records, May–December 1939, Box 8, Reel 7, NWTUL Papers; "For Immediate Action," September 22, 1939, Folder: International Relations and Peace, 1938–43, no. 5, Box 94, Group I, NCJW Records.

42. Marguerite Wells to state presidents, September 27, 1939, Folder: Neutrality Act—Request for Action 1939, Box 424, Series II, LWV Papers.

43. "A Plea for Calm," September 27, 1939, Folder 2, Box 1712, Series IV, LWV Papers.

44. "You Can Help While Congress Debates," October 7, 1939, Folder 3, Box 1712, Series IV, LWV Papers.

45. Ibid.

46. "Summary: Activity regarding Neutrality Legislation, September 19–November 10," November 30, 1939, Folder 3, Box 1713, Series IV, LWV Papers.

47. Marguerite Wells to state League presidents, September 19, 1939, Folder: Neutrality Act—Request for Action 1939, Box 424, Series II, LWV Papers.

48. "Statement on Neutrality," October 10, 1939, Box 13, Records of the Committee on the Cause and Cure of War, Schlesinger Library, Radcliffe Institute for Advanced Study, Cambridge, Massachusetts (hereafter cited as CCCW Papers).

49. Ibid.

50. Fanny Brin to Chairmen of International Relations and Peace, October 10, 1939, Folder: International Relations and Peace, 1938–43, no. 5, Box 94, NCJW Records.

51. Rogow, *Gone to Another Meeting,* 226–27. Rogow's biographical sketch of Brin notes that she was "[b]est known for her peace work" (227) and gives no sense of the greater complexity of Brin's views.

52. *New York Times,* October 14, 1939, 10.

53. Ibid.

54. Dorothy Thompson, "Lindbergh Foresees New World Order Devised by Nazis," *Washington Post,* October 18, 1939, 11.

55. Dorothy Thompson, "Col. Lindbergh's Imperialism," *Washington Post,* October 23, 1939, 7.

56. Marguerite Wells to state League presidents, October 25, 1939, Folder 2, Box 1712, LWV Papers.

57. Statement of Policy Concerning Neutrality and Peace, October 30, 1939, Box 13, CCCW Papers.

58. Margaret Stone to individual members and donors, October 26, 1939, Folder: Headquarters Records, May–December 1939, Box 8, Reel 7, NWTUL Papers.

59. Marguerite Wells to state League presidents, November 3, 1939, Folder 31, Box 31, Wright Papers.

60. Quoted in National League of Women Voters report "The Conduct of Foreign Policy," July 1940, Box 3, Sue Hamilton Cooper Papers, University of Washington Archives (hereafter cited as Cooper Papers).

61. Executive Committee 1939, Reel 10, WILPF Papers.
62. Ibid.
63. National Board Resolutions, October 1939, "Re: Mediation and World Government," Reel 9, WILPF Papers.
64. Quoted by Carrie Foster, "The Women and the Warriors: Dorothy Detzer and the WILPF" (Ph.D. diss., University of Colorado, Boulder, 1984), 581–82.
65. Report of National Executive Secretary, Dorothy Detzer, National Board Meeting, January 20–21, 1940, Reel 10, WILPF Papers.
66. Ibid.
67. Dorothy Thompson, "War to End War," *Washington Post,* November 20, 1939, 9.
68. Dorothy Thompson, "The Isolationist's Dilemma," *Washington Post,* December 6, 1939, 11.
69. Divine, *Reluctant Belligerent,* 82.
70. Dorothy Thompson, "Roulette with Destiny," *Washington Post,* January 19, 1940, 9.
71. Freda Kirchwey, "Politics and Peace," *The Nation,* January 17, 1940, 242.
72. Josephine Schain to Marguerite Wells, October 26, 1939, Folder "Cause and Cure of War," Box 440, Series II, LWV Papers.
73. "American Far Eastern Policy," Foreign Policy Problem, January, 1940, Folder: Circular Letters, Government and Foreign Policy, Box 37, Series III, LWV Papers.
74. "Fanny Brin to local Chairmen of International Relations and Peace, January 7, 1940," Folder: International Relations and Peace, 1938–1943, no. 5, Box 95, NCJW Records.
75. Folder: Broadcasts, Box 7, Speeches and Writings, Schain Papers.
76. The effectiveness of these efforts, of course, was highly questionable, but Americans often had an exaggerated belief in their success. For a brief survey of U.S.-Chinese relations, see Michael Schaller, *The U.S. and China in the Twentieth Century* (New York: Oxford University Press, 1979).
77. "International Relations Committee minutes," December 15, 1939, Series V: International Relations Committee, Reel 104, AAUW Archives.
78. "Recommendation to the Findings Committee of the National Conference on the Cause and Cure of War voted at the meeting of the Commission on the Far East, January 16, 1940," Box 13, CCCW Papers.
79. Ibid.
80. Marguerite Wells to State League Presidents, January 25, 1940, Folder 1, Box 1, Wright Papers, 83-M110.
81. Wells to State League Presidents, March 22, 1940, Folder 1, Box 1, Wright Papers, 83-M110.
82. Marguerite Wells, memo to Mrs. Wright, chairman of Government and Foreign Policy, March 20, 1939, Folder: Cause and Cure of War, Box 440, Series II, LWV Papers.
83. "Report of the Committee on International Relations to the National Board of Directors, February 15, 1940," Series V: Reports of the Chairman to the Board of Directors, Reel 104, AAUW Archives.
84. Dorothy Thompson, "Lord Lothian's Speech," *Washington Post,* January 8, 1940, 7.
85. Ibid.
86. Dorothy Thompson, "This Is Iniquitous," *Washington Post,* November 29, 1939, 11.
87. Dorothy Thompson, "V—There Is a Tide," *Washington Post,* December 27, 1939, 7.

88. Ibid.

89. Freda Kirchwey, "Munich Bears Fruit," *The Nation,* September 9, 1939, 260.

90. Freda Kirchwey, "The Great Debate," *The Nation,* December 23, 1939, 699.

91. Dorothy Thompson, "Mr. Welles' Mission," *Washington Post,* March 4, 1940, 9.

92. Freda Kirchwey, "Politics and Peace," *The Nation,* February 17, 1940, 242. See also Dorothy Thompson, "The President's Latest Move," *Washington Post,* February 12, 1940, 7.

93. Anne O'Hare McCormick, "The Neutral Front: Its Role in War and Peace," *New York Times,* November 18, 1939, 16.

94. Anne O'Hare McCormick, "Embittered Neutrals May Finally Force War's End," *New York Times,* November 13, 1939, 18.

95. Dorothy Thompson, "There Is a Tide, Chapter III," *Washington Post,* December 15, 1939, 21.

96. Dorothy Thompson, "There Is a Tide (Chapter Two)," *Washington Post,* December 13, 1939, 11.

97. Ibid.

98. Ibid.

99. Dorothy Thompson, "The President's Latest Move," *Washington Post,* February 12, 1940, 7.

100. Dorothy Thompson, "The Second Beer Hall Putsch," *Washington Post,* November 10, 1939, 15.

101. Dorothy Thompson, "A Bad Chess Player," *Washington Post,* November 15, 1939, 13.

102. Dorothy Thompson, "On the Record: Hitler as Stooge for Stalin Is History's Supreme Irony," *Washington Post,* February 7, 1940, 9. In this column, Thompson also dismisses fears about American boys being sent to France as "an eventuality of which there is not the least likelihood."

103. Dorothy Thompson, "The President's Latest Move," *Washington Post,* February 12, 1940, 7.

104. Anne O'Hare McCormick, "British Mood Swiftly Alters, Their Confidence Restored," *New York Times,* April 6, 1940, 16.

Chapter 4. Blitzkrieg

1. Freda Kirchwey, "Can We Stay Neutral?" *The Nation,* April 20, 1940, 503.

2. Kirchwey to Villard, April 30, 1940, Folder 136: "Oswald Garrison Villard, 1933–1949," Box 8, Freda Kirchwey Papers, Schlesinger Library, Radcliffe Institute for Advanced Study, Cambridge, Massachusetts (hereafter cited as Kirchwey Papers).

3. Ibid.

4. "Minutes of the 1940 Convention," p. 189, Reel 18, LWV microfilm.

5. Ibid., 227. The vote was 204 to 56.

6. *Washington Post,* May 4, 1940, 6.

7. Dorothy Thompson, "Roosevelt Was Right," *Washington Post,* May 15, 1940, 15.

8. Ibid.

9. *New York Times,* May 17, 1940, 10.

10. Robert Dallek, *Franklin D. Roosevelt and American Foreign Policy,* 221–22.

11. Freda Kirchwey, "America Is Not Neutral," *The Nation*, May 18, 1940, 614.
12. Ibid.
13. Ibid.
14. *New York Times*, May 20, 1940, 8.
15. Ibid.
16. Anne Morrow Lindbergh, *War Within and Without: Diaries and Letters of Anne Morrow Lindbergh, 1939–1944* (New York: Harcourt Brace, 1980), 96.
17. Ibid., 100.
18. Ibid., 81.
19. Ibid., 84.
20. *New York Times*, May 19, 1940, 16.
21. Dorothy Thompson, "Revising Our Concepts," *Washington Post*, May 20, 1940, 9.
22. Press Release, May 20, 1940, Box 36, Committee to Defend America by Aiding the Allies Papers, Mudd Library, Princeton, New Jersey (hereafter cited as CDA Papers); *New York Times*, May 20, 1940, 11.
23. *Washington Post*, May 23, 1940, 10.
24. Ibid.
25. For both figures see Folder: National Committee Members, Box 11, CDA Papers.
26. See Folder: press releases, May–June 1940, Box 36, CDA Papers.
27. *New York Times*, May 23, 1940, 19.
28. Ibid.
29. Ibid.
30. Ibid.
31. Ibid., 21.
32. "Statement of Policy in the Field of International Relations," May 23, 1940, Folder: HQ Records, May–December 1940, Box 8, Reel 8, NWTUL Papers.
33. Agnes Nestor to Elizabeth Christman, May 29, 1940, Folder: HQ Records, May–December 1940, Box 8, Reel 8, NWTUL Papers.
34. Margaret Stone to Agnes Nestor, June 23, 1940, Folder: HQ Records, May–December 1940, Box 8, Reel 8, NWTUL Papers.
35. *New York Times*, May 23, 1940, 18.
36. Quoted by *New York Times*, May 28, 1940, 13.
37. Dorothy Thompson, "If the Allies Lose," *Washington Post*, May 24, 1940, 11.
38. Dallek, *Franklin D. Roosevelt and American Foreign Policy*, 222–23.
39. Freda Kirchwey, "Supposing Hitler Wins," *The Nation*, May 25, 1940, 640.
40. Ibid., 641.
41. Thompson, "If the Allies Lose," 11.
42. Ibid.
43. Lindbergh, *War Within and Without*, 86.
44. *New York Times*, May 29, 1940, 11.
45. Press Release, June 1, 1940, Box 36, CDA Papers.
46. Ophelia Demaree to Louise Wright, May 31, 1940, Folder: Government and Foreign Policy, States: Maryland to Wyoming, Box 452, Series II, LWV Papers.
47. Dorothy Thompson, "The World Germanica," *Washington Post*, May 31, 1940, 13.
48. Freda Kirchwey, "Let in the Refugees!" *The Nation*, June 1, 1940, 669.
49. Dorothy Thompson, "Unearned Increment," *Washington Post*, June 3, 1940, 9.

50. Morrow, "Does America Deserve a Miracle?", Box 57, Morrow Papers.
51. Lindbergh, *War Within and Without,* 97.
52. Ibid., 99.
53. Ibid., 104.
54. Dallek, *Franklin D. Roosevelt and American Foreign Policy,* 228.
55. Dorothy Thompson, "Letter to Congress," *Washington Post,* June 5, 1940, 11.
56. Freda Kirchwey, "Saving the Front Line," *The Nation,* June 8, 1940, 695–96.
57. "Speech by Dorothy Kenyon," June 8, 1940, Dorothy Kenyon Papers, Sophia Smith Collection, Smith College, Northampton, Massachusetts (hereafter cited as Kenyon Papers).The copy of this speech in this collection contains no indication of the location or audience.
58. *New York Times,* June 10, 1940, 36.
59. *New York Times,* June 11, 1940, 6.
60. Warren F. Kimball, ed., *Churchill and Roosevelt: The Complete Correspondence,* vol. 1, *Alliance Emerging* (London: Collins, 1984), 43.
61. Mark Lincoln Chadwin, *The Hawks of World War II* (Chapel Hill: University of North Carolina Press, 1968), 280.
62. *New York Times,* May 11, 1940, 22.
63. Freda Kirchwey, "A Democratic Program of Defense," *The Nation,* June 15, 1940, 724.
64. Ibid.
65. Villard to Kirchwey, June 13, 1940, Folder 136: Oswald Garrison Villard, 1933–1949, Box 8, Kirchwey Papers.
66. Kirchwey to Villard, June 19, 1940, Folder 136: Oswald Garrison Villard, 1933–1949, Box 8, Kirchwey Papers.
67. Oswald Garrison Villard, "Valedictory," *The Nation,* June 29, 1940, 782.
68. Freda Kirchwey, "Escape and Appeasement," *The Nation,* June 29, 1940, 773.
69. Ibid., 774.
70. *New York Times,* June 13, 1940, 17.
71. *New York Times,* June 14, 1940, 19.
72. *New York Times,* June 16, 1940, 37.
73. Press Release, June 21, 1940, Box 36, CDA Papers.
74. Marguerite Wells to state presidents, June 21, 1940, Folder: Government & Foreign Policy, May 1940–42, Box 451, Series II, LWV Papers.
75. "Foreign Policy Problem: America's Choice Today," July 1940, Folder 5, Box 1712, Series IV, LWV Papers.
76. Freda Kirchwey, "What Next?" *The Nation,* June 22, 1940, 743–44.
77. David Cannadine, ed., *The Speeches of Winston Churchill* (London: Penguin, 1990), 177.

Chapter 5. Fifty Ships and a Third Term

1. Dallek, *Franklin D. Roosevelt and American Foreign Policy,* 243.
2. "For Release Saturday, August 10," Folder: Press Releases—August 1941, Box 37, CDA Papers.
3. Ibid.; this press release actually describes Candace Stimson as sister of the secretary of the navy, Henry A. Stimson, but I have assumed this was an error.
4. "Lead Sentences for News Story," September 5, 1940, Folder: Women's Division Correspondence, September 1940–June 1941, Box 29, CDA Papers.

5. "Executive Committee minutes, April 19, 1941," Folder: Executive Committee Minutes, February–June 1941, Box 10, CDA Papers.

6. See Boxes 36 and 37 for press releases, CDA Papers.

7. "Lead Sentences for News Story," September 5, 1940, Folder: Women's Division Correspondence, September 1940–June 1941, Box 29, CDA Papers.

8. Letter to Claire Franklin, September 11, 1940, Folder: Women's Division Correspondence, September 1940–June 1941, Box 29, CDA Papers.

9. "Policies to check with National Executive Committee," Folder: Executive Committee Minutes, August 2, 1940, Box 10, CDA Papers.

10. A. R. Crawford to Harold Weston, August 14, 1940, Folder: Women's Division Correspondence, June–August, 1940, Box 29, CDA Papers.

11. "Plan for National Poster Contest," September 9, 1940, Folder: Women's Division Correspondence, September 1940–June 1941, Box 29, CDA Papers.

12. Press Release, October 25, 1940, Box 36, CDA Papers.

13. See Box 29, CDA Papers, two folders of Women's Division Correspondence for many examples of this.

14. Folder: Women's Division Correspondence, September 1940–June 1941, Box 29, CDA Papers. See particularly the form letter, dated September 16, 1940, aimed at members of the AAUW and A. R. Crawford's memo to Frances Thomas about national lists for the LWV and the Committee on the Cause and Cure of War.

15. Frances Thomas to Jean Patterson, February 10, 1941, Folder: Women's Division Correspondence, September 1940–June 1941, Box 29, CDA Papers.

16. Letter to Jean Patterson, September 13, 1940, Folder: Women's Division Correspondence, September 1940–June 1941, Box 29, CDA Papers.

17. Letter to Roger Greene, December 15, 1940, Folder: Correspondence—Roger S. Greene—Patterson, Jean, Box 4, CDA Papers.

18. "Memorandum," n.d., Women's Division Correspondence, September 1940–June 1941, Box 29, CDA Papers. The "emergencies" envisaged were legislative ones rather than substantive physical crises.

19. Ibid.

20. CDA press releases estimated the figure variously at 750,000, 450,000 and 650,000. Folders: Press Releases, September and October 1940, Box 36, CDA Papers. All the following information about the Minute Americans comes from press releases dated August–October 1940, Box 36, CDA Papers.

21. Release Afternoon Papers Sept. 18, Folder: Press Releases—September 1940, Box 36, CDA Papers.

22. For Release Saturday (September 28), Folder: Press Releases—September 1940, Box 36, CDA Papers. The success rate drops to 58 percent if one includes uncompleted calls.

23. Hadley Cantril, "America Faces the War: A Study in Public Opinion," *Public Opinion Quarterly,* September 1940, 391.

24. "Plan for Organization For American Minute Women," Folder: Women's Division Correspondence, September 1940–June 1941, Box 29, CDA Papers.

25. John Keegan, *The Second World War* (London: Arrow, 1990), 91.

26. Dorothy Thompson, "Clarity at Last," *Washington Post,* July 8, 1940, 7.

27. Keegan, *Second World War,* 92.

28. Churchill to Roosevelt, June 15, 1940, in Kimball, *Churchill and Roosevelt,* 51.

29. Churchill to Roosevelt, July 31, 1940, in Kimball, *Churchill and Roosevelt,* 57.

30. Ibid.

31. *New York Times,* July 30, 1940, 13.
32. "Address by Mrs. Kermit Roosevelt," August 11, 1940, Folder: Press Releases, August 1940, Box 32, CDA Papers.
33. Chadwin, *Hawks of World War II,* 85–86.
34. Churchill to Roosevelt, August 15, 1940, in Kimball, *Churchill and Roosevelt,* 60.
35. Ibid.
36. Divine, *Reluctant Belligerent,* 95.
37. Freda Kirchwey, "Help Britain Win!" *The Nation,* August 10, 1940, 105.
38. Ibid., 106.
39. "Gallup and Fortune Polls," *Public Opinion Quarterly,* December 1940, 713.
40. Memorandum from Anne Johnstone, August 29, 1940, Folder: Government and Foreign Policy, 1940–1942, Box 451, Series II, LWV Papers.
41. Telegram from Louise Wright, August 30, 1940, Folder: Government and Foreign Policy, 1940–1942, Box 451, Series II, LWV Papers.
42. "Radio Talk—Hands Across the Sea Series," August 30, 1940, Folder: HQ Records, May–December 1940, Box 8, Reel 8, NWTUL Papers.
43. Ibid.
44. Press Release, September 10, 1940, Folder: Press Releases, September 1940, Box 36, CDA Papers.
45. Keegan, *Second World War,* 101.
46. Letter from Foreign Policy Chairmen Huddilston of Maine, Weyl of Pennsylvania, Eaton of Massachusetts, Andrus of Maryland, Ferguson of Texas and Burger of Oklahoma to the National Board, Folder: Govt & Foreign Policy, May 1940–1942, Box 451, Series II, LWV Papers.
47. Wells to Burger, May 22, 1940, Folder: Govt & Foreign Policy, May 1940–1942, Box 451, Series II, LWV Papers.
48. Louise Wright to Chairmen of Government and Foreign Policy, December 10, 1940, Folder: Circular Letters, Government and Foreign Policy, Box 38, Series III, LWV Papers. Such circulars served to inform the chairs of local foreign policy committees of the status of the League agenda, so that they might interpret and explain the League's position to local members.
49. Anne Hartwell Johnstone to Louise Wright, Dec. 2, 1940, Folder: Govt & Foreign Policy, May 1940–1942, Box 452, Series II, LWV Papers.
50. Ibid.
51. Divine, *Reluctant Belligerent,* 100.
52. Ibid.
53. "Neutrality Statement Before Senate Foreign Relations Committee," April 13, 1939, Folder 1, Box 1712, Series IV, LWV Papers.
54. Quoted by Divine, *Reluctant Belligerent,* 101.
55. Dorothy Thompson, "The New Pact," *Washington Post,* September 30, 1940, 7.
56. Ibid.
57. Louise Wright to Chairmen of Government and Foreign Policy, December 10, 1940, Folder: Circular Letters, Government and Foreign Policy, Box 38, Series III, LWV Papers.
58. Louise Wright to Marguerite Wells, December 16, 1940, Folder 2, Carton 1, Wright Papers.
59. "International Relations Digest, Jan. 1941," vol. 1, no. 4, Folder: International Relations and Peace, 1938–43, no. 4, Box 94, Group I, NCJW Records.
60. Michael Wreszin, Villard's biographer, highlights the contradictions in his thinking on fascism and the war, arguing that "Villard even cast doubt upon the sincerity of his pacifism by suggesting that the European democra-

cies were obligated to resist the Fascist and Nazi terror but at the same time denying American obligation. He became more concerned with keeping America out of war than with keeping war out the world." Michael Wreszin, *Oswald Garrison Villard: Pacifist at War* (Bloomington: Indiana University Press, 1965), 5.

61. Kirchwey to Villard, October 4, 1940, Folder 136, "Oswald Garrison Villard, 1933–1949," Box 8, Kirchwey Papers.

62. Villard to Kirchwey, October 5, 1940, Folder 136, "Oswald Garrison Villard, 1933–1949," Box 8, Kirchwey Papers.

63. Kirchwey to Villard, October 7, 1940, Folder 136, "Oswald Garrison Villard, 1933–1949," Box 8, Kirchwey Papers.

64. Michael Wreszin notes the primacy of the peace issue in Villard's thinking, quoting his endorsement of the socialist candidate, Norman Thomas, in the 1936 presidential election: "Each of us has a paramount issue. Mine is the question of war and peace and the saving of civilization." *Oswald Garrison Villard,* 247.

65. Quoted by Stephen B. Oates in *To Purge This Land with Blood: A Biography of John Brown* (Amherst: University of Massachusetts Press, 1984), 355. My thanks to Tracy McKenzie for this reference.

66. National Board Meeting Minutes, October 30, 1940, Folder 4, Box 9, Reel 10, WILPF Papers.

67. Ibid.

68. Ibid.

69. "Report," October 23, 1940, Folder: Katherine Jackson, October 1940–August 1941, Box 13, Fight for Freedom Committee Papers, Mudd Library, Princeton, New Jersey (hereafter cited as FFF Papers).

70. "Report by Helen Everitt," October 17, 1940, Folder: Women's Division, (1 of 2), Box 37, FFF Papers.

71. "Report on women's activities, February 11, 1941," Folder: Women's Division, (1 of 2), Box 37, FFF Papers.

72. Press Release, December 5, 1940, Folder: Women's Division, (1 of 2), Box 37, FFF Papers.

73. "Report for Ulric Bell on Women's Committee for Action, December 30, 1940," Folder: Women's Division, (1 of 2), Box 37, FFF Papers.

74. "Report on Women's Activities, January 9, 1941," Folder: Women's Division, (1 of 2), Box 37, FFF Papers; my italics.

75. A. C. Gumbrecht to Maury Paul, Society Editor, *New York Journal American,* July 1940, Folder: Press Releases, July–August 1940, Box 36, CDA Papers.

76. This figure is given in the "Report on Women's Activities, January 9, 1941," Folder: Women's Division, (1 of 2), Box 37, FFF Papers.

77. "National Committee on International Relations and Peace minutes," November 8, 1940, Folder: International Relations and Peace, 1938–43, no. 3, Group I, Box 94, NCJW Records.

78. "Resolutions Adopted or Reaffirmed at the 16th Triennial Convention, New York City," November 1940, Folder: International Relations and Peace, 1938–43, no. 4, Box 94, Group I, NCJW Records.

79. "International Relations and Peace Committee Report," November 10, 1940, Folder: International Relations and Peace, 1938–43, no. 3, Box 94, Group I, NCJW Records.

80. Ibid.; my italics.

81. "Newsletter: Aid to Britain," September 30, 1940, Folder: Newsletters—1940–41, Box 452, Series II, LWV Papers.

82. "Draft of interview for approval by Strauss," October 28, 1940, Folder

110, Nat'l LWV, Correspondence, 1940–1943, Box 6, Anna Lord Strauss Papers, Schlesinger Library, Radcliffe Institute for Advanced Study, Cambridge, Massachusetts (hereafter cited as Strauss Papers).

83. "Memorandum on conference between Mrs. Johnstone, Miss Kirlin and Mr. Feis of the State Department," November 7, 1940, Folder: Government & Foreign Policy, Defense "Lend-Lease Bill," Box 451, Series II, LWV Papers.

84. "Board Meeting Minutes, Friday November 15, 1940," Part I: Board Meeting Minutes, Reel 7, LWV microfilm.

85. "Edna Gellhorn to Louise Wright," December 1940, Folder 2, Box 1, Wright Papers, 83-M110.

86. Divine, *Reluctant Belligerent,* 103.

87. Freda Kirchwey, "Wendell Willkie's Speech," *The Nation,* August 24, 1940, 145.

88. Quoted in ibid.

89. Dallek, *Franklin D. Roosevelt and American Foreign Policy,* 248–49.

90. Freda Kirchwey, "There Is No Alternative," *The Nation,* August 3, 1940, 85.

91. Freda Kirchwey, "The Draft Bill," *The Nation*, September 7, 1940, 185.

92. Dorothy Thompson, "Miss Thompson Comes Out For Roosevelt," *Washington Post,* October 9, 1940, 11.

93. Dorothy Thompson, "The Axis and the Campaign," *Washington Post,* October 14, 1940, 9.

94. Dorothy Thompson, "The Axis and the Campaign," *Washington Post,* October 18, 1940, 13.

95. "Lindbergh Assails 'Present' Leaders," *New York Times,* October 15, 1940, 8.

96. "Text of Willkie's Address in the City Stadium at Newark," *New York Times,* October 8, 17.

97. "Wendell Willkie's Talks on the Radio and in Garment Center During His Tour of City," *New York Times,* October 9, 1940, 18.

98. "Willkie's Address on America's World Role," *New York Times,* October 18, 1940, 12.

99. "Text of President Roosevelt's Speeches in Philadelphia and Wilmington," *New York Times,* October 24, 1940, 14.

100. "Text of the Speeches Made by Wendell L. Willkie," *New York Times,* October 25, 1940, 14.

101. "Texts of President Roosevelt's Addresses in Boston and Hartford," *New York Times,* October 31, 1940, 14.

102. Freda Kirchwey, "To the President-Elect," *The Nation,* November 9, 1940, 437.

103. Dallek, *Franklin D. Roosevelt and American Foreign Policy,* 250.

104. Lindbergh, *War Within and War Without,* 145 n.

105. Ibid., 143.

106. Anne Morrow Lindbergh, *The Wave of the Future: A Confession of Faith* (New York: Harcourt, Brace, 1940), 19.

107. Ibid., 34.

108. Ibid., 25.

109. Anne Lindbergh to Mina Curtiss, September 21, 1940, in *War Within and Without,* 146.

110. Lindbergh, *Wave of the Future,* 15, 17.

111. Clare Boothe, "Half a Worm: A Confession of Weakness," October 17, 1940, Folder 1, Box 302, Literary File, Clare Boothe Luce Papers, Library of Congress (hereafter cited as Luce Papers).

112. Lindbergh, *Wave of the Future,* 8–9.

113. Alzada Comstock, "The Distant Drum," *AAUW Journal,* vol. 34, no. 2, 1940, 69, Series III, E. Publications, 1900–1976, Reel 25, AAUW Archives.
114. Lindbergh, *Wave of the Future,* 19.
115. Clare Boothe, "Half a Worm: A Confession of Weakness," October 17, 1940, Folder 1, Box 302, Literary File, Luce Papers.
116. Anne O'Hare McCormick speaking on *America's Town Meeting of the Air,* November 18, 1940. Eleanor Troy Williams, ed., *Bulletin of America's Town Meeting of the Air,* 6, no. 1 (1940): 13–15.
117. Clare Boothe, "Half a Worm: A Confession of Weakness," October 17, 1940, Folder 1, Box 302, Literary File, Luce Papers.
118. See the series of Thompson columns "There Is a Tide," from mid to late December 1939.
119. Freda Kirchwey, "Religion and Democracy," *The Nation,* November 30, 1940, 522.
120. Ibid.
121. Keegan, *Second World War,* 134.

Chapter 6. The Arsenal of Democracy

1. Hadley Cantril, *Public Opinion, 1935–1946* (Princeton, N.J.: Princeton University Press, 1951), 410.
2. Warren F. Kimball, *The Most Unsordid Act: Lend-Lease, 1939–1941* (Baltimore: Johns Hopkins University Press, 1969), 191–92, 194.
3. Marguerite Wells to Louise Wright, December 4, 1940, Folder 2, Carton 1, Wright Papers.
4. Ibid.
5. Louise Wright to Marguerite Wells, December 16, 1940, Folder 2, Carton 1, Wright Papers.
6. Quoted by Dallek, *Franklin D. Roosevelt and American Foreign Policy,* 255.
7. "Report on women's activities, December 19, 1940," Folder: Women's Division, (1 of 2), Box 37, FFF Papers.
8. Ibid.
9. "White Group Split Denied by Director," *New York Times,* December 29, 1940, 10.
10. Ibid.
11. *New York Times*, January 7, 1941, 12.
12. Quoted by Dallek, *Franklin D. Roosevelt and American Foreign Policy*, 256–57.
13. *New York Times,* December 31, 1940, 4.
14. Marguerite Wells to Louise Wright, December 30, 1940, Folder 2, Box 1, Wright Papers, 83-M110.
15. "Memorandum to the National Board," January 3, 1941, Folder 6, Box 1, Wright Papers, 83-M110.
16. "Mrs. Field to Marguerite Wells," January 6, 1941, Folder: Board Referenda, 1940–41, Box 440, Series II, LWV Papers.
17. Ibid.
18. Harriet Eliel to Marguerite Wells, January 7, 1941, Folder: Board Referenda, 1940–41, Box 440, Series II, LWV Papers.
19. Jeannette Cheek to Marguerite Wells, January 12, 1941, Folder: Board Referenda, 1940–41, Box 440, Series II, LWV Papers; my italics.

20. Freda Kirchwey, "Order of the Year," *The Nation*, January 4, 1941, 6.
21. "President Roosevelt's Message to Congress," *New York Times*, January 7, 1941, 4.
22. Ibid.
23. "Minutes of Executive Committee Meeting," January 7, 1941, Folder: National Committee, Executive Comm. Minutes, Box 15, CCCW Papers.
24. Margaret Stone to members of the executive board, January 9, 1941, Folder: HQ Records, January–April 1941, Box 8, Reel 8, NWTUL Papers.
25. Ibid.; italics in the original.
26. Margaret Stone to League secretaries and International Relations Chairmen, January 28, 1941, Folder: HQ Records, January–April 1941, Box 8, Reel 8, NWTUL Papers.
27. There was only one dissenting vote. "Minutes of the National Committee on International Relations and Peace," February 21, 1941, Folder: International Relations and Peace, 1938–43, no. 3, Box 94, Group I, NCJW Records.
28. Fanny Brin to Peace Chairmen, February 6, 1941, Folder: Foreign Policy—General 1941, Box 85, Group I, NCJW Records.
29. Ibid.
30. Freda Kirchwey, "President Roosevelt Reports," *The Nation*, January 11, 1941, 34.
31. Louise Wright to Marguerite Wells, January 13, 1941, Folder: Board Referenda, 1940–41, Box 440, Series II, LWV Papers.
32. Marguerite Wells to State Presidents, January 16, 1941, Folder: Lend-Lease Miscellaneous, Box 457, Series II, LWV Papers; my italics.
33. Marguerite Wells to Louise Wright, January 15, 1941, Folder 5, Box 1, Wright Papers, 83-M110.
34. "Text of Lease-Lend Bill," *New York Times*, January 11, 1941, 1, 3.
35. Ibid., 3.
36. "Opposition Starts," *New York Times*, January 11, 1941, 1.
37. Ibid.
38. *Chicago Sunday Tribune*, January 12, 1941, 1.
39. Dorothy Thompson, "Non-Belligerency," *Washington Post*, January 13, 1941, 9.
40. Ibid.
41. Anne O'Hare McCormick, "The President's Powers and the New World Order," *New York Times*, January 13, 1941, 14.
42. *New York Times*, January 24, 1941, 7.
43. Dorothy Thompson, "Footnote to Lindbergh," *Washington Post*, February 3, 1941, 7.
44. Dorothy Thompson, "Are We Dumb?" *Washington Post*, February 5, 1941, 7.
45. *Chicago Tribune*, January 28, 1941, 10.
46. *Chicago Tribune*, February 19, 1941, 12.
47. House Committee on Foreign Relations, *Lend-Lease Act: Hearings on H.R. 1776*, 77th Cong., 1st sess., 1941, 644–45, 647.
48. Ibid., 645.
49. Ibid., 648.
50. Ibid., 650.
51. Ibid., 653.
52. Ibid., 656–57.
53. Ibid., 658.
54. Ibid., 659.

55. Ibid., 660.
56. "Mrs. Van Loon's report from Washington, January 24, 1941," Folder: Women's Division, (1 of 2), Box 37, FFF Papers.
57. "Kay Jackson to Mrs. Fred B. Preston," February 11, 1941, Folder: Women's Division, (1 of 2), Box 37, FFF Papers.
58. "Report on women's activities, January 23, 1941," Folder: Women's Division, (1 of 2), Box 37, FFF Papers.
59. "Mrs. Van Loon's report from Washington, January 24, 1941," Folder: Women's Division, (1 of 2), Box 37, FFF Papers.
60. Freda Kirchwey, "The 'Loyal Opposition,'" *The Nation,* January 25, 1941, 89–90.
61. Gallup and Fortune Polls, *Public Opinion Quarterly,* June 1941, 326.
62. Press release with transcript of Thompson's speech on CBS, n.d., Folder: Lend-Lease Bill, January–March 1941, Box 32, FFF Papers.
63. Senate Foreign Relations Committee, *Hearings on the Bill to Promote the Defense of the United States,* 77th Cong., 1st sess., 1941, 632.
64. Ibid.
65. Ibid., 633.
66. Ibid., 632–33.
67. Ibid., 822–23.
68. *New York Times*, February 16, 1941, E9.
69. See the chapter on Curtis in Glen Jeansonne, *Women of the Far Right: The Mothers' Movement and World War II* (Chicago: University of Chicago Press, 1996), 57–72.
70. Senate Foreign Relations Committee, *Hearings on the Bill to Promote the Defense of the United States,* 824.
71. Ibid., 825.
72. Ibid., 769–70.
73. Ibid., 770.
74. Ibid., 773.
75. Jeansonne, *Women of the Far Right,* 79.
76. Senate Foreign Relations Committee, *Hearings on the Bill to Promote the Defense of the United States,* 714.
77. Ibid., 715.
78. Ibid., 716.
79. "Minority Report on Lease-Lend Bill," *New York Times,* February 1, 1941, 5.
80. "Woman Disturbs House Bill Debate," *New York Times,* February 6, 1941, 7.
81. Ellin Berlin speech, February 6, 1941, Folder: Lend-Lease Bill, January–March 1941, Box 32, FFF Papers.
82. Ibid.
83. Ibid.
84. Ibid.
85. Transcript of broadcast on CBS, February 9, 1941, Folder: Committee to Defend America, Jan–Feb 1941, Box 24, FFF Papers.
86. Ibid.
87. Ibid.
88. Ibid.
89. Charles Eade, ed., *The War Speeches of the Rt. Hon. Winston S. Churchill,* vol. 1 (London: Cassell, 1951), 350.
90. Ibid., 352.
91. Anne O'Hare McCormick, "Impact of Two American Visitors on Mr. Churchill," *New York Times*, February 10, 1941, 16.

92. Ibid.
93. "Special Washington Letter," February 18, 1941, Folder: Women's Division, (1 of 2), Box 37, FFF Papers.
94. Dorothy Thompson, "'The American Century'," *Washington Post,* February 21, 1941, 13.
95. Ibid.
96. Freda Kirchwey, "Luce Thinking," *The Nation,* March 1, 1941, 229.
97. Ibid., 230.
98. Dorothy Thompson. "Should the English Speaking Democracies Unite Now?" *Bulletin of America's Town Meeting of the Air,* vol. 6, no. 1 (New York: Columbia University Press, 1941).
99. Freda Kirchwey, "Luce Thinking," *The Nation,* March 1, 1941, 230.
100. Ibid.
101. "Effigy of Writer Seized in Capital," *New York Times,* February 24, 1941, 7.
102. "Glass Is Beseiged by Sit-Down Women," *New York Times,* March 1, 1941, 7.
103. "'Crusader' Gibes at Senator Glass," *New York Times,* March 2, 1941, 17.
104. "Two Women Are Fined for Senate Disorder," *New York Times,* March 7, 1941, 22.
105. "Mrs. Paul Douglas—Article for the Hyde Park Herald," March 1941, Folder: Government & Foreign Policy—Lend-Lease—states—Calif., Conn., Ga., Ill., Box 452, Series II, LWV Papers.
106. "Speech of Mrs. Hattie Caraway," February 27, 1941, Folder: Subject Files: Lend-Lease—Correspondence, Box 8, CDA Papers.
107. Ibid.; my italics.
108. "Women's Committee for Action to Mrs. Smashpipes," n.d., Folder: Speakers—FFF, Box 35, FFF Papers.
109. Ibid. In the absence of a date, this petition can be located only in the early months of 1941. I found no indications of its success or failure.
110. "Press release, January 13, 1941," Folder: Women's Division, (1 of 2), Box 37, FFF Papers.
111. "Form letter from Dorothy Overlock, January 7, 1941," Folder: Women's Division, (1 of 2), Box 37, FFF Papers.
112. "Report on women's activities, January 9, 1941," Folder: Women's Division, (1 of 2), Box 37, FFF Papers.
113. "Report on women's activities, February 20, 1941" Folder: Women's Division, (1 of 2), Box 37, FFF Papers.
114. Press Release, March 6, 1941, Folder: Press Releases, November 1940–April 1941, Box 37, CDA Papers.
115. "Time Limit on Speeches Sought," *New York Times,* March 8, 1941, 6.
116. "Gibson Disputes Wheeler Charge," *New York Times,* March 3, 1941, 8.
117. "America First Group Would List Donors," *New York Times,* March 6, 1941, 11.
118. "Last Stand Made by 'Peace Women,'" *New York Times,* March 9, 1941, 18.
119. "Speaks in Favor of Lease-Lend Bill," *New York Times,* March 9, 1941, 25.
120. "Final Step Swift," *New York Times,* March 12, 1941, 1.
121. Eade, *The War Speeches of the Rt. Hon. Winston S. Churchill,* 1:365.
122. "Statement of Policy, March 17, 1941," Folder: Policy Statements, November 1940–February 1942, Box 38, CDA Papers.
123. Mark Lincoln Chadwin, *The Hawks of World War II* (Chapel Hill: University of North Carolina Press, 1968), 156–57. Moreover, although the decision to form the new organization was taken in February, it was by then

clear that the Committee to Defend America's all-aid-short-of-war goal was about to be achieved. With lend-lease secure, war was the next step.

124. *New York Times,* April 20, 1941. Hobson thus turned a common isolationist argument from the lend-lease debate on its head. Many opponents of the bill had criticized its supporters for cowardice since they declared that it was America's war at the same time that they emphasized that the bill would keep the United States out of the war.

125. "Report on women's activities," April 8, 1941, Folder: Women's Division, (1 of 2), Box 37, FFF Papers.

126. "Kay Jackson to Mrs. Logan," February 19, 1941, Folder: Women's Division, (1 of 2), Box 37, FFF Papers.

127. "Undated release," Folder: Katherine Jackson, October 1940–August 1941, Box 13, FFF Papers.

128. The husbands of two others are listed. Also there is a Mrs. Kinsey Schmuck on the WAC and a Miss Ruth Kinsey Schmuck in the membership lists. Box 70, FFF Papers.

129. "Gallup and Fortune Polls," *Public Opinion Quarterly,* June 1941, 323–25.

130. Ibid., 325–27.

131. *New York Times,* March 9, 1941.

132. Cantril, *Public Opinion,* 976.

133. Peter Cusick, Executive Secretary of the Fight for Freedom Committee, to Anna Lord Strauss, April 25, 1941, Folder 194: Gen. prof. Correspondence, 1940–1941, Box 9, Strauss Papers.

Chapter 7. The Battle of Production

1. "Statement of Policy," May 7, 1941, Folder: Statements of Policy, November 1940–February 1942, Box 38, CDA Papers.

2. "This is the time TO FIGHT for freedom," Folder: This is the time to fight for freedom leaflet, Box 58, FFF Papers.

3. These names were drawn from a list of Committee to Defend America National Committee members, Box 11, CDA Papers; from a Fight for Freedom membership list dated April 28, 1941, Box 70, FFF Papers; and the Fight for Freedom's "This is the time TO FIGHT for freedom" leaflet, Box 58, FFF Papers. They represent only a fraction of the overlap between the two organizations.

4. Resolution offered by Miss Lillian A. Wells, New York City, at the 1941 Biennial Convention, May 7–9, 1941, Series II, Reel 9, AAUW Archives.

5. "1941 Biennial Convention," May 7–9, 1941, Series II, Reel 9, AAUW Archives.

6. Mrs. Harry Merrett of Madison, Wis., speaking at the 1941 Biennial Convention, May 7–9, 1941, ibid.

7. Mrs. R. C. Dexter of Boston, Mass., speaking at the 1941 Biennial Convention, May 7–9, 1941, ibid.

8. "Margaret Stone to National Board," May 6, 1941, Folder: HQ Records, May–December, 1941, Box 8, Reel 8, NWTUL Papers.

9. "Agnes Nestor to Margaret Stone," May 26, 1941, ibid.

10. "Convoy ballot," May 1941, ibid.

11. "Margaret Stone's report to the National Board Meeting," December 8–10, 1941, ibid. The report does not relate whether the response was favorable.

12. Branch figures are attached to the Annual Meeting Minutes for 1941, Reel 11, WILPF Papers. The national figures come from the national organization secretary's report.

13. Ibid.

14. Appendix to Annual Meeting Minutes, 1941, ibid.

15. Executive Committee Minutes, November 19, 1941, ibid. It seems likely that this is the same branch as that anonymously mentioned in the National Board Minutes of October 18, 1941, as wishing to "dis-associate itself from the state and national branches of the W.I.L." Ibid.

16. Executive Committee Minutes, November 19, 1941, ibid.; my italics.

17. "General Council Minutes," Thursday, May 8, 1941, Reel 7, LWV microfilm. When the National Board met after the General Council there was some disagreement as to what this resolution meant. Seven board members believed that it meant the League should not act on any legislation dealing with the issue of transportation; six believed that it indicated a desire to focus on production at the present time, but that the League might take action on the transportation question at a later date as deemed necessary by the National Board. See "National Board Minutes," May 10, 1941, Reel 7, LWV microfilm.

18. Marguerite Wells to Louise Wright, December 4, 1940, Folder 2, Carton 1, Wright Papers.

19. "National Board Minutes," Monday, May 5, 1941, Reel 7, LWV microfilm.

20. "Marguerite Wells to state league presidents," May 13, 1941, Folder: Battle of Production, Box 439, Series II, LWV Papers.

21. "The Battle of Production: It Can Be Won," June 20, 1941, Folder 1, Box 7, Cooper Papers. This pamphlet was first issued in April, before the campaign in general had been developed. It was revised on May 19, June 7, and June 20.

22. "Battle of Production flier," Folder 3, Box 6, Cooper Papers.

23. "Suggested Movie Screen Flashes," June 20, 1941, Folder 1, Box 1713, Series IV, LWV Papers.

24. "Virginia Mannon to Marguerite Wells," June 26, 1941, Folder: Battle of Production Campaign Publicity, Box 439, Series II, LWV Papers.

25. "Harding/Wells interview," June 5, 1941, Folder: Battle of Production, Box 439, Series II, LWV Papers.

26. "Louise Wright radio speech," July 15, 1941, Folder: Battle of Production Campaign Publicity, Box 439, Series II, LWV Papers.

27. *Alert,* March 18, 1941, newsletter of the Woman's Division of the Committee to Defend America, Folder: Newsletter Woman's Division, Box 35, CDA Papers.

28. Grace Manners to local chapter chairmen, March 13, 1941, Folder: Women's Division Correspondence, September 1940–June 1941, Box 29, CDA Papers.

29. "National Woman's Division Sponsors National Song Contest," n.d., ibid.

30. Folder: Musical Scores, Song Contest Winner, n.d., Box 34, CDA Papers.

31. I have not come across any example of this argument, only numerous references to it in League papers and statements.

32. "Win the Battle of Production Campaign," May 13, 1941, Folder: Battle of Production, Box 439, Series II, LWV Papers.

33. "Short talk on the Battle of Production—Illinois LWV," June 1941, Folder 5, Carton 1, Wright Papers.

34. "Louise Wright radio speech," July 15, 1941, Folder: Battle of Production Campaign Publicity, Box 439, Series II, LWV Papers.
35. Lindbergh, *War Within and Without,* 208.
36. See *Public Opinion Quarterly* for 1941 for a variety of polls asking this question.
37. Freda Kirchwey, "War Is Not the Issue," *The Nation,* May 3, 1941, 518.
38. Ibid.
39. Freda Kirchwey, "Now We Must Act," *The Nation,* May 24, 1941, 601.
40. "Mothers, S.O.S." Folder: Subject Files, America First Memoranda, 1941, Box 7, CDA Papers.
41. Press release, May 8, 1941, Folder: Press Releases, May 1941, Box 37, CDA Papers.
42. "Lindbergh Warns of America's Fall," *New York Times,* May 4, 1941, 1.
43. "War Choice Denied, Lindbergh Holds," *New York Times,* May 11, 1941, 31.
44. Freda Kirchwey, "If Lindbergh Is Right," *The Nation,* May 10, 1941, 546.
45. "Texts of the Addresses by Lindbergh and Wheeler," *New York Times,* May 24, 1941, 7.
46. Ibid.
47. "War Choice Denied, Lindbergh Holds," 31.
48. Press release, May 26, 1941, Folder: Press Releases, May 1941, Box 37, CDA Papers.
49. "Pre-Speech Appeal Made to President," *New York Times,* May 28, 1941, 20.
50. "Text of the President's Address Depicting Emergency Confronting the Nation," *New York Times,* May 28, 1941, 2.
51. Dallek, *Franklin D. Roosevelt and American Foreign Policy,* 266.
52. Press release, n.d., Folder: Subject Files Fight for Freedom Committee, May–June 1941, Box 8, CDA Papers.
53. Dorothy Thompson, "Neutrality Act, '37, Godsend to Hitler," *Spokesman-Review,* June 18, 1941, 4.
54. Freda Kirchwey, "Hitler's Political Front," *The Nation,* July 5, 1941, 5.
55. Quoted by Lindbergh, *War Within and Without,* 199.
56. Lindbergh, *War Within and Without,* 207.
57. "Lindbergh Called Nazi Tool by Ickes," *New York Times,* July 15, 1941, 13.
58. Dorothy Thompson, "There Is a Tide," *Washington Post,* December 11, 1939.
59. Dorothy Thompson, "The Wave of the Future Has Passed into Hands of Churchill and Roosevelt," *Spokesman-Review,* June 29, 1941, 4.
60. Freda Kirchwey, "We Have but One Aim," *The Nation,* June 28, 1941, 740–41.
61. Divine, *Reluctant Belligerent,* 135.
62. Dallek, *Franklin D. Roosevelt and American Foreign Policy,* 276.
63. Freda Kirchwey, "In Rising Wrath," *The Nation,* August 9, 1941, 104–5.
64. Ibid.
65. Anne O'Hare McCormick, "Cross-Currents Converging on Washington," *New York Times,* June 16, 1941, 14.
66. Freda Kirchwey, "Shall We Declare War?" *The Nation,* July 26, 1941, 64–65.
67. Dorothy Thompson, "Present World Situation and America's Stake in It," *Spokesman-Review,* September 3, 1941, 4.
68. Divine, *Reluctant Belligerent,* 140.

69. Quoted by Dallek, *Franklin D. Roosevelt and American Foreign Policy,* 283.
70. Freda Kirchwey, "Prelude to Action," *The Nation,* August 23, 1941, 153.
71. Dallek, *Franklin D. Roosevelt and American Foreign Policy,* 287.
72. "The President's Speech," *New York Times,* September 12, 1941, 1, 4.
73. Dallek, *Franklin D. Roosevelt and American Foreign Policy,* 288.
74. "Lindbergh Sees a Plot for War," *New York Times,* September 12, 1941, 2.
75. Lindbergh, *War Within and Without,* 221.
76. Quoted in ibid., 222.
77. Ibid.
78. Ibid., 226.
79. "America First Says Race Is Not Issue," *New York Times,* September 25, 1941, 4.
80. Freda Kirchwey, "The Roosevelt Strategy," *The Nation,* September 20, 1941, 243.
81. Ibid.
82. Thompson, "Questions, by Dorothy Thompson, to be Answered by the American People," *Spokesman-Review,* October 5, 1941, 4.
83. Rose Chayes to Miss Finney, September 23, 1941, Folder: Women's Division, (1 of 2), Box 37, FFF Papers.
84. Rose Chayes to Miss Finney, October 3, 1941, Folder: Women's Division, (1 of 2), Box 37, FFF Papers.
85. "Why the Women of Fight for Freedom should go to Washington," Folder: Women's Division, (1 of 2), Box 37, FFF Papers.
86. "Address by Mrs. Philip Morgan," September 10, 1941, Folder: Speeches, September–December 1941, Box 58, FFF Papers.
87. Ibid.
88. Ibid.
89. "Repeal of the Neutrality Act," October 23, 1941, Folder 1, Box 1713, Series IV, LWV Papers.
90. "Survey of Board opinion on Neutrality Repeal," October 1941, Folder: Government and Foreign Policy, May 1940–1942, Box 451, Series II, LWV Papers.
91. "Repeal the Neutrality Act," *International Relations Digest,* vol. 2, no. 2, October 1941, International Relations and Peace, 1938–43, no. 3, Box 94, Group I, NCJW Records.
92. Ibid.
93. Freda Kirchwey, "Neutrality Is a Sham," *The Nation,* October 4, 1941, 297.
94. Freda Kirchwey, "End of a Myth," *The Nation,* November 22, 1941, 502.
95. Divine, *Reluctant Belligerent,* 153.

Chapter 8. "Brave Women and Fair Men"

1. "Rose Chayes to Mrs. Tillett," October 28, 1941, Folder: Women's Division, (2 of 2), Box 37, FFF Papers.
2. "Memorandum," n.d., Folder: Women's Division, (2 of 2), Box 37, FFF Papers.
3. "Memorandum to Ulric Bell," November 25, 1941, Folder: Women's Division, (2 of 2), Box 37, FFF Papers.
4. "Undated memorandum," Folder: Women's Division, (2 of 2), Box 37, FFF Papers.

5. "Brave Women and Fair Men," November 21, 1941, Morrow Papers. All quotations in the following paragraphs come from this speech.

6. Dorothy Thompson, "It Had to Come and There Was Nothing Unexpected About It," *Spokesman-Review,* December 14, 1941, 4.

7. Anne O'Hare McCormick, "For Americans the Question Period Is Over," *New York Times,* December 8, 1941, 22.

8. McCormick's imagination clearly failed her when she wrote, "It cannot be charged by any one that we have provoked this 'incident.' The president or the 'warmongers' cannot be accused of seeking to involve us in this conflict." Ibid. She did not anticipate the revisionists.

9. Freda Kirchwey, "Fruits of Appeasement," *The Nation,* December 13, 1941, 599.

10. Ibid., 600.

11. Anne O'Hare McCormick, "Hitler Was Forced to Declare War on the Ultimate Enemy," *New York Times,* December 13, 1941, 22.

12. Louise Wright to Marguerite Wells, December 9, 1941, Folder: Government and Foreign Policy, May 1940–1942, Box 451, Series II, LVW Papers.

13. "Chicago to Chicago—Legislative Review," Folder 1, Box 4, Cooper Papers.

14. Rose Schneiderman and Elisabeth Christman to Franklin Roosevelt, December 10, 1941, Folder: HQ Records, May–December 1941, Box 8, Reel 8, NWTUL Papers.

15. Rose Schneiderman and Elisabeth Christman to Franklin Roosevelt, December 10, 1941, Folder: HQ Records, May–December 1941, Box 8, Reel 8, NWTUL Papers.

16. "Nothing to Fear—Much to Do," *AAUW Journal* 35, no. 2 (January 1942): 67–84.

17. Margaret Hope Bacon, *One Woman's Passion for Peace and Freedom: The Life of Mildred Scott Olmsted* (Syracuse, N.Y.: Syracuse University Press, 1993), 223.

18. National Board, "Statement on Pearl Harbor," December 10, 1941, Reel 11, WILPF Papers.

19. Lindbergh, *War Within and Without,* 243.

20. Chadwin, *Hawks of World War II,* 266 n.

21. Freda Kirchwey, "Saving the Front Line," *The Nation,* June 8, 1940, 968.

22. "President Praises Women Backing Bill," *New York Times,* March 6, 1941, 11.

Bibliography

Manuscript Collections

Library of Congress
- Clare Booth Luce Papers
- Papers of the National League of Women Voters
- Records of the National Council of Jewish Women

Seeley G. Mudd Library, Princeton University
- Papers of the Committee to Defend America by Aiding the Allies
- Papers of the Fight for Freedom Committee
- Papers of the American Union for Concerted Peace Efforts

Schlesinger Library, Radcliffe Institute for Advanced Study
- Vera Micheles Dean Papers
- Freda Kirchwey Papers
- Helen Hill Miller Papers
- Anna Lord Strauss Papers
- Marguerite Wells Papers
- Louise Wright Papers; and addendum 83-M110.
- Papers of the National Conference on the Cause and Cure of War

Sophia Smith Collection, Smith College
- Elizabeth Cutter Morrow Papers
- Dorothy Kenyon Papers
- Peace Collection
- Josephine Schain Papers

University of Washington Archives
- Sue Hamilton Cooper Papers

Microfilm Collections

Records of the Women's International League for Peace and Freedom United States Section, 1919–1959. Wilmington, Del.: Scholarly Resources, 1988.

American Association of University Women Archives, 1881–1976. Sanford, N.C.: Microfilm Corporation of America, 1980.

Papers of the National Women's Trade Union League. Microfilm of Library of Congress collection.

Papers of the League of Women Voters, 1918–1974. Frederick, Md.: University Publications of America, 1985.

Government Publications

U.S. Congress. House. Committee on Foreign Affairs. *A Bill to Promote the Defense of the United States,* 77th Cong., 1st sess., 1941.
U.S. Congress. Senate. Committee on Foreign Relations. *A Bill to Promote the Defense of the United States,* 77th Cong., 1st sess., 1941.

Newspapers and Periodicals

Bulletin of America's Town Meeting of the Air
Chicago Tribune
The Nation
New York Times
Public Opinion Quarterly
Spokane Spokesman-Review
Washington Post

Published Sources

Cannadine, David, ed. *The Speeches of Winston Churchill.* London: Penguin, 1990.
Cantril, Hadley. *Public Opinion, 1935–1946.* Princeton, N.J.: Princeton University Press, 1951.
Eade, Charles, ed. *The War Speeches of the Rt. Hon. Winston S. Churchill.* Vol. 1. London: Cassell, 1951.
Kimball, Warren F., ed. *Churchill and Roosevelt: The Complete Correspondence.* Vol. 1, *Alliance Emerging.* London: Collins, 1984.
Schewe, Donald B., ed. *Franklin D. Roosevelt and Foreign Affairs, Second Series, January 1937–August 1939.* Vol. 13. New York: Clearwater, 1969.
Zevin, B. D., ed. *Nothing to Fear: The Selected Addresses of Franklin Delano Roosevelt, 1932–1945.* Cambridge, Mass.: Houghton Mifflin, 1946.

Secondary Sources

Alonso, Harriet Hyman. *Peace as a Women's Issue: A History of the U.S. Movement for World Peace and Women's Rights.* Syracuse, N.Y.: Syracuse University Press, 1993.
———. *The Women's Peace Union and the Outlawry of War, 1921–1942.* Knoxville: University of Tennessee Press, 1989.
Alpern, Sara. *Freda Kirchwey: A Woman of "The Nation."* Cambridge, Mass.: Harvard University Press, 1987.
As, Berit. "A Materialistic View of Men's and Women's Attitudes Towards War." *Women's Studies International Forum* 5, nos. 3–4 (1982): 355–64.
Bacon, Margaret Hope. *One Woman's Passion for Peace and Freedom: The Life of Mildred Scott Olmsted.* Syracuse, N.Y.: Syracuse University Press, 1993.
Berkin, Carol R., and Clara M. Lovett, eds. *Women, War, and Revolution.* New York: Holmes and Meier, 1980.

Buhite, Russell D., and David W. Levy, eds. *FDR's Fireside Chats.* Norman: University of Oklahoma Press, 1992.

Bussey, Gertrude, and Margaret Tims. *Women's International League for Peace and Freedom.* London: George Allen and Unwin, 1965.

Campbell, D'Ann. *Women at War with America: Private Lives in a Patriotic Era.* Cambridge, Mass.: Harvard University Press, 1984.

Carroll, Berenice A. "Feminism and Pacifism: Historical and Theoretical Connections." In *Women and Peace: Theoretical, Historical and Practical Perspectives,* edited by Ruth Roach Pierson. New York: Croom Helm, 1987.

Chadwin, Mark Lincoln. *The Hawks of World War II.* Chapel Hill: University of North Carolina Press, 1968.

Chatfield, Charles. *For Peace and Justice: Pacifism in America, 1914–1941.* Knoxville: University of Tennessee Press, 1971.

Clavadetscher, Carl Julius, Jr. "An Analysis of the Rhetoric of the Committee to Defend America by Aiding the Allies." Ph.D. diss., University of Oregon, 1973.

Cole, Wayne S. *America First: The Battle Against Intervention, 1940–1941.* Madison: University of Wisconsin Press, 1953.

———. *Roosevelt and the Isolationists, 1932–1945.* Lincoln: University of Nebraska Press, 1983.

Conway, Jill. "The Woman's Peace Party and the First World War." In *War and Society in North America,* edited by J. L. Granatstein and R. D. Cuff. Papers presented at the Canadian Association for American Studies Meeting, Montreal, Fall 1970. Toronto: Thomas Nelson and Sons, 1971.

Crapol, Edward, ed. *Women and American Foreign Policy: Lobbyists, Critics, and Insiders.* 2d ed. Wilmington, Del.: Scholarly Resources, 1992.

Dallek, Robert. *Franklin D. Roosevelt and American Foreign Policy, 1932–1945.* New York: Oxford University Press, 1979.

Divine, Robert. *The Illusion of Neutrality.* Chicago: University of Chicago Press, 1962.

———. *The Reluctant Belligerent: American Entry into World War II.* 2d ed. New York: Knopf, 1979.

Doenecke, Justus D., and John E. Wilz. *From Isolation to War, 1931–1941.* Arlington Heights, Ill.: Harlan Davidson, 1991.

Dye, Nancy Schrom. "Rose Schneiderman." In *Notable American Women: The Modern Period.* Cambridge, Mass.: Belknap Press of Harvard University Press, 1980.

Elshtain, Jean Bethke. *Women and War.* New York: Basic Books, 1987.

Elshtain, Jean Bethke, and Sheila Tobias, eds. *Women, Militarism, and War: Essays in History, Politics, and Social Theory.* Savage, Md.: Rowman and Littlefield, 1990.

Enloe, Cynthia. *Bananas, Beaches, and Bases: Making Feminist Sense of International Politics.* Berkeley: University of California Press, 1990.

Foot, Rosemary. "Where Are the Women?" *Diplomatic History* 14 (September 1990): 615–22.

Foster, Carrie. "The Women and the Warriors: Dorothy Detzer and the WILPF." Ph.D. diss., University of Colorado, Boulder, 1984.

———. *The Women and the Warriors: The U.S. Section of the Women's International League for Peace and Freedom, 1915–1946.* Syracuse, N.Y.: Syracuse University Press, 1995.

Foster, Catherine. *Women for All Seasons: The Story of the Women's Inter-*

national League for Peace and Freedom. Athens: University of Georgia Press, 1989.

Fowler, Robert Booth. *Carrie Catt: Feminist Politician.* Boston: Northeastern University Press, 1986.

Gilligan, Carol. *In a Different Voice: Psychological Theory and Women's Development.* Cambridge, Mass.: Harvard University Press, 1982.

Guinsburg, Thomas N. *The Pursuit of Isolationism in the United States Senate from Versailles to Pearl Harbor.* New York: Garland, 1982.

Herbst, Susan. *Numbered Voices: How Opinion Polling Has Shaped American Politics.* Chicago: University of Chicago Press, 1993.

Higonnet, Margaret Randolph, Jane Jenson, Sonia Michel, and Margaret Collins Weitz. *Behind the Lines: Gender and the Two World Wars.* New Haven, Conn.: Yale University Press, 1987.

Huston, Nancy. "Tales of War and Tears of Women." *Women's Studies International Forum* 5, nos. 3–4 (1982): 271–82.

Jeansonne, Glen. "Furies: Women Isolationists in the Era of FDR." *Journal of History and Politics* 8 (1990): 67–96.

———. *Women of the Far Right: The Mothers' Movement and World War II.* Chicago: University of Chicago Press, 1996.

Jeffords, Susan. *The Remasculinization of America: Gender and the Vietnam War.* Bloomington: Indiana University Press, 1989.

Jeffreys-Jones, Rhodri. *Changing Differences: Women and the Shaping of American Foreign Policy, 1917–1994.* New Brunswick, N.J.: Rutgers University Press, 1995.

Johnson, Walter. *The Battle Against Isolation.* Chicago: University of Chicago Press, 1944.

Jonas, Manfred. *Isolation in America, 1935–1941.* Ithaca, N.Y.: Cornell University Press, 1966.

Keegan, John. *The Second World War.* London: Arrow, 1990.

Kimball, Warren F. *The Most Unsordid Act: Lend-Lease 1939–1941.* Baltimore: Johns Hopkins University Press, 1969.

Kraditor, Aileen. *The Ideas of the Woman Suffrage Movement, 1890–1920.* New York: Columbia University Press, 1965.

Kurth, Peter. *American Cassandra: The Life of Dorothy Thompson.* Boston: Little, Brown, 1990.

Langer, William L., and S. Everett Gleason. *The Challenge to Isolation: The World Crisis of 1937–1940 and American Foreign Policy.* New York: Harper, 1952.

Leigh, Michael. *Mobilizing Consent: Public Opinion and American Foreign Policy, 1937–1947.* Westport, Conn.: Greenwood Press, 1976.

Lindbergh, Anne Morrow. *War Within and Without: Diaries and Letters of Anne Morrow Lindbergh, 1939–1944.* New York: Harcourt Brace, 1980.

———. *The Wave of the Future: A Confession of Faith.* New York: Harcourt Brace, 1940.

McEnaney, Laura. "He-Men and Christian Mothers: The America First Movement and the Gendered Meanings of Patriotism and Isolationism." *Diplomatic History* 18, no. 1 (December 1994): 47–57.

Oates, Stephen B. *To Purge This Land with Blood: A Biography of John Brown.* Amherst: University of Massachusetts Press, 1984.

Papachristou, Judith. "American Women and Foreign Policy, 1898–1905: Exploring Gender in Diplomatic History." *Diplomatic History* 14 (September 1990): 493–510.

Pierson, Ruth Roach, ed. *Women and Peace: Theoretical, Historical and Practical Perspectives.* London: Croom Helm, 1987.

Platt, Rorin Morse. *Virginia in Foreign Affairs, 1933–1941.* New York: University Press of America, 1991.

Pois, Anne Marie. "The Politics and Process of Organizing for Peace: The United States Section of the Women's International League for Peace and Freedom, 1919–1939." Ph.D. diss., University of Colorado, Boulder, 1988.

Rainbolt, Rosemary. "Women and War in the United States: The Case of Dorothy Detzer, National Secretary WILPF." *Peace and Change* 4 (September 1977): 18–21.

Reardon, Betty A. *Women and Peace: Feminist Visions of Global Security.* Albany: State University of New York Press, 1993.

Robertson, Nan. *The Girls in the Balcony: Women, Men, and* The New York Times. New York: Random House, 1992.

Rogow, Faith. *Gone to Another Meeting: The National Council on Jewish Women, 1893–1993.* Tuscaloosa: University of Alabama Press, 1993.

Rosenberg, Emily S. "Gender." *Journal of American History* 77 (June 1990): 116–24.

Ruddick, Sara. *Maternal Thinking: Toward a Politics of Peace.* Boston: Beacon Press, 1987.

Rupp, Leila J. *Mobilizing Women for War: German and American Propaganda, 1939–1945.* Princeton, N.J.: Princeton University Press, 1978.

Schaller, Michael. *The U.S. and China in the Twentieth Century.* New York: Oxford University Press, 1979.

Schott, Linda. "The Woman's Peace Party and the Moral Basis for Women's Pacifism." *Frontiers* 8 (1985): 18–24.

Schneider, James C. *Should America Go to War? The Debate over Foreign Policy in Chicago, 1939–1941.* Chapel Hill: University of North Carolina Press, 1989.

Schwar, Jane Harriet. "Interventionist Propaganda and Pressure Groups in the United States, 1937–1941." Ph.D. diss., Ohio State University, 1973.

Scott, Joan W. "Deconstructing Equality-Versus-Difference: Or, the Uses of Poststructuralist Theory for Feminism." *Feminist Studies* 14 (March 1988): 33–50.

Sheean, Marion Turner, ed. *The World at Home: Selected Writings of Anne O'Hare McCormick.* New York: Knopf, 1956.

Steinson, Barbara J. *American Women's Activism in World War I.* New York: Garland, 1982.

———. "'The Mother Half of Humanity': American Women in the Peace and Preparedness Movements in World War I." In *Women, War, and Revolution,* edited by Carol R. Berkin and Clara M. Lovett. New York: Holmes and Meier, 1980.

Stiehm, Judith Hicks. "The Protected, the Protector, the Defender." *Women's Studies International Forum* 5, nos. 3–4 (1982): 367–76.

Stoper, Emily, and Roberta Ann Johnson. "The Weaker Sex and the Better Half: The Idea of Women's Moral Superiority in the American Feminist Movement." *Polity* 10 (winter 1977): 192–203.

Swerdlow, Amy. "Ladies' Day at the Capitol: Women's Strike for Peace Versus HUAC." *Feminist Studies* 8 (1982): 493–520.

———. *Women Strike for Peace: Traditional Motherhood and Radical Politics in the 1960s.* Chicago: University of Chicago Press, 1993.

Thompson, Dorothy. "Women, Peace and History: Notes for an Historical

Overview." In *Women and Peace: Theoretical, Historical and Practical Perspectives,* edited by Ruth Roach Pierson. New York: Croom Helm, 1987.

Ware, Susan. *Holding Their Own: American Women in the 1930s.* Boston: Twayne, 1982.

Warren, Frank A., III. *Liberals and Communism: The "Red Decade" Revisited.* Bloomington: Indiana University Press, 1966.

Wheeler, Michael. *Lies, Damn Lies, and Statistics: The Manipulation of Public Opinion in America.* New York: Liveright, 1976.

Wilson, Joan Hoff. "'Peace Is a Woman's Job . . .' Jeanette Rankin and American Foreign Policy: Her Lifework as a Pacifist." *Montana: The Magazine of Western History* 30 (April 1980): 39–53.

———."'Peace Is a Woman's Job . . .' Jeanette Rankin and American Foreign Policy: The Origins of Her Pacifism." *Montana: The Magazine of Western History* 30 (January 1980): 28–41.

Wreszin, Michael. *Oswald Garrison Villard: Pacifist at War.* Bloomington: Indiana University Press, 1965.

Young, Louise M. *In the Public Interest: The League of Women Voters, 1920–1970.* New York: Greenwood Press, 1989.

Index